Reelin' in
the Years

Also by Mark Radcliffe

Showbusiness
Northern Sky
Thank You For the Days

REELIN' IN THE YEARS

THE SOUNDTRACK OF A NORTHERN LIFE

MARK RADCLIFFE

SIMON &
SCHUSTER

London · New York · Sydney · Toronto

A CBS COMPANY

First published in Great Britain by Simon & Schuster UK Ltd, 2011
A CBS COMPANY

1 3 5 7 9 10 8 6 4 2

Simon & Schuster UK Ltd
1st Floor
222 Gray's Inn Road
London WC1X 8HB

www.simonandschuster.co.uk

Simon & Schuster Australia
Sydney

A CIP catalogue record for this book is available
from the British Library.

ISBN: 978-0-85720-050-1

Typeset by M Rules
Printed in the UK by CPI Mackays, Chatham ME5 8TD

For my Mum and Isla May

CONTENTS

INTRODUCTION

In 1973 I went to the record department of Kendal Milne's in Manchester and bought the Steely Dan LP *Can't Buy A Thrill*. A classic album, it has ten great songs on it and none greater than 'Reelin' In The Years' with its immortal twin-guitar trickery. That title inspired this book, which is about music and buying records throughout my life, but also about how the world around me, and you, has changed over that time. I've chosen one song from each year I've been alive. They might not always be the best or most popular tunes of that year, but they all seem to capture a moment.

Hopefully they're not too obscure, either, as I thought it would be better when you're reading this to be able to bring at least some of them to mind. So in a way it's a bit like one of my radio shows: songs with talking in between.

Think of it as a miscellany, a treasury, a compendium or simply the addled ramblings of a middle-aged disc jockey filling in what would otherwise be dead air, or blank pages, between the records.

1958

CLIFF RICHARD – 'MOVE IT'

It's 1958. A gleaming black Austin A40 with, get this, leather seats, leaves the maternity unit car park at Townleys Hospital in Farnworth near Bolton. Trundling past the Co-op, avoiding the rain-hooded grandmas who periodically step into the road to see if the bus is coming, it turns left onto Bradford Road. Pausing at the traffic lights by Green Lane Park, just by the ornate bungalow with its sea-shell-encrusted wishing well sitting precociously on the crazy paving, it waits patiently for amber to fully give way to green before proceeding over the junction. A few yards further on it cautiously negotiates a left-hand turn into Hampton Road before coming to a standstill outside the small but neat semi-detached at number two.

Whilst the driver, my dad, performs his elaborate post-flight checks, his passenger, my mum, steps out onto the pavement holding a bundle of me in a crocheted shawl. Not unreasonably she feels exhaustion but also a sense of elation which, she now admits, may have been the result not only of the successful delivery of her first-born but also the successful delivery of her first fridge.

At around the same time as these momentous events are unfolding in the Northwest, Ian 'Sammy' Samwell and his mate board a Hertfordshire bus and head into central London, composing what I consider to be the first British rock'n'roll song on the journey. These events may appear unrelated to the casual observer (which, for a book like this, is the only sort of observer that can reasonably be expected), but I've come to see a connection. My life in the hurly burly of rock'n'roll radio could not have happened if, at the risk of stating the obvious, I hadn't been born. Nor could it have happened if British rock'n'roll hadn't been born either. As luck would have it, both of these occurrences took place in this momentous year.

It's generally accepted that the first rock'n'roll record was 'Rocket 88' recorded in 1951 by Ike Turner and his Kings of Rhythm. Strictly speaking a rhythm and blues song, it had a new, aggressive, distorted sound allegedly resulting from rainwater getting into Ike's amplifier in the boot of his car. Another version of the tale has the same amp falling from a roof rack and suffering significant damage. Whichever you choose to believe it seems that the birth of rock'n'roll owes something to Ike Turner's very casual attitude to automobile maintenance and/or road safety. A trip down to the Memphis branch of Halfords would surely have resulted in the purchase of some of those little stretchy rope things, which would have secured the precious roof-rack cargo. Let's give Ike the benefit of the doubt, as the long-suffering Tina often did, and say it was half-day closing.

The first big rock'n'roll hit arrives in 1954 with 'That's All Right' by Elvis, and yet the other hit parade stalwarts are such rockabilly rebels as Doris Day, Johnnie Ray, Vera Lynn, Rosemary Clooney and Winifred Atwell. Things don't improve much the following year, as Slim Whitman avoids ripping it up with 'Rose Marie' and antediluvian, nylon-haired future disc jockey Jimmy Young fails to mobilise a nation's disenfranchised youth with such riotous calls to arms as 'Unchained Melody' and 'The Man From Laramie'. There had to be a sense among the young that there was more to music than this.

In late 1955, after its use in the film *Blackboard Jungle*, 'Rock Around The Clock' hits the UK hit parade and the tipping point for rock'n'roll in Britain approaches. Reedy-voiced dustman progeny Lonnie Donegan has a smash with 'Rock Island Line' in early '56, having recorded it two years earlier, laying claim to being the first UK artist to make a rock'n'roll disc. Though it undoubtedly marks a turning point in the story of UK pop, I'm not persuaded that as a real rock'n'roll record it's fit for purpose. It is undoubtedly a rolling (mile)stone in UK pop history but it's still a skiffle record performed with a bit more bite. You could also argue that it couldn't be a rock'n'roll song as it was already a blues number made popular by Huddie Ledbetter, better known as Lead Belly due to his acute constipation.

Toothsome, bequiffed, loose-legged leprechaun Tommy Steele enters the fray in 1956 when 'Rock With The Caveman' charts. Steele, who gives very good Scrooge these days, can probably claim to be Britain's first rock'n'roll star and in fact may have a boast that no other UK recording artist can claim. Legend has it that he had a day out in London with Elvis. It is commonly accepted that Presley's only time on UK soil came at Prestwick Airport in 1960, but according to theatrical impresario Bill Kenwright, The King made a secret trip to the capital to hang out with young Tommy. Kenwright reveals that the two rock'n'rollers took in a trip to the Houses of Parliament, before presumably hooking up with Dick Van Dyke and some of his chimernee sweep mates for a good old Cockernee knees-up dahn at the Old Bull and Bush with a young Chas and Dave and The Krays. Or something. Kenwright's claims have proved hard to verify, as member of the Memphis mafia and tricky Scrabble hand Lamar Fike subsequently claimed it was he who flew to London to hang out with thumb-sized Tom, though it's hard to work out why unless he had been despatched by private jet from Graceland to pick up some jellied eels, mash and liquor to embellish one of Elvis's bumper baps.

In 1957 the rock'n'roll imports become a regular feature of the charts, as Elvis, Buddy Holly, Chuck Berry, Little Richard and Jerry Lee Lewis enjoy regular success – but where is the home-grown superstar who's going to galvanise the generation of disaffected young Englanders who are desperate to get swinging in readiness for the fast-approaching sixties? Who can we call on to outrage the fuddy-duddies and moisten a million pubescent gussets? Well, Ian 'Sammy' Samwell is sitting next to him on that bus.

'We had been playing at a pub called The Five Horseshoes in Hoddesdon,' says Sir Cliff Richard, generously taking time out from his hectic musical and wine-making schedule to chat to me from his Caribbean retreat, 'and Ian came in and said he liked what we were doing and he could play a bit of guitar.'

So it was that Samwell joined Cliff's pre-Shadows backing band The Drifters and we are very close to history being made.

Often, Cliff and his mates would ride into town to check out the skiffle scene on the celebrated coffee bar circuit revolving around The 2i's on Old Compton Street. Cliff was in fact a member of The Dick Teague Skiffle Group, where he met a fellow rock'n'roll enthusiast in drummer Terry Smart, leading to the formation of The Drifters. On one trip to the West End they carried their equipment into a booth at the back of the HMV shop on Oxford Street where bands could lay tracks down and have them pressed on the spot onto acetate discs, which they would then hawk around the record companies. Here Cliff and his mates cut the versions of 'Lawdy Miss Clawdy', made famous by Elvis, and Jerry Lee Lewis's 'Breathless' that got them that all-important audition with Norrie Paramor at EMI. And the song they played live in his office to clinch the deal? 'Move It', of course.

'Ian had written half of "Move It",' Cliff tells me in a post-tour croak. 'He completed it on the way into town on the 715A Green Line bus that went right through to Oxford Circus. Thirty-eight years later he sent me the second verse but now when I do it Bruce Welch (The Shadows' rhythm guitarist) says to me, "You shouldn't sing the new verse 'cos people remember that old verse that you sang twice".'

I ask Cliff if he thought it was a great number on first hearing.

'Oh, definitely,' he replies immediately. 'I thought I was starting with something that sounds like a classic rock'n'roll song and it has become that.'

We're agreed on that, but what about my theory that it marks the beginning for rock'n'roll in the UK? Cliff acknowledges the groundwork laid by Lonnie Donegan, Terry Dene and Tommy Steele, though he says that he never really considered the latter to be a real rock'n'roll singer as he was more of 'a theatrical performer, which he became'. That must mean that I'm right then, eh, Sir Cliff?

'I really do believe that "Move It" was the first rock'n'roll record made outside America.'

Thank you. I rest my case.

'In fact,' he continues, despite sounding in need of a bit of the old Buttercup Syrup, 'when I first met Hank and Bruce they thought I was American.'

Which leads us to the inevitable comparisons with Elvis.

'Elvis had a sensuality that the press latched on to. The movements that he did – hip swinging and stuff. Then those of us who came after were called "Britain's answer to Elvis" and there wasn't one. He was unanswerable. I learned that really quickly and I thought, I can't afford to be just another copy of Elvis, so I moved into ballads. But I never stopped singing rock'n'roll. And then the press said I had "smouldering eyes". I didn't know I had but when I read that I started to smoulder. I wasn't aware of smouldering before they said that.'

Once the classic line-up of The Shadows settled, Ian Samwell left the live stage to concentrate on composing. He would go on to have an illustrious writing and production career with, among others, The Small Faces, Dusty Springfield, Grateful Dead, Frank Zappa and Joni Mitchell. He passed away in 2003 but his classic song lives on.

'I've sung it at pretty much every concert since the day I recorded it,' rasps Cliff, who must be very glad he's not recording today with his throat the way it is. 'I've got one or two songs that could be rated as classic pop rock records: "Devil Woman", possibly "We Don't Talk Anymore" and definitely "Move It". Anyone could sing them, but I got them first.'

Life for Cliff Richard changed the day Ian 'Sammy' Samwell walked into The Five Horseshoes. 'But for that meeting,' he has said previously, 'I would still be Harry Webb, clerk.'

It was 1958 and the world was in many ways changing rapidly for everyone. Mr and Mrs Radcliffe got a new son and a new refrigerator. The first regular transatlantic flights began. The microchip was invented, although the introduction of parking meters would have more of a direct impact on the lives of Britons for some years yet. The Preston bypass was opened in December, becoming Britain's first stretch of motorway. This was indeed a sign of what the future held in store as it was closed for roadworks in January 1959. No matter, we had the net gains of jet planes, fast lanes, unlimited ice cubes and Cliff encouraging us to 'Move It'. The young ones were on the march and, though it would be some time yet before I would be aware of these seismic shifts, I had a pretty dramatic year myself as I swapped the security of the womb for the hustle, bustle and bright lights of downtown Farnworth. And we're off!

1959

THE DAVE BRUBECK
QUARTET – 'TAKE FIVE'

It's easy to forget now just how important jazz was in usher-
ing in a new world of possibilities in the fifties. I've never
been what you might call a committed jazz aficionado
though in my student days I was a regular visitor to city
centre jazz clubs in Manchester like The Band on the Wall.
Admittedly this was because they were the only places where
you could get a drink after ten-thirty at night, unless you
wanted to go to a swanky, neon and chrome-encrusted dis-
cotheque and pay five pounds for a glass of Harp lager while
being sneered at by Maltese businessmen.

And though being tempted by the cheap and seemingly
unrestricted supply of alcohol might seem a pretty lame
reason to be drawn to this twilight musical world, it often
seemed that many of the participating musicians were thinking the same way. They might have been keen to display
their instrumental gifts, but they were just as keen to get
sloshed. And in this regard they had some heavyweight role
models. The litany of drink and drug abuse in jazz is tragic
but nevertheless impressive. Some of the key names of the
genre had well-publicised battles with the booze and the
dope: Bix Beiderbecke, Billie Holliday, Art Blakey, Lester
Young, Charlie Parker, Dexter Gordon, Stan Getz, John

Coltrane, Chet Baker and Miles Davis to name but a few. Even cute old Louis Armstrong was once busted for the possession of marijuana, though you would have thought that toking on fat joints was a very poor choice of hobby for a professional trumpet player. But that seemed to be at least partially the point. These guys were the first group of musicians to live life with scant regard for their own health. They invented the rock'n'roll lifestyle before rock'n'roll had even been invented, and then once rock'n'roll came along decided they didn't like it much anyway.

So modern jazz represented a dark and dangerous shadowland that must have seemed deliciously tantalising for the hipsters, flipsters and finger-poppin' daddies of that time. How cool it would have been to be sitting alongside some skeletally beautiful Parisian ingénue in a fugged-up subterranean dive on La Rive Gauche, dressed in your matching polo-necks and nodding knowingly to the serpentine squalls of the smoky saxophone.

How close that scene seemed to my dad reclining in his Parker Knoll armchair in a cardigan whilst sipping a Dubonnet and listening to Dave Brubeck is hard to say. To be fair to him, though, the most celebrated figures in British jazz seemed a long way from the nefarious netherworld occupied by the American blotto bad boys of bebop as well. In England the big three, in terms of television appearances, were Kenny Ball, George Chisholm and Acker Bilk. All were very much exponents of trad jazz, which was vital in paving the way for skiffle and pop, but all seemed devoid of the remotest whiff of danger, though Ball looked like he might have enjoyed sinking a pint or two, which was presumably why he sweated so much and was – as all trumpeters performing 'When The Saints Go Marching In' seem to do – constantly mopping his over-moist face with a sopping handkerchief.

Kenny Ball and his Jazzmen went on to have major chart hits in the early sixties with such tunes as 'Midnight In Moscow', 'Casablanca' and 'Hello Dolly'. Successful as they were, they couldn't compete with West Country clarinet-toting crown prince Acker Bilk, who was the first Brit to hit number one on the Billboard charts in America with his 1961 classic 'Stranger On The Shore'. Bilk's trademarks were a bowler hat, goatee beard and gaudy waistcoat and, along with Ball and top turn of the trombone Chisholm, they were a staple of TV light entertainment.

But that was the problem. 'Proper' jazz didn't want to be part of the mainstream; it was designed to be an alternative to it. Certainly it was hard to imagine my grandma Doris being as pleased to see Miles Davis on *The Black and White Minstrel Show* on Saturday night television in the slot normally occupied by the Goon-ish Glaswegian George Chisholm. Why would they hire black artists anyway when they had a regular supply of white ones they could just apply face paints to?

The other reason why Miles Davis wouldn't have slotted easily into the format is that he would have insisted on playing an extended piece that might have taken several listenings before revealing to Doris, puffing on her Senior Service and rooting for Polo mints in her personal portmanteau, anything she might recognise as a tune. This was where the ground-breaking modern jazzers differed from their English cousins. Chisholm, Ball, Bilk and their ilk were all consummate musicians and, at time of writing, both Kenny and Acker are still on the road, which is a testimony to their skill and continuing popularity. But Miles and his mercurial monomaniacs dared to be different. Dared to make music that shattered the rules of what had gone before. Laudable though this was, it is the main reason why jazz has struggled to get coverage in the mainstream media. To most people, it's a tough listen. To be blunt, jazz is less popular these days because not many people like it. Even Jazz FM had to change its name so as not to scare people.

So, why don't people like it? Well, you would have to say that sometimes the musicians themselves are to blame. Basically, just as a group of downhill slalom Olympic skiers utilise all their dexterity at high speed to avoid any obstacle, so a group of jazzers often utilise all their dexterity at high speed to avoid any tune. They will also make this experience more painful by playing as many notes as possible in order to show off to each other. 1959 saw the first edition of *Juke Box Jury* on television, where a panel passed judgement on a series of pop records declaring each one to be either a 'hit' or a 'miss'. If it had been launched as 'Jazz Juke Box Jury' there wouldn't have been any 'hits'. There is nothing more certain than if you put four brilliant players in a room together they will, if left to their own devices, resort to mind-bending self-indulgence. Or, to give it its technical term: jazz rock, which skilfully manages to incorporate the worst bits of both genres. No wonder they have to have a late bar, eh?

The two foremost proponents of jazz rock have been the critically lauded groups Weather Report and the Mahavishnu Orchestra. Both boast musicians whose mastery of their instrument is not in question. The Report's Joe Zawinul, Wayne Shorter and Jaco Pastorius are legends of the piano, sax and bass. Mahavishnu's Jan Hammer and Billy Cobham's credentials as a keyboard player and drummer respectively are impeccable. Their leader John McLaughlin knows notes and chords on the guitar that haven't been invented yet. But can any of you hum me one of the big numbers of either band? How many times, outside of secure psychiatric institutions, has someone said out loud: 'What this party needs is a bit of jazz fusion to liven things up. Stick Mahavishnu's "*Between Nothingness and Eternity*" on, Baz, and crack open another Party Four'? Well, I've no entirely reliable statistics to answer that question but a rough estimate would be somewhere below the one mark.

We're all familiar with the old probability scenario of the monkeys and the typewriters and that if left alone long enough they will come up with the works of Shakespeare. Theoretically, this is not only possible but certain. Jazz is following a similar paradigm. If enough college-scholarship-trained musos make as much unlistenable, atonal din for an unspecified period, they will eventually come up with a song that someone might want to listen to. But in these greener days this seems wilfully wasteful. I mean, Chuck Berry just went into his bedroom with a guitar and three chords and wrote dozens of classic songs that formed the backbone of the rock'n'roll revolution. Much more environmentally sound. And anyway, isn't the chimps and the word processor scenario flawed? Even if they did come up with the works of Shakespeare, haven't the works of Shakespeare already been come up with? By Shakespeare?

Nevertheless, the coolest music of the late fifties is provided by the masters of American jazz and the coolest tune of them all is 'Take Five' by The Dave Brubeck Quartet from their *Time Out* album. Nineteen fifty-nine should be celebrated for the introduction of the Mini and Barbie and possibly this record. With its desperately hip abstract sleeve by Neil Fujita it was the first LP I can remember seeing in our house as a kid. It was stacked amongst my dad's classical discs and my mum's Andy Williams collection in the white melamine hi-fi cabinet, and seemed to hint at a happening scene somewhere in another world. I would later watch with nostalgia and glee as the same sleeve came to life in the video to the Donald Fagen song 'New Frontier'. 'Take Five' was written by Paul Desmond, who was the quartet's marvellously fluid saxophonist, and boasts a truly memorable tune over a restless 5/4 vamp. There's also a celebrated extended drum break by Joe Morello.

It seems simultaneously cool and yet engaging, effortless yet somehow forceful. I imagine if you were a hep-cat or beatnik inhabiting dimly lit, smoke-filled bars in a black-and-white striped T-shirt and black hipsters, it provided just the right soundtrack for the new Bohemia. And after hearing it, the bar would still have been open. The new world must have seemed so beguiling and seductive in those heady days. Sadly the dream would become tarnished and sullied as the realisation dawned that the bar was open late not only to avoid the audience being driven out into the cold night air by the contemporary cacophony, but also to enable the musicians to get so sloshed that avoidance of the tune would be, like the monkeys at the qwerty keyboard, a certainty.

1960

THE SHADOWS – 'APACHE'

The Fender Stratocaster is one of the 'big four' electric guitars. There are many design classics that would make it into a top twenty but, like the Premier League before Liverpool got a bit rubbish, there is an established big four: the Gibson Les Paul and SG, and the Fender Telecaster and Stratocaster. The Fenders are commonly abbreviated to the Tele and the Strat. The Gibsons are never abbreviated to the Les and the S. Don't ask me why, although it's probably to do with being cool. It sounds very hip to be 'picking up a Strat', less dashing to be 'strapping on a Les'. And be careful if you decide to Google that.

Every high-end guitar has a serial number and it is alleged that David Gilmour is the owner of Fender Stratocaster number 00001, manufactured in 1954. There are those who challenge this by saying there wouldn't actually be a number one as the serial numbers are created in a more complicated way than simple number ascendancy, but it doesn't really matter because the most important Strat in England has the serial number 34346. This was the first Strat in the UK and was ordered from the American catalogue, and paid for, by the king of rock'n'roll himself Cliff Richard for his bespectacled chum Hank Marvin.

It's pretty much impossible to overstate the influence of

Hank Marvin on guitarists, and indeed spectacle wearers. Plank spankers as varied as Mark Knopfler, Pete Townshend, Jimmy Page, The Edge, Brian May and Frank Zappa have all paid tribute to his trailblazing on the axe, as the guitar is sometimes known on account of its resemblance to ... errmm ... an axe. It's worth noting, however, that whilst it is theoretically possible to sharpen the edge of a 'Les' in order to chop logs, this is a time-consuming and expensive solution to the firewood conundrum. There is a cheaper, readily sharpened product on the market that is better suited to this purpose. It's called an axe.

But whilst more or less every 'axe-hero' has been inspired by Hank somewhere along the way, he's been less of a role model when it comes to stagecraft. Certainly when Townshend was windmilling his arms in a Kwik-Fit boiler suit and shattering guitars on Keith Moon's head, it seemed a very long way from little Hank with his big glasses and cheesy grin doing that funny little cross-step shuffle that was a central feature of The Shadows' live experience. In fact, aside from the exemplary playing, it was pretty much the only feature, although this was still one more than The Beatles had.

And let's not be too hasty in disregarding Hank's trademark glasses. Wearing cool specs in rock is a very difficult trick to pull off. The only people who have really managed it are Buddy Holly, Roy Orbison, Elvis Costello, John Lennon and Jarvis Cocker. Charismatic if occasionally cantankerous Captain Mainwaring-alike Elton John is probably pop's most celebrated spectacle wearer, but much as I admire his albums of the early seventies, you couldn't describe him as cool, could you?

I myself would have worn glasses for years had vanity not led me to one of those laser eye clinics. It was particularly annoying to be wearing specs when playing gigs with my group

The Family Mahone, as they were always steaming up and sliding down my nose. Due to the generous fortune of genetics my proboscis is of sufficient length to allow just about a song's worth of slippage, and thereby prevent the eyewear from clattering off my perspiring face and onto the drums. If there was an extended playout to the song I could usually play the kit with one hand whilst pushing the frames back up to the bridge area as, for the kind of music we play, one hand is often sufficient. I was reminded of this when an Irish group from Scotland, Snow Patrol, cancelled a string of gigs as their drummer had broken an arm. Having heard a lot of their music this seemed a feeble excuse, as surely playing the drums for Snow Patrol could be undertaken by someone with one arm. After all, that plucky lad with the shaggy perm seems to manage perfectly well in Def Leppard.

You may of course be asking why I had to wear glasses at all because, whatever the optimum number of limbs a drummer needs, he certainly doesn't need to see very far as he's only hitting things that are quite big and also quite close. My problem was that I am also the singer and, at my advancing age, can't remember the words. Indeed, I can't go to the shops for milk, bread and a paper without writing a list. Even this is not an infallible approach if you then forget where you put the list. So the words to the songs had to be printed out and placed on a music stand ... which I couldn't read without a little help from the Northwich branch of Specsavers.

So it was that I found myself lying under a laser in a clinic in South Manchester experiencing for the first time the smell of my burning corneas. No, really. They don't tell you about that. You actually lie there with the stench of your own smouldering eyeballs filling the air. It feels like you've taken quite a leap of faith at that point, I can tell you. The aftermath is even more alarming as you stumble around a waiting room with vision so blurred that not only can you not read

Woman's Realm, but you can't even see the table on which the illegible *Woman's Realm* is sitting.

Gradually, however, the mists begin to clear. The day after the operation I came out of the front door of the BBC on Oxford Road in Manchester. It was one of those bright, dry spring days that are such a feature of the Mancunian climate. Looking up the road I could see the Central Library about half a mile away and the Doric pillars of its familiar portico were standing there in perfect focus. It was quite a moment.

Of course, nothing lasts forever and my short-range vision is now pathetic. This means that the gig lyric sheet problem has resurfaced with all its attendant pitfalls. At one recent concert at the charmingly appointed Crown Hotel ballroom, Nantwich, I finished a slow song and introduced the following speedier number with the words: 'Right, back to the thrash metal.'

During the interval it was pointed out to me by one astute punter that it was pretty much impossible to say that convincingly while putting on your reading glasses.

If I'd just followed the lead of Hank, such embarrassments could have been avoided. That's the thing about Hank – he's iconic because of his playing *and* his unique look. That's why he's one of the very few real-life people who have become part of Cockney rhyming slang. If you're a barrow boy, or other occupation beloved of Londoners, like Manchester United supporter, and lunchtime is approaching you might well profess to be 'Ank Marvin, or starvin'. Other public figures to have had this honour similarly bestowed include Ruby Murray (curry), Pete Tong (wrong), Ayrton Senna (a tenner), Claire Rayner (a trainer) and, though I'm struggling to remember what he is rhyming slang for, Gary Glitter. Pint of bitter, was it?

The bonus of pulling off the spectacles thing, though, is that people generally assume you are intelligent. Like Brains off *Thunderbirds*. And in fact in the 1966 film *Thunderbirds are Go*, Cliff and The Shadows appear in marionette form playing at the Swinging Star Club. In puppet outer space! How cool is that? They've got little Strats and Vox amplifiers and everything.

What basically happens is that Alan Tracy, pilot of Thunderbird 3, escorts counter-espionage plywood posh totty Lady Penelope to this intergalactic nightspot where they encounter the highly strung miniature Cliff and The Shads doppelgängers. This is a big night for Alan as despite resembling the ideal location for a seventies porn film, Tracy Island offers few romantic opportunities for the red-blooded, foot-high wooden international crime fighter. In his puppet biography he is said to enjoy exploring the rocks and potholes around the island. Well, needs must I suppose, although Alan might be said to be better off than most of the Tracy clan when it comes to female attention. He has an admirer in Tin-Tin, the relatively hot-looking balsa daughter of the Tracys' faithful factotum Kyrano. Perhaps it's just as well, then, that Alan's big night with M'Lady turns out to be a dream when he falls out of his marionette bed.

In some part Alan's romantic flight of fancy was probably driven by a sense of inadequacy when compared to Scott and Virgil, who got to do most of the impressive assignments. Scott was always first on the scene in the speedy Thunderbird 1, whilst Virgil would be the backup heavy artillery with whatever pod of equipment they'd decided to attach to Thunderbird 2. Poor Alan, despite having a rocket with much cooler fins than T1, would then be despatched to sort of see that everything was going OK. Pretty demeaning work for a guy who's been to puppet Colorado University. Even so, he's probably better off than Gordon, whose job is to look after Thunderbird 4. Which is a submarine. That's restricting how many times you're going to be called out for a start, isn't it? You're really just hanging around hoping for international puppet terrorist threats of an aquatic nature, which are few and far between for obvious reasons. Marina from *Stingray* aside, how many puppets do you know who are good swimmers?

Having said that, you'd still rather be Gordon than poor old John Tracy stuck up in space in Thunderbird 5 on his own all the time. What he did for amusement and relaxation we're perhaps better not asking.

Brains, as his name suggests, was the brains of the outfit. Just like Hank in The Shadows. And if Brains kept the operation ticking over so that a generation of lads dreamed of becoming a Thunderbird, then Hank inspired the same generation to pick up the guitar.

1961

THE MARCELS – 'BLUE MOON'

So it's 1961 and there's all that shenanigans going on in the Bay of Pigs down Cuba way, The Beatles play at The Cavern for the first time, the farthing ceases to be legal tender and a rare foray into the deep south beckons for the intrepid Radcliffe clan.

The impact of the disappearance of the farthing I don't remember as having a massive impact on my life, but then I was only three and would not have foreseen the gradual removal of the classic pre-decimal pocket-money stalwarts that I would come to depend on, such as the ten-shilling and pound notes, the half-crown, the two-shilling piece, the six-pence and the thrupenny bit. So beloved were the pre-decimal coins that they pretty much all had nicknames. The thrupenny bit was referred to as a 'joey', a sixpence was a 'tanner', a shilling was known universally as a 'bob' and a two-shilling piece was a florin. Combinations of these would weigh down the pockets of my grey shorts for years to come, with a genuine threat of exposing myself after birthdays or Christmas, when the tonnage of shrapnel tested fully the resolve of the elasticated waistband.

Really, readers who have known only decimal currency will have no idea of the weight small boys were forced to haul around. It was practically child labour. I may have been born a generation or so late enough to avoid being press-ganged into the navy or forced up chimneys, but I still had to laboriously tramp around town in search of sweet shops with a 'penny tray', bowed down with coinage weighing a couple of hundredweight (or 'cwt', to use its wilfully perverse abbreviation).

The one area of underage exploitation that was fully in place throughout my childhood, and was directly related to currency, was 'Bob-A-Job' week. Finally abolished as recently as the late nineties, this was a period around Easter where Scouts and Wolf cubs were forced to trudge the streets in search of gruelling manual work in return for a shilling per task. Occasionally this would lead to an attractive, cheerful, lonely or bored, negligee-wearing housewife with an elaborate blonde demi-wave getting you to rake the fire grate out before plying you with cherryade and macaroons. But more often than not it would entail slaving for several hours cutting back a briar patch that had last seen secateurs sometime around the Crimean War, while some brown-toothed battle-axe in a nylon housecoat and fluffy slippers looked on sternly whilst puffing on a Park Drive. And all for a shilling which was then sunk into Scout funds to pay for new pennants on sticks that you could hit Brownies over the head with at church parade.

Of course, I was a mere thirty-six months old and so wouldn't be directly involved in this barbaric nonsense for a few years yet, but it all began in 1961 with the disappearance of the farthing. It was a tiny coin with a cute wren on the 'tail' side and was worth a quarter of a penny. Or about 0.1p in new pence. That might not sound a lot, but in those days it was enough to get you a cup of beef tea at a league football match, a quarter of floral gums or even perhaps an offcut of tripe.

At this point in my life I was actually living in London, as my dad had taken a job as assistant editor of the *John O'London's Weekly* review. Founded in 1919, this august publication was an unashamedly high-brow literary monthly which had boasted contributions in the past from the likes of W. Somerset Maugham, Max Beerbohm, Winston Churchill and Arnold Bennett. It had a regular section devoted to grammar and common usage. *Nuts* magazine it wasn't. When it finally closed the editor Webster Evans declared: 'People prefer to read trash.' And the tabloid press was born.

We were living in a small, rented flat in Finchley on the corner of the millionaire's row called Bishop's Avenue where Lakshmi Mittal and the Sultan of Brunei currently have modest pieds-à-terre. I've just had a look at what's on the market there now and there's a nice-looking, ten-bedroom family home for a mere 40 million pounds. Wow, in old money that's 38 billion farthings! Really, it is. I worked it out with a calculator.

Our small, dingy flat was in a small, dingy block at the end of this ludicrously priced boulevard and my very first memories stem from this brief London period. I recall going for tea with an old lady, whom my mum later told me was called Miss Cadwallader, in the flat above us with its tall dresser stacked with willow pattern china. I was taken to see the Trooping of the Colour but remember preferring to mount my own military spectacle by sailing matchsticks in a puddle. I can honestly say I could taste the fog in the park as I walked alongside my parents, who were carrying a roll of linoleum observed by darting squirrels. These are my earliest recollections and remain crystal clear. I also remember a song. A song with an opening that, once heard, no one could forget.

My father was a very big fan of the Marx Brothers and his enthusiasm for their unique blend of badinage and slapstick instilled a similar penchant for their capers in me. At some point I first saw their 1939 classic *At the Circus* and so must have heard the song 'Blue Moon' as it appears in that movie. Composed by musical heavyweights Richard Rodgers and Lorenz Hart for the 1934 *Manhattan Melodrama* starring Clark Gable and Myrna Loy, it was a popular song way before it received the 'doo-wop' treatment in the early sixties.

Doo-wop has its roots in a cappella singing and, though following a tradition that may well begin with Negro spirituals and barbershop, really came into its own in the late fifties and early sixties. Ghetto youth gangs, usually though not exclusively male, short of something to do and somewhere to go, would gather on the sidewalks of New York and other major American cities and teach themselves to sing in harmony. This may be the only recorded example in the history of the human race of something useful coming out of kids hanging around on street corners. What a quaint and cosy vision of gang culture that conjures up. How delightful to get yourself lost in the mean streets of the Bronx and to happen upon a posse of hoodlums who, instead of threatening you with a flick-knife and demanding your wallet and mobile phone, would serenade you with a medley of the greatest hits of The Inkspots. Without groups like this there would have been no Smokey Robinson and The Miracles, Temptations, Four Tops and Drifters, and pop would have been all the poorer for that.

Of course, it took me a while to realise this. When I was young I used to get incensed at combos like The Stylistics, who would clog up *Top of the Pops* with their simpering falsettos and matching salmon-pink spangly jerkins. The bastards. There I was, glued to the screen, waiting for either a 'proper' band like Status Quo or Deep Purple, or the mercifully underdressed dance troupe Pan's People. Five cheaply clothed, clumsily choreographed clowns doing synchronised hand gestures and singing 'Betcha By Golly, Wow' just didn't have the same galvanising effect on the adolescent psyche.

One of their dirges was titled 'Na Na Is The Saddest Word'. Well, apart from anything else, it's just not true. I can think of lots of words that are sadder than 'Na Na': misery, lonely, penniless, homeless, 'ladies and gentlemen, please welcome The Stylistics'. All of these words would make you feel sadder than 'Na Na'. And is 'Na Na' even a real word anyway? Or is it two words? And if it is, the title of the song becomes a grammatical nightmare. Hadn't these chaps ever read *John O'London's*? Webster Evans must have been turning in his grave.

The Stylistics were a Pennsylvanian outfit, hailing from Philadelphia, as were The Marcels, who came from Pittsburgh. They took the Rodgers and Hart ballad 'Blue Moon' and gave it the full throttle doo-wop treatment, creating one of the most memorable openings to a song ever as Fred Johnson's bass voice springs into life with the immortal opening refrain which goes something like:

Bam-be-de-bam-de-bom-de-bom-bom-de-de-bam-de-
de-bam-de-bum-de-dum-bum-de-de-
bubbybombom-Blue Moon.

In fact, these vocal soundings are central to the whole ethos of the genre, which takes its name from the 'doo-wop, doo-wah' backing vocal motif that crops up in literally hundreds of records.

That song would have been one of the songs of my early life and I would think fondly enough of it if that was the only time it had touched me. How wonderful, then, in later life to have stood on the terraces at Maine Road, urging on Manchester City as forty thousand of us bellowed the same song, adopted as an anthem for our boys in sky blue and sung at all our games to this day as we implore our band of plucky international multimillionaires to do it for Sheikh Mansour and the lads. I assume the club has now bought the rights to the song. We appear to be in the process of buying pretty much everything else including, one hopes, the Premier League title. Hey, don't blame us. We didn't put it up for sale.

So 'Blue Moon' is a song close to my heart. It's part of my life now, and it was a massive hit at the time I was living in London as a toddler. But here's a bit of a family mystery. I've checked the dates from this period with my dad because, though I was a bright three-year-old and was reading the literary reviews in my cot nightly, taking particular interest in the grammar and usage sections, I couldn't be entirely sure on timelines. It was 1961, The Marcels were on the wireless and my father was assistant editor of *John O'London's*. Looking up some background on this publication I was surprised to learn that it closed in 1954. So where was he going every day? I can only assume that he was in fact working for MI5, but there's no point asking him because he'll have signed the Official Secrets Act, won't he?

CHUBBY CHECKER – 'LET'S TWIST AGAIN'

The twist was one of those dance crazes that took the world by storm, not least because it involved movements that blokes could do as well. I don't care what anybody says, men are not genetically programmed to dance properly. Be honest, when you see those marvellously lithe, athletic, male ballroom dancers with their silky blouses slit to the navel, thrusting their perfectly rounded arses out in those weird high-waisted trousers, your admiration is combined with the feeling that it's just not right somehow. A man just doesn't naturally feel comfortable wiggling his hips and grinning like an imbecile with freshly pomaded hair. You have to decide to do it, and embrace a whole new set of rules as to what masculinity entails.

I was once asked to be a contestant on *Strictly Come Dancing* and it astonishes me now that I actually considered it. That I even thought for one second that I might be able to pull off the paso doble in tight Lycra is as horrifying as it is preposterous. I'm full of admiration for the guys who can go on and master it, but I know now that it could never be me. Firstly, I would never remember the steps. Secondly, I would look a cretin in the skimpy chemises and spray-on pantaloons. Thirdly, I wouldn't be able to conceal my contempt for the feeble jokes of doddering dance-hall fancy-dan Bruce

Forsyth. Mainly, though, I couldn't do it because I couldn't convince myself it was the right thing to be doing. It just seems like something that should be left to women.

And yet, I know I'm wrong. Whilst staying at a hotel in Carlisle recently I slipped into the ballroom where elderly couples were taking a spin round the sprung dance floor. They were moving with a stately, slow elegance that seemed to hark back to an age of greater gentility and refinement, and I was struck by the loveliness of it all. All the women had put on their best frocks and jewellery and were wearing sparkly shoes they'd brought just to dance in. The men, too, boasted a smattering of cummerbunds, bow ties and patent pumps. Even the old chaps with impressive beer bellies and Bri-Nylon-shrouded man boobs seemed to achieve a certain light-footed grace. I was so taken with it all I might just have been tempted to join in had I not been short of a partner, ignorant of all the steps, and wearing full hiking kit due to being on a walk across Hadrian's Wall. Lengthways, before you ask. I only mention this as that very question was put to me on my return by a mate of mine called Taxi Mike. It is worth bearing in mind, however, if you want to say you have walked Hadrian's Wall but are short of time. I have walked it lengthways and it was eighty-four miles and took me just under a week. Up by Housesteads Fort you can walk across the wall instead. It is a distance of a few feet and will take you about ten seconds and you will still, technically, have 'walked Hadrian's Wall'.

My generation seem to have been the first where the male of the species was not expected to know how to dance. Certainly my dad and my grandfathers knew the basics of ballroom and wouldn't have had any trouble in that department when taking a girl out dancing. These days, people don't even bother learning any proper steps when they're having the first dance at their own wedding. They just hold on to each other for safety, cringing with embarrassment as everyone watches them swaying slightly ahead of the beat as the DJ spins 'Three Times A Lady' or 'The Lady In Red' or something else with 'Lady' in the title (though probably not 'The Lady Is A Tramp'). My wife and I were so traumatised by the thought of this public display of incompetence that we had folk dancing at our wedding with a caller to tell you what to do. This meant we were joined on the floor by several couples, as all of these folk dances involve swapping partners, having their origins in the lively swinging scene of the Middle Ages when stinky serfs would toss their turnips into the middle of the hut before heading off to the old straw mattress with a different whiffy wench.

My earliest attempts at dancing with a girl were untutored but at least spirited. Hilary Wardle and I would hold one hand at the end of an outstretched arm whilst shaking our bushy mops of hair wildly until our heads were in danger of falling off. Not quite the American Smooth, admittedly, but that dance is notoriously unsuited to 'Fireball' by Deep Purple anyway.

Growing up on rock music in its various sub-genres meant that organised dancing with recognised moves just didn't exist. There was 'headbanging' and that was it. On Saturday nights I would often join the crush in the seatbelt-free Fiat 500 belonging to Chris Ecob's girlfriend Susan and make the trip over the moors to the since mythologised Wigan Casino. However, I didn't go to execute the backdrops and twirls of the Northern Soul aficionado, but to flail my mullet to Motorhead or Slaughter & The Dogs. After the band had gone off at around ten-thirty, the lights would come up, the bar would close, and roll-up puffing, greasy-haired mugwumps would sweep the dance floor clear of Newcastle Brown bottles, Embassy Regal packets and saturated beer mats as we filed sweatily down the narrow staircase before stumbling out into the starchy Lancashire air. There to greet us, in their baggy trousers with a change of shoes and vest in their Adidas holdalls, would be the massed ranks of the Northern Soul army. How it wasn't a pitched battle every week I'll never know. I would always see soul boys I was on chummy terms with at school and though we barely acknowledged each other in those situations, as that would have been highly inflammatory, I think it must have dissipated the sense of threat somehow. Also, I think that secretly we leather and denim macho-uniformed rockers knew that in a fight, the soul lads would be harder, even though they were wearing effeminate knitwear.

Later on I began to regret that I hadn't participated in the Casino's 'All-Nighter' scene as I came to love the music, once I grew up sufficiently to be able to drop my rock tribalism, and would have liked to be able to do at least one dance properly. However, the Northern Soul dance floors I did witness seemed to be full of people dancing largely by themselves or in large groups of men. This seemed to be missing out on the main purpose of being able to dance, beyond losing yourself in the sounds, which was to feel more comfortable with, and even possibly impress, girls. Hip-hop dancing would seem to suffer from the same problem. It's all very impressive in an Olga Korbut sort of way, but it's very difficult to chat someone up when you're spinning on your head. Unless she's doing the same, and even then it's going to be a snatched conversation each time your face whizzes past hers.

Perhaps this explains the popularity of line dancing. Blokes feel more comfortable when the women are restricted to the same few prescribed moves, thereby limiting their natural grace. Once you've got that slapping the back of your heel and waving an imaginary lasso, you're pretty much there. My only observation is that when I see people doing it, they don't appear to be having a lot of fun. They look rather like soldiers on the parade ground, terrified of putting a foot wrong. And it's still no good for getting closer to women, as you're constantly turning round and staring at the backs of their heads. For most men, having females turn their backs on you can be achieved without the need to learn any dance steps.

There have been other organised group dances. 'The Birdy Song', by the presciently named Tweets, which involved some feverish 'bingo wing' flapping, and Black Lace's 'Agadoo' with its attendant pineapple pushing, whatever that might be, were guaranteed floor-fillers for all mobile discos. You have to ask yourself, though, do you really want to try and strike up a conversation and fledgling relationship with a woman who will be seen in public dancing to music like that?

A better one was The Gap Band's 'Oops Upside Your Head', which despite appearing to make little sense to the keen English student, involved a long seated line being formed in which girls you didn't know would sit between your splayed legs and grind away to the beat. Well, it was a start, wasn't it?

My only other close association with a communal dance came during the punk era, when I became no less useless at the pogo than any other numpty. This was primarily because it consisted of jumping up and down. It has yet to make an appearance on *Strictly Come Dancing*. I guess you had to be there, but when joined by a couple of hundred like-minded souls in front of a stage stalked by The Clash or The Damned or The Heartbreakers it felt utterly euphoric. Of course, unlike the Viennese Waltz the pogo is a dance that you can't continue into middle and indeed old age, as my new-wave chum Jamie realised when he found himself a few years ago springing up and down at a gig by The Lurkers dressed in his office suit and holding his briefcase.

During the course of one of my radio programmes I had an email from a teenage lad on his birthday asking if I had any advice for a fifteen-year-old, so I asked the listeners if they could oblige. Almost immediately came a response from a thirty-something woman with three suggestions that seemed to make perfect sense: smell nice, don't be afraid to ask out the prettiest girl, and learn to dance. These were things, it seemed to me, that every adolescent should know. Even the cheapest aftershave is a preferable aroma to teenage perspiration; the most attractive women often receive fewer offers as blokes assume they've got no chance (which they probably haven't, but you never know); and your ability to acquit yourself on the dance floor with some aplomb is going to come as a nice surprise to any partner at some point, isn't it?

The Twist was one of those rare dances that didn't require a lot of skill, but could be done as a couple, as you were at least facing each other. The moves, which were open to personal interpretation, were roughly akin to wiggling your toes from side to side as if on wet sand whilst simultaneously drying your back with a beach towel. In the early sixties it was a global phenomenon and the soundtrack was provided by Chubby Checker.

Chubby Checker was a gentleman from Philadelphia called Ernie Evans who took on his portly stage persona in homage to the similarly broad in the beam Fats Domino. His first hit came in 1961 with 'The Twist', which he then followed up with 'Let's Twist Again' and 'Slow Twistin'' in 1962 before unleashing 'Twist It Up' the following year. The keen-eyed amongst you may notice a pattern emerging there. However, if you're about to dismiss Chubby as a bit of a one-twist pony you're ignoring his album output, which included *Twist With Chubby Checker, For Twisters Only, Let's Twist Again, Twistin' Round The World, For Teen Twisters Only,*

Don't Knock The Twist, Your Twist Party and *It's Pony Time.*
Where this pony thing came from I have no idea, though one
can't imagine his manager being thrilled at the sudden out-
break of equestrian enthusiasm.

To be fair to The Chubster, he did also make a folk and a
psychedelic record as well as some ill-advised limbo-related
waxings before returning to the charts in 1975 with a reissue
of 'Let's Twist Again'. He then joined forces with others
who shared his 'glandular problems' when he hooked up
with The Fat Boys in 1988 to bring us 'The Twist (Yo
Twist)', milking the cash cow into the hip-hop period.

And though *It's Pony Time* has yet to enjoy a significant
artistic reappraisal we have a lot to thank Chubby for. Not
only did he popularise a dance everybody could do, but he
became one of the very few fat pop stars. This is still a touchy
subject as, despite Checker's best efforts, if you want to be a
'proper' rock star, you have to be thin. I know this sounds
cruel, but if you're thinking of getting into it, it is worth
bearing in mind. When you're young it doesn't appear to be
much of a problem, but as you get older, if you want to
remain convincing as a real rock'n'roller you will have to be
either very fortunate genetically or exist on very little food.
The rocking paunch is never, ever a good look. I know there
will be those who accuse me of irresponsibility here in an age
of rampant eating disorders, and I would defend myself by
saying I'm talking thin and not skeletal, but it is just one of
those things. Jockeys can't be fat either, and no one slags
them off for not being 'good role models'. Rock stars also get
a hard time because they're often no strangers to drugs (and
this might well help them to remain skinny). But they're
hardly glamorising sticking a needle in your arm, are they?
Enough of them have died doing heroin and it's hard to see
how they could warn more effectively about the dangers of
drugs than by dying. How does that glamorise narcotics? It's

like saying the portrayal of cancerous lungs on cigarette packets is glamorising smoking.

No, if you want to be a rock star, like David Bowie or The
Rolling Stones, be prepared to be hungry a lot of the time.
Richard Ashcroft of The Verve was once reputed to eat a
small can of ravioli every other day. He's now a well-adjusted,
happily married family man. But he's still thin. He's worked
at it all his life and if you don't think you have this kind of
dedication and discipline, choose another career. Pub landlord, sumo wrestler or proprietor of a fetid caravan selling
cheeseburgers in lay-bys are all occupations in which a degree
of heftiness is positively encouraged. You'd have to be suspicious of a skinny publican, wouldn't you? If I want to see thin
people I'll go to the gym. When I go to the pub I want to
drink guilt free, which means seeing people working there
who are much fatter than I am.

Things may change in the future, of course. Genetic engineering would seem to suggest that it will soon be possible to
buy a footballer with a couple of spare legs. This would seem
to be a perfectly sensible way forward and presumably can't
come soon enough for Fernando Torres – if you're going to
pay upwards of 25 million pounds for a striker then a million
or so for a couple of stand-by limbs would seem to be a no-
brainer. Though it will probably be feasible to order another
one of those as well. And so one can foresee a time when a
rocker will be able to have a spare torso to ensure slenderness
in perpetuity.

In the meantime, size matters. Basketball players have to be
tall, although what the point in basketball is I'm not really
sure. The players are very tall and put a ball in a basket that is
very high up. What's the point in that, then? You might as
well have a professional getting-stuff-off-the-top-shelf at WH
Smith's league.

And dwarves have to be small. You can't take the kids to

the panto and see Snow White attended upon by seven strapping rugby players. Dwarves are, in fact, I'm reliably informed, in rather short supply for seasonal theatre. My sister-in-law Victoria produced a pantomime at Radlett in Hertfordshire and was unable to afford the going rate; she had to make do with kids, cushions up the tabards and the old whiskers and spirit glue. This seems rather unfair to me. Surely a dwarf should be cheaper than a full-sized actor at that time of year. When I go and buy my Christmas tree I pay by the foot.

At the time of writing Chubby Checker is still on tour and will be twisting on stage somewhere as you read this. That's good to know, isn't it? Way to go, big man!

1963

PETER, PAUL AND MARY –
'PUFF THE MAGIC DRAGON'

In 1963 the vilified Dr Richard Beeching presented his brilliant plan for the future of the railways by recommending closing almost half of the nation's stations and decommissioning around four thousand miles of track. These swingeing cuts were not only unpopular but also failed to deliver the required savings as the plan hinged on travellers used to hopping on at their local stations getting in their cars and boarding at larger terminals. Quite evidently, if you get in your car you're more likely to stay in it and just drive to where you're going. Especially in those days when rush hours in most town centres consisted of a couple of Morris Oxfords, a van delivering ink for fountain pens, a rag and bone man on a horse and cart and three gents on bicycles tipping their trilbies to promenading ladyfolk.

Nowadays, of course, the government will do anything to dissuade you from taking your car into a city centre – unless it's a Toyota Pious – especially if you're the owner of a four-wheel-drive vehicle. This group of motorists are charged more road tax and higher congestion charges than drivers of other cars, and are constantly lambasted for their non-environmentally friendly habit. Except when it snows, when they're expected to act as an extra emergency service.

Of course if Beeching hadn't decimated the rail network we might not need cars at all now, although in the interests of balance, let's not forget the eminent doctor's achievements. Since 1963 was also the year of the 'Great Train Robbery', there had to be a far lower chance of this ever happening again if there was a lot less railway to do it on. Well, so far so good.

If Dr Beeching had been in charge of the Isle of Wight he'd have probably axed the narrow-gauge railway and its celebrated steam engine *Puffing Billy*. Thankfully it was there for a young Londoner called Edward White to see when he went on his holidays in the forties and fifties. He would later go on to become an admired composer of light classical music and perhaps his most celebrated composition was named after the huffing and chuffing little locomotive he recalled so fondly. His other big number was called 'The Runaway Rocking Horse', which seems a tricky concept to grasp as by the very nature of being on rockers the nag's capacity for running anywhere would appear to be limited. 'Puffing Billy', on the other hand, was a piece of music which would instil a sense of glee in a generation of young-sters as it was the familiar theme tune to *Children's Favourites* on the BBC Light Programme.

Broadcast on a Saturday morning at nine, it was presented by Derek McCulloch, universally known as Uncle Mac, later inspiring the nickname of the lead singer of Echo and The Bunnymen. The show would be renamed *Junior Choice* after the launch of Radios 1 and 2 and would be hosted from 1968 by the venerable Ed 'Stewpot' Stewart, one of only three radio presenters to adopt an item of kitchenware as part of their stage name, the other two being 'Diddy' David Baking Tin and Ken 'Rolling Pin' Bruce. Oh, and Mary Anne Hob(b)s.

Children's Favourites really was an appointment to listen for millions of kiddies as it was one of the very few programmes on radio or television that acknowledged our existence at all, let alone catered specifically to us. Given the great leap forward in televisual entertainment for the young that has brought us the luxury of constant *Hannah Montana*, it's hard for my kids to think of a world in which you would get an hour of worthy *Blue Peter*-style programming before the early evening news and a short puppet show at lunchtime as part of the daily 'Watch with Mother' slot.

For many years the weekly schedule of these remained unchanged. On Mondays we got the dull one out of the way with *Picture Book*, which basically consisted of a posh lady with elaborate coiffure reading stories whilst a bolted-together dachshund called 'Sausage' bounced around a bit. The ante was upped a bit on Tuesday when Andy Pandy, Looby Loo and the imaginatively named teddy 'Teddy' entertained us, passing the baton on to Bill and Ben the Flowerpot Men on Wednesday. Thursday brought woodland adventures with Rag, Tag and Bobtail, a hedgehog, mouse and rabbit, before the week was rounded off with *The Woodentops*. A traditional farming family, they were a kind of visually realised, and only marginally more wooden, version of mystifyingly popular radio sacred cow-pat *The Archers*. These programmes might not sound like much, but they were actually well written, told credible stories and had engaging characters, which explains why *Andy Pandy* and *Bill and Ben* were later remade, with no strings attached. And let's not forget that 1963 was the year *Doctor Who* was launched as well. Not that I've ever been a fan. Let's be honest, the Daleks were a pretty unintimidating foe. If under attack from a Dalek then just nip upstairs and there's very little it can do, as a Dalek climbing a staircase is about as likely as a rocking horse running away. Unless, of course, your house has a Stannah stairlift, in which case you're in trouble.

The songs played regularly on *Children's Favourites* are still available today on CDs bearing the programme's catchphrase 'Hello, Children Everywhere', and I daresay you can download them onto your My First iPod or Early Learning Centre MP-3 player. They included such classics as 'Nellie The Elephant', 'The Laughing Policeman', 'Right Said Fred', 'The Big Rock Candy Mountain', 'Teddy Bears' Picnic', '(How Much Is) That Doggie In The Window?' and a smattering of hymns just to make sure we didn't get too carried away. The idea of an hour's unadulterated fun was deemed far too decadent and 'All Things Bright And Beautiful' being slipped into the playlist would remind the youngsters of the dangers of moral turpitude. In my time at Radio 1 I did suggest this as a production note to Westwood, him being a bishop's son and all, but he doesn't seem to have taken any notice.

There were also songs that seemed, well, just weird. An extended piece called 'Sparky's Magic Piano' told of a lad whose keyboard could talk to him. 'Little Red Monkey' by Jimmy Edwards, Dick Bentley and Joy Nichols remains so deeply, deeply strange that I have found it even more unsettling in adulthood. It makes 'The Singing Ringing Tree' seem like Fifi and the Flowertots. There are those who maintain that some of these apparently innocent songs actually contain veiled references to recreational drug use, which leads us on to 'Puff The Magic Dragon'.

Written by room-mates Pete Yarrow and Leonard Lipton at Cornell University it has its origins in a poem called 'Custard the Dragon' by Ogden Nash. It became a huge hit when recorded by Yarrow with Paul Stookey and Mary Travers as Peter, Paul and Mary. Though consistently denied by the writers, there are just too many possible allusions to drugs for the denial to ring true for many people. 'Chasing the dragon' is a heroin-related phrase that has passed into common usage. Having a 'puff' on a joint became a common experience for many people in the early sixties. A spliff needs rolling and Puff's human friend is Little Jackie Paper, which you would have to say does seem an unusual name. Of course, the song is unarguably about loss of innocence, but you could construe that taking mind-bending narcotics for the first time represents exactly that. And the whole thing does seem curiously hallucinogenic.

Look, I can only take Pete Yarrow at his own word and it's worth remembering that as the counterculture gained momentum, the Establishment became obsessed with finding just these sorts of hidden messages within popular songs that might corrupt the world's impressionable youth. The Byrds' classic description of the joys of aeroplane travel 'Eight Miles High' fell foul of the authorities. 'High' had to mean under the influence of something, didn't it? Well, possibly or possibly not, though with David Crosby in the band you'd have to have some sympathy with the powers that be. Jefferson Airplane's 'White Rabbit' was subjected to similar scrutiny, which hardly seemed fair as any dubious imagery was gleaned from *Alice in Wonderland* and you'd have to work pretty hard to find druggy allusions in something as innocent as a caterpillar smoking a hookah sitting on an edible mushroom that makes you feel as if you've changed size.

If you look at pictures of Peter, Paul and Mary now it's hard to think of them as leading figures of the hippy scene. Peter and Paul look like two lanky, geeky, sober-suited relatives of Basil Fawlty flanking the virginal blonde ingénue Mary. However, they were scenesters. They had emerged from the louche yet radicalised Greenwich Village coffee house scene and had scored – no pun intended – a massive hit with 1963's definitive protest song, Bob Dylan's 'Blowin' In The Wind'. Other classic records of that year included The Cascades' 'Rhythm Of The Rain' and Roy Orbison's

'In Dreams', but truly great as these were, they harked back to doo-wop and the dawn of rock'n'roll. Peter, Paul and Mary were looking to the future. Their apparently innocuous image had to mean there was something subversive going on behind the scenes, right? For a start, there were two blokes and one woman and many people took that as evidence of some kind of debauched *ménage à trois*. After all, these were permissive times and, when you start to look closely, they were all at it: Jimmy Edwards, Dick Bentley and Joy Nichols; Bill, Ben and Little Weed; Andy Pandy, Teddy and Looby Loo. Come on, you're not trying to pass that off as coincidence, are you? It was the swinging sixties, for goodness' sake, though it's hard for me to be absolutely certain what was going on as I was listening to 'All Things Bright And Beautiful' at the time.

1964

THE ANIMALS – 'THE HOUSE
OF THE RISING SUN'

1964 was a big year for the pop aficionado as not only did Radio Caroline start to broadcast from a disintegrating Danish passenger ferry anchored off Felixstowe, but *Top of the Pops* was transmitted from a disintegrating church hall anchored off Oxford Road in Manchester.

Radio Caroline was named with obvious logic after John F. Kennedy's daughter, as America's first family could often be found taking flotilla holidays on the limits of Britain's territorial waters in rusting Scandinavian tugboats. A revolution in radio, it presented a pop programming challenge to the pre-existing Radio Luxembourg, a curious station that had been set up in the twenties to broadcast military-music concerts to the Grand Duchy's avid militaristic hordes and, because of its geographical position, had accidentally been heard by most of Europe. Well, kind of. How well I remember sitting by the bay window of my parents' house in Albert Road, Bolton, on Tuesday nights in the early seventies to listen to the UK Top 30 rundown with my mate Roger Milne. We were obsessed with the charts and used to write that week's listings down in a little notebook in a futile attempt to give ourselves some cachet at school the next day – while I was never going to score a hat-trick for the football team, I did know that The Strawbs had gone in at number twelve. Bizarrely, accumulating just this kind of seemingly pointless trivia has turned out to be a lot more useful to me throughout my working life than anyone could possibly have predicted. And where's the star striker of the football team now, eh? Well, he's a leading barrister and QC, but you know where I'm coming from.

. The ongoing challenge in accumulating this vital information, though, was the notoriously unreliable Luxembourg signal. You could just be poised, Cratchit-like, propelling pencil in hand, to inscribe the all-important top three into the ledger when the DJ's voice would disappear into the ether. Nightmare scenario. The system we devised to minimise the risk of this happening was that we would take turns to act as chief clerk while the other held the transistor radio up to the window in order to be able to hop from one foot to the other if the signal became crackly, as wiggling the apparatus about usually made the programme audible again. That way we could be sure that Lieutenant Pigeon's 'Mouldy Old Dough' had indeed hit the top spot. How could you have slept otherwise?

Naturally, as a six-year-old I was still far more concerned with *Children's Favourites* than pirate radio, and much more engaged with another new television programme called *Play School* than *Top of the Pops*. However, the one song that you couldn't really avoid was 'House Of The Rising Sun', the origins of which are pretty much impossible to pin down for sure. Probably an old English folk song in its earliest incarnation, The Animals' organist Alan Price reckoned it had something to do with a Soho brothel of the sixteenth century. There are also numerous American versions dating from the 1930s onwards before it resurfaces on Bob Dylan's debut album. Its lineage then extends beyond the celebrated Animals version with an acid rock treatment released in 1969 by the Detroit band Frijid Pink.

The song's meaning is also hard to nail down. There's definitely some jiggery and indeed pokery that has gone on here. The talk of the 'ball and chain' would lead you to assume that the narrator, who can be male or female, Joan Baez having had a notable crack at it, is in prison after having committed a murder. Thankfully for Eric Burdon, lead vocalist of The Animals, the death penalty ceased to be enforced in the UK this very year so he could sing with impunity. Common consent, though, places the action firmly in a house of ill repute, possibly the one run in New Orleans by Madame LeSoleil Levant in the 1860s, if that's not a bit too convenient. However, the warning is clear for any young boy, you can easily get yourself in a lot of bother by knocking around knocking shops and knocking off women. Just ask Wayne Rooney.

Formed in Newcastle upon Tyne, The Animals are an interesting act in the history of British beat music. In fact, with their hard-edged sound and glowering looks, they could be said to be the first 'rock' as opposed to 'pop' band. They were certainly the first group I can remember seeing who you really thought you wouldn't like to meet in a dark alley. The Beatles were exciting but looked cuddly and cute. The Rolling Stones tried to snarl and sneer but couldn't disguise their inherent prettiness and you'd have fancied your chances in a fight as they were all tiny. The Kinks were modishly handsome and wore frilly shirts. The Hollies looked very chummy and seemed to lean towards a sort of hippy vibe, which was confirmed when Graham Nash left to embrace the Laurel Canyon scene in general and Joni Mitchell in particular. The Animals were different. They were called The Animals, for starters. Guitarist Hilton Valentine, drummer John Steel and Alan Price all had a twitchy, shifty look and would have been ideal to play weasels in a Brit-beat stage show of *The Wind in the Willows*. Lead singer Eric Burdon looked positively feral and resembled one of those blokes with the collar of their leather jacket turned up who smoked fags and took your money whilst riding the waltzer with effortless cool whenever the fair came to town. Bass player Chas Chandler had something of a baby face by comparison, though it would have been a risky gambit to regard him as a soft touch, as he was as big as the rest of the group put together. Chandler would in fact come to be an important figure in the story of rock, managing not only glam god-fathers Slade, but also discovering and looking after Jimi Hendrix. Musically The Animals had a real gritty edge, but they also proved you didn't have to be a male model to be in a successful band, and how grateful we were for that.

The original line-up of the group didn't last all that long as Price departed, financially secure thanks to his arrangement of their definitive version of 'House Of The Rising Sun'. In a rather unexpected turn of events Valentine and Burdon began to spend a lot of time in America, where they enthusiastically threw themselves into the counterculture both creatively and chemically. Valentine, who lives and plays in the States to this day, had started to take other 'paths to enlightenment' whilst still a member of The Animals. On one occasion they were in New York to play the prestigious Madison Square Garden, which, by the way, isn't in Madison, isn't square and isn't a garden. As the day wore on the other guys in the group became aware that Hilton hadn't been seen for a while. When he reappeared shortly before the biggest gig they'd ever played, it was clear to all that the North Shields guitarist had taken a puff on the magic dragon and maximised other recreational possibilities. Valentine later described playing a solo and seeing coloured stars cascade through the air every time he hit a certain note and so, with infallible logic, he just stayed on that note as it 'sounded great to me'.

★

That the early line-up of The Animals didn't last long doesn't matter. Their place in the ann(im)als of rock is assured. They had their 'moment in time'. And, in fact, the song with which they're most associated marks a moment in time for me too, as it was the first song I ever played in a group. If two of us counts as a group.

Jimmy Leslie was a chubby lad with unruly hair who shared my passion for pop and rock when we were at Bolton School in the late sixties and early seventies. Often we would find ourselves standing side by side in front of the stage when big lads from the sixth form performed with their bands at school discos. For years we would do this, as we wanted to be close enough to see how they were doing it, to understand how you made that noise happen. Other boys were obsessed with motorbikes and would strip the engines down and put them back together to see how they worked. We were just the same with bands. We broke them down into their constituent parts so we could build our own when the time came.

Jim lived in a small, meticulous semi up near a local lake called Doffcocker Lodge with his painter and decorator father and his petite, blonde mother who was, as were most of the mums I knew, a housewife. As Jim was an only child he not only had a large bedroom to himself, but also free run of the parlour, which was the downstairs front room used only when family came to tea. Here he kept his Eko Ranger 6 acoustic guitar and his Kemble upright piano. His dad, also called Jim, was a classical music and hi-fi buff and so there was the luxury of a top-of-the-range record player as well, with stereo speakers and everything.

One Sunday afternoon I put my snare drum and stand, hi-hat cymbal and a pair of hand-painted bongos that had been bought on holiday in Calella into the canvas bag I kept at home to use for my morning paper round and cycled up to

Jimmy's house. We set the basic drum kit up in the bay window, the bongos strapped to the snare drum with an elasticated belt, a stool with vinyl covering brought through from the kitchen, and sat down to play together.

This, as anyone who's ever been in a band will tell you, is a nerve-racking experience. You have dreamed of the moment and built up to it for so long that, like a first date or first kiss, you are petrified of it going wrong. Even now, and I formed my most recent band The Big Figures as recently as 2009, playing the first note of the first song together is something of a leap of faith. We had decided to try 'House Of The Rising Sun' because Jim knew it on the piano and I knew the words and figured that the rhythm was straightforward enough. As soon as we started to play together something really magical happened. For the first time you actually got to feel the joy of performing music with someone else. We grinned at each other in the way that musicians often do when appreciating the connection they've made. It really felt amazing. It was almost like losing your virginity. Look, I'm not trying to paint this as a Lennon and McCartney moment or anything, it's not like either of us went on to great musical careers, but for me, and I can only assume for Jim too, the world shifted slightly on its axis.

Over the next few weeks we invited others into our sanctum. And that was another great discovery. That a band was your own gang where you set the rules yourselves. Neither of us had had the skills to get into the football team and whilst I see now that Jim was something of a loner in some respects, I certainly didn't feel disenfranchised from mainstream school life. But this was our club designed specifically to make us feel special because it played to our strengths. So Andy Wright and Chris Ecob, later bass player and roadie, were made to stand in that small sitting room and admire the first moments of The Berlin Airlift, with guitarist Ross

Warburton only weeks away from making his own little dent in Bolton rock legend.

The life and times of The Berlin Airlift are well documented in my first book *Showbusiness: The Diary of a Rock'n'Roll Nobody* and so it would be daft to go through it all again here. But looking back at those two tousled teenage T. Rex fans, I realise that things were never quite the same for me again after that afternoon. Of course, there was every chance that if I hadn't forged that bond and formed a band with Jim, I'd have done it at some point with someone else. But that's how it did happen and seeing as music and bands have constituted pretty much my entire social life for the past thirty-five years, I think of this as a key point in my life, where I just knew I was on the cusp of something very special.

Rather like The Animals, the original line-up of The Berlin Airlift didn't stay together very long. It soon became apparent that Jim and I both wanted to be the leader of the band, and so he left to form Zwolff. Strangely, I would come to play with his new band whilst still leading the group we'd formed together as if, like doomed lovers, we could stay neither together nor apart.

We are apart now as, very sadly, Jimmy is no longer with us. The last time I saw him was in our thirties and he had gained a lot of weight and lost a lot of hair. Looking back on those schooldays now I begin to see how, despite The Animals' best efforts, he worked hard to morph himself into what we all thought a rock star should look like. He grew his fine, mousey-brown hair to shoulder length and, presumably through half starving himself, shed half his body weight. As a stocky lad he had endured the familiar jibes, and he didn't want to go through the same thing in public when he walked out on stage. Funnily enough, and I wonder now if this was connected to his determination to stay thin, I don't remember him drinking much. When the rest of us discovered cider and keg bitter, he abstained. Sad then that in later life he became a publican and, in what are by no means unique circumstances, once he made a late start on the booze he couldn't stop.

Sorting through some old photographs the other day I came upon the only one I have of Jim. He's four years old and standing in Trafalgar Square with a pigeon on his head. I find it sad looking at that little boy knowing now how comparatively short a time he had to live, and so I just want to say, Jim, that I was glad to have known you and glad that we did the stuff that we did.

1965

THE KINKS – 'SEE MY FRIENDS'

I'm not consumed with trying to work out how I'll be remembered when I'm gone, to the extent that I'll be remembered at all outside my close family and friends, although if you're reading this now in the distant future by thought-transference pellet or whatever the means of disseminating books and information is now, then great. How are things in the year 3000? Was it like the finest scientific minds of our generation McFly said it would be? Are you really living underwater?

I have occasionally thought that if I could die having written The Miracles' classic 'The Tracks Of My Tears' then I could slip away contentedly knowing I had made a lasting contribution to the culture of my times, as it's pretty much as perfect a pop song as you could imagine. I didn't write that song, of course, as not only was I seven but I didn't know anyone at Tamla Motown records because they had failed to open a Bolton office. I did later co-write the unheralded punk classic 'Breakfast In Bondage' with Phil 'Wammo' Walmsley, but I'm not sure on my deathbed I will consider that as being in the same league. It's a snapshot of its period, however, and on a strictly personal level, you understand, transcends its times as keenly as Smokey Robinson's pocket symphony of perfection.

That's why I love Ray Davies's work so much. You can listen to his songs and feel what it was like to be in swinging sixties London at that moment. For me, far more so than with The Beatles – whom I admire greatly, of course, but their songs up to this point seem to be made of simpler stuff somehow. I'm not suggesting that the records they were making were anything less than wonderful, but they were relatively simple pop songs about, predominantly, girls. Nothing wrong with that, although you can see that by the end of the year, when they release *Rubber Soul*, that the future is about to be changed forever. The creative adventure is beginning and gathers momentum with *Revolver* the following year before leaving earth orbit completely with *Sgt. Pepper* in 1967. In mid 1965, though, they're more absorbed with playing at Shea Stadium where they are screamed at by, predominantly, girls.

Ray Davies was already penning songs like 'A Well Respected Man', 'See My Friends' and 'Dedicated Follower of Fashion' as he documented suburban struggles and life's real characters as he came across them. Admittedly he would never go on the sonic journey that The Beatles took, but musical experimentation would have detracted from his beautifully measured homespun vignettes, and the sound of The Kinks was nothing if not influential. The distorted guitar figure running through 'You Really Got Me' courtesy of Dave Davies could be said to be the first heavy metal riff, and 'See My Friends' is pretty much the first Western record to flirt with Indian sounds. Certainly they were well-respected men on the London scene, with The Who in particular being big fans. In fact when The Kinks were inducted into the UK Music Hall of Fame, which still doesn't actually seem to exist despite having a raft of inductees, they were presented with the honour by Pete Townshend, although it's perhaps only right to mention that

The Who themselves were similarly honoured that night along with Bob Dylan, Jimi Hendrix, Joy Division/New Order, Pink Floyd, Black Sabbath and some bloke who played records on the radio called John Peel.

That's not in any way to suggest that The Who's regard for Ray and co was anything less than sincere. The Who's incredibly gifted bassist John Entwistle, when pushed to name his favourite bass player, plumped for The Kinks' recently deceased Pete Quaife for the drive he gave the band. Certainly it seemed entirely right that if we were going to have a UK Music Hall of Fame, whether it be a mythical Valhalla or a warehouse on an industrial estate on the outskirts of Hemel Hempstead, The Kinks ought to be in it.

I was there at Alexandra Palace that night presenting a radio programme from a truck backstage. My mobile studio was a compact and not particularly bijou space where the taupe shag-pile carpeting on the walls boasted nearly as many dubious stains as the taupe shag-pile carpeting on the floor. Other inductees (including New Order, Pink Floyd's David Gilmour and Nick Mason and a full complement of 'Sabs', of whom more later) appeared on our show but it was when I found myself in our dismal padded cell with all four original members of The Kinks that I really became starstruck.

During the course of my career I have met Ray Davies several times, not least when he performed a much-loved duet of 'Waterloo Sunset' with Damon Albarn on a Channel 4 programme I hosted called *The White Room*. Ray has always had something of a reputation as being a prickly customer and not tolerating fools with any great equanimity. I have to say that I have never found him to be anything less than charming, interesting and interested. However The Kinks, and the Davies siblings in particular, do have a reputation for being argumentative and fractious with each other and there's always a chance that a toxic atmosphere might come to pervade any live interview. When they arrived in the studio there didn't seem to be any real sign of that. Dave Davies, though friendly, seemed fragile as he was recovering from the effects of a stroke. Ray was amiable and animated but was keeping a watchful eye on his baby brother. Drummer Mick Avory seemed relaxed and friendly and so we seated them at the relevant microphones and prepared to chat. However, as the record playing on air began to fade the studio door crashed open to reveal a stocky, flustered figure wearing a polo shirt and blazer looking rather like the bar steward at a rugby club. It was Pete Quaife, who spat: 'Oh, so this is where you all are, is it?' causing a sharp intake of breath from all assembled and a noticeable bristling on the part of Mick Avory. It was wonderful. I was with the founder members of The Kinks, and they were still needling each other.

Back in 1965 there was plenty of arguing going on as well. Mods and rockers routinely arranged to meet up at seaside resorts for a breath of sea air, fish and chips served in newspaper and a collective bout of mindless violence. Instinctively throughout my life I've aligned myself with the rockers, as rock music was very much the soundtrack to my youth. On reflection in later years this is an allegiance I've come to question. Looking at the photographs now it's clear that the mods are far, far cooler and much more in tune with the times. The Post Office Tower was opened as the new icon on London's skyline this year and it's much more of a mod building than a rocker one. And it had a revolving restaurant at the top where you could imagine mods in pristine tonic suits sipping frothy coffees as they gazed imperiously down on scruffy rockers shuffling into backstreet boozers in search of cheap snakebite.

Seeing them now it's quite clear that the mods have style

in spades whereas the rockers just looked like they should be carrying spades. It's also true to say that being a mod is something you can carry into middle and indeed old age. Look at Charlie Watts. Good haircut, sharp suit, Gretsch drums. It's my belief that you should get smarter as you get older. I mean, everybody loves to see a dapper old chap in a trilby and bow-tie. Nobody wants to see a pensionable scruff in jogging bottoms and cheap trainers. And old rockers are the worst of the lot. They have matted grey ringlets tied into a flimsy ponytail down the back with just a few strands plastered to the top of the head and combine this tonsorial nightmare with a pair of ill-fitting stonewashed jeans and a tour T-shirt purchased at a Budgie gig at the De Montfort Hall, Leicester, in 1973. Come on, lads, get a grip. Who wants to see that? I've nothing against Budgie, and in fact clock an earful of 'Breadfan' on occasion, but it can be appreciated just as easily whilst wearing a good shirt from Ted Baker. No one over the age of thirty should, irrespective of man boobs, be wearing a T-shirt outside of the gym or DIY activities. And if you must wear one in some mistaken belief that it makes you look trendy, which it doesn't, then for goodness' sake make sure it's plain, as any kind of logo design is best left to toddlers or teenagers. Not you, old man.

In 1965 the choice of clothing for seven-year-olds was severely limited. There was no GapKids or anything like that. Posh children could be fitted out in the relevant department of a department store but would come out looking like a minor member of the Royal Family in patent buckled shoes and a coat with a velvet collar. The rest of us wore Ladybird clothes, which appeared to have undergone their last stylistic overhaul sometime in the Victorian era. If they'd been any more old-fashioned we'd have been turned out in junior doublet and hose. In the fifties, of course, this didn't matter as all the adults were wearing dowdy clothing too – England

was still pretty much a monochrome country in those days
and not just on the telly. Once the Carnaby Street revolution
in fashion began to gain momentum, however, we became
aware of just how much our Ladybird clothes made us look
like characters from Ladybird books. Thankfully everybody's
mum could sew and could run up a pair of paisley infant bell-
bottoms and a junior seersucker waistcoat during the thirteen
days that Goldie the London Zoo eagle was on the loose,
possibly getting a close look at the mods at the top of the Post
Office Tower.

The songs of The Kinks, who despite having massively
influenced the course of rock were intrinsically more mod,
perfectly mirror those times. 'See My Friends' may not be
their most celebrated hit, but hearing it takes me right back
to those days as a young boy waking up to the power of pop
and the trials of friendship. The first friend I can remember
having was called Paul Tadpole. Well, I daresay that wasn't his
real surname, but that's what I called him as our early bond-
ing experiences were shared leaning over a small pond with
jam jars dangling from bits of string. Calling him Paul
Tadpole then seemed entirely appropriate and it was a way of
referring to mates through the activities we shared that I carried on for many years through my friendships with Barry
Lego, Roger Subbuteo and Alan Woodpecker-Cider.

Friendships are key to any childhood and more than anything I wanted me and my pals to have the life of Rupert
Bear. I have always been utterly captivated by Rupert's
adventures in and around Nutwood. To this day I get the
Rupert Annual for Christmas and have always read the latest
batch of adventures by the end of Boxing Day. I now have
every *Rupert Annual* since 1950, which is a collection I'm
ridiculously proud of, despite having been unwilling to fork
out the crazy prices asked for the editions dating from the
thirties and forties. The character was created by Mary

Tourtel and launched in the *Daily Express* in 1920. When I
was offered a column in that newspaper in the nineties I had
no hesitation in accepting because, despite the fact that it was
not a publication to which I had ever subscribed, it was the
home of Rupert. And besides, they were paying a pound a
word.

Talking here of 1965, I pulled the relevant *Rupert* book
from the shelf and found that it used to belong to my sister
Jaine, as her name and our address are written in my mum's
handwriting in the inside front cover. I can't really think
why. It's not like she was planning to take it anywhere
although, if she had, it's likely that someone would have
taken the trouble to post it back to her. That was how things
were in those days as I recall, and it was certainly how things
were for Rupert. The world he inhabits is in some ways an
idealised England, allowing for the fact that much of the
landscape is inspired by the beloved Snowdonia of long-time
illustrator Alfred Bestall. And yet, it would be a mistake to
dismiss it as a work of pure imagination. That world of vil-
lages and woodlands, forests and seaside caves, was vividly
believable for thousands of children, reflecting in a very real
way aspects of their own lives. Admittedly we didn't take to
the skies in airships to meet the clerk of the weather or fly
through the night sky in our dressing gowns with Jack Frost,
but that was what was so bewitching. We did roam the
woods and hillocks and streams just like Rupert did, and so
there had to be the possibility that at any moment we could
meet a sprite made out of twigs just like Raggity, hadn't
there?

More than this, though, it was about the security of having
your own gang and you could argue that Rupert's associates
presage the arrival of multiculturalism. Animals and humans
mix easily, walking on their hind legs and talking the same
language. The heroic bear's immediate chums are Bill the

badger, Algy Pug, Podgy Pig, Gregory the guinea pig and Edward Trunk the elephant. It's a fantastic demonstration of an integrated society. If an elephant can play happily with a guinea pig then anybody can get along, right? Ethnic minorities are welcomed and revered for their knowledge, as the Chinese conjuror and his daughter Tiger-Lily were relieved to discover when they emigrated from their homeland. Old people or beasts like the Professor, Gaffer Jarge and the Wise Old Goat here are afforded requisite respect. People with disabilities like the Professor's dwarf assistant Bodkin have a valued role to play. The controversial area of policing is left in the canine hands, or paws, of Constable Growler. This seems eminently sensible and, in the constant discussions of spending cuts in the modern day force, how economical it could have proved if we had looked at this as a practical idea. I mean, how much could we have saved in the war against drugs if the investigating officer was also a sniffer dog?

So if that idea does get adopted at some future time, you'll know whose idea it was, and though I still won't have written 'The Tracks Of My Tears' or 'See My Friends', I'll still feel I've made a lasting contribution to the world I lived in.

1966

THE MONKEES – 'I'M A BELIEVER'

1966 was a big year for kids' television with the appearance of three major new programmes. *Star Trek* was launched, which never really grabbed me despite having been a keen *Thunderbirds* watcher and so interested by space travel that I would later tell my school careers teacher Mr Pollard that I wanted to be an astronaut or poet when I grew up. They didn't have pamphlets on either of those, which left both of us rather stumped as to what to do next. I eventually left with a brochure on the Royal Navy which proved excellent raw material for the construction of paper aeroplanes. I suppose if I'd been taking it seriously I should have at least attempted to make a paper *Ark Royal* to land them on but my failure to do so marked out my intrinsic unsuitability for serving in Her Majesty's Forces. Well, that and my pathetic level of fitness and inability to take orders from anybody.

Star Trek would also come to let me down badly when I attempted to pass my physics O level by watching several episodes back-to-back on the basis that it was all science. Unfortunately that year's paper posed not one question on transporter beams or warp drives. I subsequently failed, so thanks for nothing, Gene Roddenberry.

The other two significant programmes launched that year which became much closer to my heart were *Camberwick*

Green and *The Monkees*. The former was an exquisite depiction of English village life meticulously created by Gordon Murray and narrated by the inimitable Brian Cant. In many ways it wasn't that far from the country idyll of the *Rupert* books, though the storylines were much less fanciful. Instead of Rupert's journeys to the skies and deep underground we were treated to the daily challenges facing Farmer Jonathan Bell, PC McGarry, Micky Murphy the baker, Dr Mopp, Captain Snort, Sergeant-Major Grout and in particular the enigmatic Windy Miller, patiently grinding corn whilst living alone in his windmill. The following year would see the Camberwick family extended with the launch of its companion piece based on the nearby market town of Trumpton. Here I first encountered the legendary firefighters Pugh, Pugh, Barney McGrew, Cuthbert, Dibble and Grub. When not tackling blazes these redoubtable three-inch-tall public servants had used their time profitably by forming their own band. A brass band, admittedly, but a band nonetheless, making them a sort of Dave Dee, Dozy, Beaky, Mick and Tich of the stop-motion world.

Many years later at the Glastonbury festival I found myself in the company of The Troggs. Founder members Reg Presley and Chris Britton were still there along with a more recently recruited bass player, who still had several years' service as a Troglodyte under his not inconsiderable belt. At one point I asked him what he'd been doing before joining the band and he told me he'd been playing with Dave Dee, Dozy, Beaky, Mick and Tich. Being an inquisitive sort of chap and a stickler for band detail and trivia, I naturally enquired, 'So, which one were you, then?' to which he replied, 'Dunno. I never asked.'

He later admitted that he was pretty sure he wasn't Dave Dee.

★

A great deal of my life has been spent playing in bands, and in fact I was in the military band at school in the key position of second trumpet, and so it's possible that my interest in playing in musical ensembles could have been started by the Trumpton fire brigade had it not been for *The Monkees*.

The Monkees were a band formed in America in response to the impact Stateside of The Beatles. Recruited through auditions, they would enjoy colossal global success but would attract sneers from pop purists and musical snobs because they were hand-picked by svengalis, and hadn't grown up together as friends. To put it another way, they were 'manu-factured'. They were 'The Prefab Four'. Adding fuel to the fire was the admission that they didn't play on their early records, though they would later fight their corner on that one and were a fully functioning group by the time the *Headquarters* album was released in 1967. I've always found this gripe a bit hard to understand. Nobody ever criticises Tamla Motown for its 'manufactured' acts, and quite rightly so. The Supremes, The Temptations and The Four Tops played no instruments and rarely contributed to the song-writing process, but created some of the most glorious pop music of all time. Does it matter that one Top, Abdul 'Duke' Fakir, didn't play sousaphone on 'Walk Away Renée'? Of course not. Would you have been more excited when seeing The Supremes live if Mary Wilson had played a blistering glockenspiel solo? No. They sang together beautifully and that was what mattered. In addition Motown employed all manner of fashion, elocution and deportment advisers to send the likes of Diana Ross through a kind of showbiz fin-ishing school. Admittedly, most of the classic Motown groups had grown up together. In fact The Four Tops were boyhood pals from Detroit who released their first record in 1953 and kept the same line-up right through until 1997 when Lawrence Payton died. And they had known struggle and adversity, as we like all bands to do. They had once been so impoverished that they couldn't afford belts and had held their trousers up with lengths of rope, which is presumably where The Levellers got the idea.

The Monkees hadn't grown up together. Keen to make sure their band couldn't be disrupted by members being sent to serve in Vietnam, they picked two recruits who had minor health problems, preventing the call-up of Mickey Dolenz and Peter Tork; an Englishman, Davy Jones; and Mike Nesmith, who had already completed his service in the US Air Force. Of the four, only Tork and Nesmith were musicians. This didn't really matter, as the creators of the brand already had access to some of the finest pop talents of the day including Glen Campbell on guitar and the compositional skills of Neil Diamond. Jones and Dolenz both had an acting background, which seemed eminently sensible as the prime motivation was to make a TV show. Jones had appeared in the West End and on Broadway as the Artful Dodger, whereas Dolenz had been a child star at the age of ten as *Circus Boy*, a light-hearted caper following the adventures of the sparky lad Corky in the aftermath of the death of his parents in a freak trapeze accident.

Rejected applicants for roles in the group included Stephen Stills, Bobby 'Boris' Pickett and Van Dyke Parks though not, as has often been rumoured, Charles Manson. Shame really. If Charlie had been a Monkee it would have saved an awful lot of trouble and perhaps the nirvana of the sixties wouldn't have become so soured and the hippy dream irredeemably tarnished.

In fact it is just possible that Charlie did play with The Monkees. I have absolutely no proof of this whatsoever, but the Manson Family were regular liggers and party-goers on the LA hippy circuit, famously moving into Beach Boy Dennis Wilson's mansion at one point. Various Monkees also had lavish houses in the area, Peter Tork playing host to a posse of informal lodgers including a personal harem and a young guitarist called Jimi Hendrix. Hendrix's first big tour would be supporting The Monkees, though he was dismissed after the first few dates as the clean-cut audience found him a tad overbearing. Manson was an aspiring singer-songwriter on this social scene and so who knows who sang with whom at which parties deep in Laurel Canyon?

The TV show was launched in September that year, a few weeks after England won the World Cup, and immediately I was hooked. Here were four guys goofing around, wearing matching groovy clothes and going everywhere in a big car together singing and having adventures. Well, that had to be a design for life, didn't it? It certainly looked like a more interesting career path to investigate than poetry, space travel or even the Royal Navy.

So taken was I by these guys that I subscribed to their very own publication, *Monkees Monthly*. Even now the excitement is palpable as I leaf through issue number four, price 2/-, the cover of which boasts not only a heart-shaped photograph of Nesmith in his trademark 'Benny off *Crossroads*' woolly hat, but also the promise of '100 Monkee concert tickets to be won' and 'lots more of Davy's secrets'. Inside it is announced that the coveted tickets are going to be allocated through a 'lucky dip' and that fifty winners will receive two tickets each as 'it's not very nice for anyone to go to a show like this by themselves'. However, the concept of a pair of tickets is still some way in the future evidently, as the selected chosen few's seats will be 'as near to each other as possible at the same concert'. Which is nicer than 'not very nice' but not as nice as sitting right by your friend.

The magazine, which is the size of your standard football programme, also boasts the in-depth interview with Mike that the cover implies. In it he talks about his poor childhood when as the only child of a divorced mother he lived in a run-down neighbourhood and was the only non-Mexican in his class at school. This, he reveals, made him appreciate what really matters in life, like food and shelter, and not material wealth. Nevertheless, he did become wealthy through the band, revealing that 'okay, now my shelter costs me 150,000 dollars', but his attitude remains unchanged. Whether the same could be said for his mother I couldn't tell you, though happily her fortunes increased dramatically when she invented liquid paper. Mike would later be the Monkee who would resist most of the group's comeback offers, showing he was staying true to his avowedly non-materialistic principles, which must have been much easier being the heir to the Tipp-Ex fortune.

Elsewhere in the fanzine there is an article titled 'Moments I Remember' by Davy Jones recalling his early days as a stableboy and trainee jockey. Davy, as the smallest and cutest, was seemingly the most adored Monkee. In fact the 'Stop Press' section leads with the news that he has passed his army medical, evidently having been resident in the States long enough to be drafted after all. Needless to say, the British fans didn't like this one bit: 'Monkee maniac Linda Hards of Twickenham got so incensed about the possibility of Davy being called up that she organized a big protest march. Hundreds of Davy fans met at Marble Arch on April 5th. Linda then led everyone round London's Hyde Park until eventually the column arrived at the American Embassy. Linda then handed in a letter addressed to President Johnson and a petition signed by two thousand people.'

And it must have worked as Davy never did serve in the armed forces, so well done President Johnson for bowing to the Monkee maniacs. That's the power of effective lobbying for you.

A rather less happy ending is in evidence in 'Monkee

Mail', however, where Vicki Creek of Northwood Hills, Middlesex, describes a school trip to the National Gallery. At one point she and her friends spot a bloke 'wearing Monkee boots, trousers and jacket. You could guess our surprise when we saw his back view. Exactly like Pete!' For several paragraphs the giggling gaggle follow in his wake until he turns round and they see that 'he didn't look anything like Pete'. Not one of the great anecdotes, is it, Vicki?

I don't have many copies of *Monkees Monthly* left now, as once I'd read each issue, I would carefully cut the photographs out and add them to the ever-growing collage pasted to the headboard of my bed. Eventually I would get a bit older and start to cut different kinds of pictures out of different kinds of magazines, and would also start playing in bands for real. And though there were moments when I would hit a cymbal and think of Barney McGrew, in my mind I was always in The Monkees.

1967

SANDIE SHAW – 'PUPPET ON A STRING'

I know what you're thinking. 1967? 'OK, so "Puppet On A String" won the Eurovison Song Contest but wasn't that the year The Beatles released arguably the most important album ever made in *Sgt. Pepper's Lonely Hearts Club Band*?' To which the answer is yes. Your perfectly reasonable supplementary question might then be why I've picked Sandie Shaw. I'll come to that.

There is absolutely nothing I can tell you about *Sgt. Pepper* that hasn't been written a thousand times before. It may well be the greatest LP of all time, and certainly changed the parameters of what a pop group could achieve. Its sheer creative fearlessness and cultural impact are hard to imagine now. For me its significance was marked as it was the first pop record I can recall my parents owning. Their records were mainly classical, musicals and my mother's favoured Andy Williams albums. Perhaps it's because the soundtrack to so much of my childhood was the honeyed Williams tones that I retain great affection for his voice to this day. Well, that and the fact that he is clearly a better singer than the grossly over-rated Frank Sinatra.

That my mum and dad had a copy of *Sgt. Pepper* was quite a big deal not only to us but to the likes of my godparents Derek and Joan, who would come round on Saturday nights to play bridge and drink Guinness. I vividly recall all of us listening to that landmark album and taking turns to handle the lavishly glossy gatefold sleeve. As a record jacket it was as much of a revolution as the vinyl artefact it contained. Designed by Peter Blake, it cost one hundred times as much to produce as a normal record sleeve, coming in at just under three thousand pounds. In 1967 a Ford Cortina cost in the region of seven hundred pounds, so if they'd eschewed the lavish artwork the four Liverpudlian pop petrol-heads could have had a Cortina each, although I think it's fair to say they were up the automotive food chain a bit by then. Blake's seminal artwork has been correctly identified as raising the stakes for record design and so legendary were the individuals immortalised on the front of that record that we can all name a selection of them without checking it on Wikipedia. I know I can: Pitt the Younger, Tommy Cooper, Dame Nellie Melba, Tom Finney, Glenn Miller, 'Babs' Windsor, 'Babs' from Pan's People, Thomas Hardy, Kenneth Williams, Millican and Nesbitt, Vlad the Impaler, Victor Mature, The Two Ronnies, Frank Randle, Noddy Holder, Jethro Tull, a bacon slicer, a mangle, a matching set of Tupperware boxes and a sackbut. Or was it a crumhorn? Not bad off the top of my head, eh?

Oh, and The Beatles are on there. Twice. In the centre they're in the brilliant satin military coats that inspired a thousand copies from Carnaby Street to a different street that was a bit farther away. They're also there in their comparatively sober-suited mop-top personas thanks to the presence of their wax likenesses from Madame Tussauds, the models holding a deep fascination then as now. It seems in many ways remarkable that you can't pass Tussauds on Marylebone Road in that there London without seeing a queue stretching round the block. With technology changing as fast as it is, and with the advent of holograms, 3-D and HD, why should we still be drawn to lifeless facsimiles sculpted from wax? You'd have thought that it wouldn't be too long before we could have clones or avatars of our favourite stars to enjoy in the comfort of our own homes, if that doesn't sound slightly pervy and conjure up middle-aged men impatiently growing their own Britneys. But it seems ages ago that scientists cloned Dolly the Sheep, so why isn't it now possible to have your very own Westlife that you could grow from a packet of seeds? I mean, it should be even easier than creating a sheep because a sheep has to withstand winter outdoors and be able to climb steep hills. The Westlife's natural habitat is on a flat stage so no real agility is required, and not one of them has ever spent the cold season on a craggy outcrop in Tipperary.

Of course, you might not think your life has been massively inconvenienced by not having your very own synthetic Shane, Kian, Nicky and errm ... Seamus, is it? But it would be a marvellous addition to any household as if you didn't like their music you could always put them on light domestic duties such as taking the bins out or worming the cat. Now, if these cloning scientists do get back to the cloning coalface anytime soon instead of slacking off and bragging about one bloody sheep, we could all have a famous pop group to help with domestic chores, to which I would just issue one word of warning: storage. If these avatars are going to be life-size you don't want to go for a very tall group like Coldplay unless you have ample full-height broom cupboards to spare. Better to go for Bon Jovi who you can just pop under the sink there.

For those of us who lived through the sixties the sleeve of *Sgt. Pepper* is an indelible image and so I was intrigued when a central part of it came up for auction recently. The painted skin from the bass drum in the middle of the picture was offered at a guide price of £150,000. This, whilst undoubtedly a lot of cash for a used drum head, seemed pretty cheap to me. I'm not suggesting for one moment that I've got that kind of money to throw about, I haven't. I'm not even saying that if I had I would spend it on this, but when you think about it, it is a genuine piece of pop history and was cheaper than a Damien Hirst spot painting which Damien probably hadn't even painted anyway. This, I concluded, had to make it a bit of a bargain, which is why I wasn't all that surprised when it sold for just over a million dollars, or 739 Cortinas in old money. It's a first edition. How incredible to own not a drum skin that looked just like the one on *Sgt. Pepper* but the very one. The only one.

Auctions of rock memorabilia have become really big business these days and I can understand how much of a buzz it must be to own a shirt that has been worn by Elvis Presley, Johnny Cash or even Shakin' Stevens. The biggest thrill of all, though, must be to own a guitar once played by a true icon. I have a 1927 Gibson L3 acoustic that looks like the model on the knee of Robert Johnson in his most famous photograph. His is an L1 and so I'm not for one minute suggesting that he could have played mine, but every time I pick it up I wonder where it has been and whose hands have been up and down the neck playing it considerably better than I can. So how extraordinary would it be to let your fingers wander the frets where the celebrated digits of Peter Tork's lodger Jimi Hendrix had been before you?

Interestingly, a notable Stratocaster of Hendrix's came up for sale in 2008. It was the one he set fire to on stage in 1967 at the Astoria on Charing Cross Road. This iconic and much copied act really changed the face of rock'n'roll performance and established the design classic of the thrill-seeking rock star who had scant regard for his, or anyone else's, safety. Hendrix was sticking two fingers up to the Establishment by demonstrating that their regulations did not apply to free spirits like him. He had no need of their rules or institutions, though to be fair he did have need of the institution of the National Health Service and the rule of free health care when he was taken to accident and emergency after the show with burns to his hands. So, he was still sticking up two fingers to 'the man', it's just that they were smouldering and he was asking 'the man' to bandage them after applying a soothing ointment. That charred guitar sold for £280,000 but, again, it represents a moment in time in a world changing fast. Monterey, the first pop festival, happened in California with appearances by The Who, Janis Joplin, Otis Redding, The Mamas and The Papas, Ravi Shankar, Simon and Garfunkel, and Hendrix himself with some oven gloves purchased from a souvenir shop at Heathrow airport. The hippy musical *Hair* hit the West End, homosexuality was decriminalised, Pink Floyd unveiled their psychedelic masterpiece *Piper At The Gates Of Dawn* and The Beatles changed rock'n'roll for ever with *Sgt. Pepper's Lonely Hearts Club Band*. So why have I picked Sandie Shaw? I'm coming to that.

As I've already said, the copy of *Sgt. Pepper* in our house was my dad's and whilst I am one hundred per cent convinced of its utter genius, it didn't feel like it was mine. Rather like Bob Dylan seemed to be someone that all my mates' big brothers liked, The Beatles were the band your father admired and so, immediately and instinctively, you felt you had to look elsewhere. If The Beatles and Dylan represented rebellion, it wasn't my rebellion. Of course, looking back on a lifetime of music from the age I am now, none of this makes any difference. As a 52-year-old, unencumbered by any sense of style or cool, I am free to enjoy whatever music I like without fear of peer pressure and ridicule. That my tribal prejudices made me come to Dylan later in life doesn't matter, it was a wonderful discovery when I was ready to make it.

But The Beatles felt, to me, like 'dad-rock' before the concept even existed. Nowadays it is a term that has passed into common usage as bands and their audiences have got progressively older without moving on to to the light classical repertoire and songs from the shows. We have to remember that rock'n'roll was only invented in the fifties and a lot of those original artists and fans are still around. It was assumed that it was a fad that would pass as the young people moved on to the next craze, but it didn't. It turned out to be an incurable addiction for everyone.

Ironically, The Beatles, whatever they may have been, were never 'Dad-rock'. 'Dad-rock' is unpretentious, no-nonsense, mid-paced, white guitar band music played in 4/4. It might have elements of country rock, punk rock, pub rock, glam rock, indie rock, classic rock, goth rock or hard rock, but not progressive rock, post rock, pomp rock, art rock, jazz rock or folk rock. It is basically music that cannot be seen to be trying too hard. I'm not saying there isn't absolutely brilliant 'dad-rock' but its ambitions are limited. It specialises in terrace anthems suited to the large arena as demonstrated by Oasis. It is pub rock that has become too popular to be played in the pub. It is resolutely workmanlike and you can watch a 'dad-rock' band and see how it's all happening, though not like you can see how the Pompidou Centre works with its elegantly externalised ducting and piping. As a building, that's far more prog rock. 'Dad-rock' is like a mill in a Northern town in the 1930s belching smoke into the atmosphere.

But The Beatles were never like that. The Rolling Stones have become 'dad-rock', as have Kiss, AC/DC, The Who, Status Quo, The Sex Pistols, ZZ Top, Paul Weller, The Police, The Stranglers, Deep Purple, Dire Straits and Bon Jovi. In Phil Lynott, Thin Lizzy may well have had the only non-white dad-rocker, and Queen, in Freddie Mercury, the only gay. I'm not trying to denigrate or devalue the work of the artists in that list, some of whose records and concerts I have enjoyed hugely and continue to do so. But having laid out the basic principles of 'dad-rock' you can see that it was never a term that could be applied to The Beatles. Whether they would have become 'dad-rock' if they had stayed around long enough is open to question, but it's hard to see how the minds that hatched *Sgt. Pepper* could ever have been content with those kinds of constraints.

So why did I pick Sandie Shaw? Well, though I had no way of understanding it at the time, she must have been my very first crush. Why else would I have squatted on the rockery in the back garden of our new home at 18 Towncroft Lane attempting to photograph her picture in the *Fab 208 Annual* with a Kodak Instamatic? Photographing a photograph so I would have an extra photograph . . . now that is the action of an ardent admirer. And inept photographer. Looking at pictures of her now from that era she has an effortless beauty, unfussy sense of style and beguiling air of mystery. She was to England what Nancy Sinatra was to America or Françoise Hardy was to France. And yet we have failed to afford her the respect she so clearly deserves. Madame Hardy is rightly stitched into the very fabric of French cultural pride, but the reputation of the divine Miss S seems forever polluted by her Eurovision triumph with the irritatingly jaunty 'Puppet On A String', and if as not only a Sandie but also a puppet fan, I can't derive great pleasure from it then what chance have the rest of you got? However, her other hits like 'Girl Don't Come', '(There's) Always Something There To Remind Me', 'Long Live Love' and the 'lost' classic 'Run' remain sublime reminders of that era. She went on to launch her own fashion range. She worked with The Smiths. She withdrew from showbiz and became a therapist. Like Chrissie Hynde, she's always had more or less the same design classic haircut. She is a hoot. She is cool. How much more persuading do you need? You're right, though. Basically I picked her to represent 1967 because I thought she was beautiful. I still do. I am a bloke, you know.

1968

THE SHOWSTOPPERS – 'AIN'T NOTHING BUT A HOUSE PARTY'

I'm particularly attached to The Showstoppers' classic for three reasons. Firstly, in sounding like there genuinely is a party going on, it does what it says on the tin. Not that it came in a tin. If you wanted a record in a tin you had to wait until 1979 when PIL released their *Metal Box* LP as three 45rpm twelve-inch discs in a film canister. The Small Faces' classic mod concept album *Ogdens' Nut Gone Flake* which was, coincidentally, also released in 1968 came in a sleeve based on a familiar round tobacco tin but wasn't available in a real one until the 2006 CD reissue. Sometimes, you just have to be patient if you want something in a tin. As the slightly modified adage goes: everything in a tin comes to he who waits. I had to wait until 2008 to receive a canned single gherkin. A gift from Olly Ralfe of the enchantingly off-kilter Ralfe Band, it still sits proudly on the office windowsill waiting for an occasion that warrants a ceremonial opening.

Other pop acts who might have been able to employ this 'disc in a tin' ploy would have been Canned Heat, Can or Suzi Quatro with her chart-topping stomper 'Can The Can'. Indeed, one wonders if Jacques Offenbach flirted with the idea when he began to see how popular 'The Can-Can' was in the dance halls of Montparnasse. In theory this would have been a possibility as the conveniently French Leon Scott had invented recorded music with the phonautograph in 1857, a year before Jacques's *Orpheus in the Underworld* from which 'The Can-Can' is taken debuted. And the concept of putting things in cans was also extant having had its origins in the battle plans of another handily French bloke called Napoleon Bonaparte, who had been asking his aides-de-camp to find ways of preserving food for his troops in the field. To my knowledge there has never been a recording of 'The Can-Can' available in a can-can, although eventually it was possible to purchase an essential component of the more modest performances of the dance, a pair of women's knickers, in a tin. And guess what? Women's knickers as we know them, or to use the correct word 'indispensables', were invented in France in 1859. What a golden age for the French that was. Agincourt must have seemed a very distant memory.

For The Showstoppers, who came from Philadelphia and featured two younger brothers of Solomon Burke, 1968 gave them their big moment. Their one smash hit may not have come in any kind of special package, but it does perfectly conjure up the atmosphere of a house party. Naturally, I can think of nothing worse than attending one of these nowadays because I have grown up. Parties are great on your birthday when you're a kid and especially great when you're a teenager and can drink cider and wrestle with girls or boys or perhaps even both according to your proclivities. It's also acceptable to have a party on a major birthday or anniversary throughout adulthood, but for the most part, once you are beyond your mid-twenties you should avoid them. You should particularly avoid hosting them, as it's pretty much impossible to get rid of people. I mean, I'm as laissez-faire as the next man. I lived through the sixties. I experienced the counterculture even if I was only ten years old in 1968. Let it all hang out, I say. If people want to come to my house for a 'happening' or 'shindig' with shoeless dancing on the hearth rug then let them, man. Please, though, let's not get carried away. I've known guests to still be sampling the Caribbean punch at gone eleven o'clock. At night! What are they, vampires?

In 1968 house parties were not a feature of Radcliffe family life in the small but comfortable three-bed semi at Towncroft Lane. The lane was an 'unmade' road, which was not at all unusual in those days. The road surface itself was riddled with potholes which my dad and other neighbours would regularly try to fill with the ashes and clinker from the living room fire. On 5 November we would light a communal bonfire that we'd built in the middle of the road as no one wanted their garden messing up, and what few vehicles passed down the street could easily swerve gently around it. One year I'd spent many hours painstakingly stuffing my dad's old Intelligence Corps army fatigues to make a really terrific 'guy' only to be horror-struck, rather like Edward Woodward in *The Wicker Man*, when I realised he was going to be consumed by flames. No one had thought to mention that bit to me. If you grow up in Shetland then you'll understand the traditions of the fire festival Up Helly Aa and will be prepared for the fact that the Viking galley you've spent long, dark months building is going to be torched at the end of Yuletide. I was not similarly enlightened and neither was my precious 'guy', who remained unburned due to the hissy fit I had. He then sat for months in the corner of our wooden garage, looking increasingly forlorn as he gradually collapsed into a heap, a broken figure having missed his moment of destiny. His final indignity was to be tossed onto the council tip.

The average price of a house in the UK in 1968 was just over four thousand pounds, or one 250th of the price for which London Bridge was sold to someone in Arizona the same year. Our average house had little to distinguish it from any other although we did have a strip of melamine-coated chipboard fastened to the kitchen wall known as the 'breakfast bar'. Here me and my brother Joe and sister Jaine could perch on chrome-legged, vinyl-seated stools to enjoy our soft-boiled eggs safe in the knowledge that we were doing so at the cutting edge of interior design. Other than that, the only notable bit of 'home improvement' I recall was the installation of a serving hatch between the kitchen and dining room to avoid the previously unavoidable, arduous, ten-yard trek weighed down with a potentially hazardous cargo of Lancashire hotpot. These portals were very much in vogue at the time and consisted of an aperture over which would be fitted double doors in the inevitable melamine chipboard so that your home could resemble a works canteen. What a great notion. I think my mother must also have coveted a Hostess Trolley which was, and still is, a heated contraption into which you deposit the food you had prepared earlier until it had lost only a little of its warmth but practically all of its flavour. We never owned one of these, preferring to take the radical route of eating food when it was ready. We did, however, take advantage of developments in heating technology by installing night storage heaters. These three-foot-long monsters dominated every room although, to be fair, their appeal was not aesthetic, but economic. The brilliant plan was that they used electricity overnight before letting out heat in the morning. This gave you a comparatively toasty ten minutes at the 'breakfast bar' of a morning for sure, but the heat then continued to radiate all day long while we were out at school and work, making the house lovely and chilly for when we came back in again at the end of the day. Genius. Perhaps that's why we didn't have any house parties.

The second reason I love this record so much is that I was introduced to it by a friend from Bolton called Steve Bridges.

He was five years older than me and so knew all kinds of cool tunes and in the years to come would introduce me to many artists I'd never heard of like Bruce Springsteen, Jonathan Richman, Southside Johnny, The Band and Ry Cooder. We would come to play all these and more in our band Zoot Suit and The Zeroids in and around our home town in the late seventies. The tape of one of those performances at Rivington Barn, the Budokan of Bolton at that time, has just resurfaced thanks to the archiving foresight of our ex-bassist Andy Wright. Listening to us perform 'House Party' now is difficult for me because not only is the sound quality poor, in case you were thinking of ordering the live album on Amazon, but mainly because Steve passed away due to pancreatic cancer a couple of years ago at the age of fifty-five. Steve was a good singer, guitarist and harmonica player with shoulder-length hair, a drooping moustache and the most lurid collection of Hawaiian shirts you've seen in your life unless, possibly, you were a Hawaiian. He came with me to buy my first real matching drum kit when we spotted it for sale in the classified adverts in the *Bolton Evening News*. It was a gold sparkle Beverley which we haggled over and got for £115. How thrilled I felt driving back over Darwen Moor with the precious cargo in Steve's Vauxhall Viva, a two-tone model being principally white but with large sections of rust, both of us yelling along to The Modern Lovers' 'Ice Cream Man'. Steve was like a big brother to me for a few years back there and so it's strange and sad to think he's no longer around. Especially when I hear 'House Party'.

The third reason I love The Showstoppers' only hit is because it was the first record I ever played as a DJ. As a teenager I'd helped a school friend called Jim Silver with his mobile disco as he traipsed around various polystyrene-roofing-tile-topped function rooms in the Bolton area. For hours on end, as some of these dismal events dragged on towards midnight for heaven's sake, we would sit behind his double decks, adjacent to the buffet table stacked with meat paste fingers, mushroom vol-au-vents and cubes of catering cheddar and pineapple chunks on cocktail sticks stuck into half a melon, and watch as giggling girls with bubble-permed hair shuffled around their patent plastic clutch bags to George McCrae before the lads thundered in when we put on 'Born To Be Wild' by Steppenwolf. To me it seemed routine work. Even though I loved music the idea that it was anything other than a job never occurred to me. It was manual labour. You humped the gear in, humped the records onto one of the turntables and then humped the gear out again. It would later become apparent that there were other kinds of humping opportunities open to the acne-riddled disc jockey, though nobody mentioned it to me at the time. It struck me then, as it does now, as highly peculiar that putting records on should be seen as sexy or impressive somehow. How can you be impressed by people doing something you can do yourself? I am speechless with admiration at the way Andy who lives over the field from me can strip down and reassemble the engine of his chunky old jeep whilst muttering about head gaskets and sumps and torpedoes and periscopes or whatever it was he was on about. Technical information tends to wash over me after a while. But putting records on is something anyone can do, so why has it proved to be so highly valued? If you go to a gig you want to see a show, don't you? You want the visceral live experience of a thrilling band. I can see that during the acid house years the drugs of choice made the beats the main point of the exercise, but surely there has to be more to a musical night out than that to ensure lasting satisfaction. I don't care how difficult these live DJ's make it look with their headphones and telephone receivers, endlessly fiddling about with twelve-inch discs on turntables in the hope that we won't notice it's all on a DAT

whilst punching the air in some sort of approximated euphoria. It will never compare to David Bowie doing Ziggy
Stardust. There is a club DJ who's very big in Paris called
Mamy Rock. By day she is known as Ruth Flowers and
comes from Bristol. Her signature look comprises spiky silver
hair, a gold bomber jacket, gaudy jewellery and impenetrable
black sunglasses. If you met her you would naturally assume
her to be related to cigar-toting Methuselah of the marathon
and Godfather of bling, Jimmy Savile, which in a manner of
speaking she is. To some degree all DJ's owe a debt of gratitude to the cotton-wool-headed jogmeister, as he more or
less invented the disco as long ago as the 1940s when he
charged people to come into the back room of a pub in
Yorkshire to watch him playing records. Not only that, for a
while he got the punters to bring the records, which is a bit
like running a restaurant and asking diners to bring their
own food (which, as a word of warning, is not a bad idea if
you find yourself perusing the menu at The Pheasant Moon
Bar and Grill, Morecambe).

The thing that people find most remarkable about Mamy
Rock is her age. She is seventy. That this should be seen as
noteworthy is odd, as being a DJ would seem to be perfect
work for a pensioner. The shifts are nice and short, it involves
no heavy lifting, you're inside 'in the warm' and you can
wear the same tracksuit you've just shuffled to Aldi to buy
Superkings in.

My dancehall DJ days began, and pretty much ended,
when I was a student at Manchester University in 1976. My
hall of residence was called Woolton and, like all the other
halls around the south Manchester Fallowfield campus,
would stage a social evening known somewhat quaintly and
anachronistically as a 'bop'. For me and my mates these
evenings would always follow the same pattern. Around
teatime we would hasten to a local hostelry called The

Friendship where we'd talk about the prettiest girls we'd seen knocking round the lecture halls whilst fortifying ourselves with several pints of Hyde's bitter, funded by the taxpayer as these were still the halcyon days of the student grant. Suitably enlivened we would then troop back to the junior common room where we would further fortify ourselves at the subsidised bar, which was a real bonus seeing as we were subsidised already, finding ourselves as fortified as newts before too long. We would then stumble into the main hall where the music was playing to watch giggling girls with unbrushed hair shuffle round their macramé shoulder bags to George McCrae before we thundered in when the DJ put on 'Born To Be Wild' by Steppenwolf.

Oddly, as we whirled the floor in a fevered, sweaty rugby scrum, the assembled females found our charms strangely easy to resist.

After a couple of months of this routine I answered the plea on the noticeboard asking for lads who would DJ for an hour to help out. I don't know why I said I would but several Saturdays later I found myself standing behind the double decks on a trestle table, facing an empty dance floor and wondering what the hell I was going to play. Rifling through the college's singles collection I came across a record on the Beacon label by The Showstoppers. Thanks to Steve, I knew this could not fail as a 'floor-filler' and slapped it on the right-hand deck before 'wowing' it in ever so slightly. Now, at this point I would love to be able to tell you that as the first bars of 'House Party' blared out of the speakers, the dance floor became filled with ecstatic undergraduate couples frugging with erotic abandon. Unfortunately, as the new recruit, I was given the first hour of the evening and the room was more or less devoid of people save a few loyal friends like Mark Chown and Rick De Nezza, who encouraged me with such comments as: 'What's this shit? Haven't you got any Zappa?'

Still, that moment marks the start of my DJ life and, though I'm not proud to admit it, I have kept that copy of 'House Party' stamped 'Property of Woolton Hall Socials' as a souvenir. And it was while spinning the discs in that draughty refectory that I came to the attention of a willowy, blonde-haired nurse from Poulton-le-Fylde called Helen Bibby. In a sense I suppose that was mission accomplished, but I'm sure Helen would back me up when I say to girls who are attracted to club DJs, you'd be better advised to view this resident egomaniac with suspicion and pay far more attention to the bloke who's in charge of the plumbing and air conditioning, as he will be of far greater use to you later in life. A good plumber is increasingly hard to find and, when all's said and done, anyone can put records on.

THE BEACH BOYS – 'COTTON FIELDS'

One of the great discoveries of my life has been the music of Nick Drake. Well, when I say discovery, it's not on a par with Howard Carter's discovery in the Valley of the Kings or anything. I mean, it took Howard about fifteen years of shifting sand and rocks before he found the tomb of Tutankhamun. I just went into a record shop to look for Drake's 1969 debut album *Five Leaves Left* and there it was, so in terms of the actual search Carter wins hands down. On the other hand, I got the number five into Bolton and walked from Moor Lane bus station to Tracks on my own, it was a solo undertaking, whereas Howard had help from hundreds of Egyptian labourers, so we'll call it one–all. I could also make the point that my expedition was entirely self-funded, which is more than you can say for Carter. Did you see me running cap in hand to Lord Carnarvon to stump up my bus fare and the price of my lunch at Ye Olde Pastie Shoppe on Churchgate? No, you did not, and so whilst Howard Carter is to be celebrated for his top-flight excavations and all that, let's not lose sight of who has the moral high ground here.

The songs and voice and guitar playing of Nick Drake are sounds that will haunt me till I die and possibly, though I cannot know what awaits me, beyond that. I have left instructions that I would like 'Northern Sky' to be played at my funeral, which I would very much like to be a really, really sad day. I know the modern way is to make these things joyous occasions and a celebration of one's life, but I would really feel much happier knowing that everyone is going to be much sadder. Those attending will be my family and friends, and the tabloid hacks hungry for any salacious detail from my inspirational life obviously, and the least you can do if you call yourself a mate is to turn up and have a bit of a weep.

The tragic early death of Nick Drake at his parents' home in Tanworth-In-Arden in 1974 has contributed to his myth and enigma and it's extraordinary to see the reputation of an artist who received so little attention in his lifetime grow subsequently to such an extent that the title track from his stark 1972 final album *Pink Moon* was used in a TV commercial for Volkswagen in 2000. To me his music will always be fascinating, mysterious, intimate, melancholic, beautiful and quintessentially English. Those who find it a bit polite are to me missing the angst and the agonies that run just below the surface of so many of our Little England suburban lives.

Naturally I would love to be able to say that I bought *Five Leaves Left* the year it came out and made an inspired choice for the first record I ever bought. I didn't. To be fair to myself, it would have been a left-field purchase for an eleven-year-old. So I bought 'Cotton Fields' by The Beach Boys instead.

I had no idea until comparatively recently that 'Cotton Fields' was originally a song by legendary Louisiana blues man Lead Belly. The lyrics reflect his impoverished share-cropper roots and had little in common with the lower-middle-class upbringing of the Lancastrian eleven-plus candidate, or indeed that of The Beach Boys, although fields of a different kind will forever be associated with this record in my mind.

Bolton School, keen that their town-dwelling pupils should get a taste of country air, had purchased an imposing, grey-rendered house called St Mark's Vicarage in Cautley, near Sedbergh, which is where Cumbria meets the Yorkshire Dales. A breathtakingly beautiful location, Cautley is perhaps best known for Cautley Spout, which is Britain's highest waterfall above ground. I say 'above ground' to head off complaints from keen waterfallers who will point out that technically the beck crashing into Gaping Ghyll creates a larger drop.

At regular intervals groups of us would be loaded into minibuses devoid of health and safety restrictions such as seatbelts and, occasionally, sufficient seats, and would be despatched to roam the fells and hike into Sedbergh to jeer at the boys of that town's famous public school who were forced to wear short trousers right up until the sixth form. Well, I guess it was character building. They were also forbidden from leaving the perimeter of the school grounds and so were unable to chase us up the village street and give us the thrashing we so richly deserved.

In the evenings we'd sit around a common room and play Scrabble and Battleships and also listen to records on an old Dansette. Those who had taken vinyl with them were therefore afforded a certain respect and though I didn't have the funds available to buy a full LP, and so wasn't quite in the rarefied company of Adrian Long with his pristine, gatefold-sleeve-clad copy of *Foxtrot* by Genesis, my ownership of The Beach Boys hit did bring me a certain cachet.

Lack of funds, though, would come to be an issue. I'm not complaining or anything but it did prove difficult to tackle substantial peaks when you'd been sent not only without any hiking boots but in regular school shoes. Now I know that hiking equipment was not so readily available at reasonable prices as it is today, and Mallory and Irvine had tackled Everest in a pair of sturdy brogues and a deerstalker while chugging on a Woodbine.

But my shoes were not sturdy brogues. They were plain black slip-ons with a wafer-thin sole ingenious in design for being entirely smooth and devoid of any grip. This would have been ideal footwear for executing Northern Soul spins on the dance floor of Wigan Casino, but proved less suitable for the ascent of Howgill Fells. However, the ascent was nothing compared to coming back down again when I invented the little-known sport of fell surfing. So treacherous was my plight becoming that two teachers, Messrs Lomax and Openshaw, had no option but to take an elbow each and more or less slide me back to base camp.

This filled me with dread, as in the unzipped pocket of my Peter Storm cagoule nestled a packet of ten Consulate menthol cigarettes, the discovery of which would mean a swift return home in considerable disgrace. Thankfully any strip-searching policy was somewhat lax in that bucolic atmosphere and I was able to recover my equilibrium back in the vicarage, where the soothing tones of Al Jardine singing about those arduous days out in the fields seemed suddenly a lot closer to home.

These days, thankfully, I am quite the well-shod rambler, and also a non-smoker I'm pleased to say. Not that an infrequent menthol cigarette habit really amounted to juvenile delinquency, especially when you consider the recreational possibilities at the Woodstock Music and Arts Fair which was taking place in upstate New York at the same time as I was ending up in a right state at Cautley Spout.

No one had ever seen anything quite like Woodstock before. Shortly before his sad and untimely heart attack and death I talked to an old colleague of mine called Cahill

O'Doherty who had actually been there. A rogueish, raffish Irish charmer with an ever-present twinkle in his eye, Cahill had been head of Radio 1 promotions and marketing when I was a young producer. Fresh out of school, he and his mate Joe had taken off to spend the summer in New York and seeing posters for this event just bought tickets, which no one ever checked, and took off on the local bus for Max Yasgur's farm to watch the likes of Creedence Clearwater Revival, Country Joe and The Fish, Sly and The Family Stone, The Who, Jefferson Airplane, Santana, Canned Heat and Jimi Hendrix. He described having to abandon any notion of motorised travel as the freeways became gridlocked, forcing him to sleep by the roadside on a picnic table before joining what he called 'a biblical stream of long-haired people with blankets over their shoulders'. Joni Mitchell's estimate of the crowd being 'half a million strong' would seem to be a fair assumption. Mike Heron of British psychedelic folkies The Incredible String Band told me of arriving at the festival to play in an open-sided military-style helicopter seated next to Ravi Shankar clutching his sitar and asking the pilot: 'What is that crop down there?' to which the answer came: 'Humans!'

As a brave new world of limitless possibilities Woodstock invented the now familiar notion of a grand musical event as a kind of gathering of the clans where like-minded souls follow a calling down the ley-lines, although it's worth remembering that the idea came not from hippy idealists but Wall Street investment bankers with a love of music but no qualms about making money. Nevertheless, it seemed to epitomise a society of sharing and freedom. Cahill talked about being given food and drink by fellow fans. He was also given blue acid – the brown stuff being best avoided as confirmed by stage announcements – directly into the mouth by a passing hairy dispensing free of charge. Waking up after snatching a few hours' rest in the open air, their heads rested on their rolled-up T-shirts, they found 'two blonde, beautiful girls rubbing suntan oil into our white Irish-skinned backs'. He also vividly recalled the appearance of Jefferson Airplane at six in the morning as dawn broke behind Grace Slick's white, cheesecloth dress as she invited the audience to enjoy their 'morning maniac music'.

Rather wonderfully, the organisation does seem to have been blissfully loose as the event was marshalled not by the police force but, as Mike Heron recalled, a hippy collective known as 'the please force'. For a few days it did seem as though there was an alternative way of life in the offing as the Age of Aquarius dawned. Celebrated in the 'Aquarius/Let The Sun Shine In' song from the musical *Hair* and a hit in this year for The 5th Dimension, the unveiling of this new astrological era promised greater love, understanding and humanity than had been evident in the Piscean period that was coming to an end. And, fascinatingly, this looking to the stars could not have been more appropriate as this was also the year, about a month before Cahill walked over the hill to Woodstock, that Neil Armstrong and Buzz Aldrin walked on the moon. Though NASA's finest couldn't have been further apart in the spectrum of society from the great unwashed and somewhat dazed Woodstock pilgrims, in a sense they were forever conjoined by the need to escape earth orbit. They were both breaking away from the old rules of what was possible and acceptable. In a manner of speaking, for a while back there, the hawks and the doves were flying together. Like Lead Belly, everyone was on a journey to new possibilities and was keen to leave their own personal cotton fields far, far behind.

1970

CANNED HEAT – 'LET'S WORK TOGETHER'

If 1969 promised the dawning of the new age then 1970 brought us all back to earth with a bit of a bump. Despite the Isle of Wight Festival picking up where Woodstock left off and attracting a crowd of 600,000, the rock'n'roll dream turned to nightmare when Janis Joplin and Jimi Hendrix died. The Beatles announced they were splitting up and John and Yoko's 'bed-ins' resulted not in lasting world peace but in a pile of very dirty laundry and a room at the Amsterdam Hilton badly in need of an airing. Not only that, but the euphoria of Apollo 11 gave way to the tension of Apollo 13. And in case you were wondering if there was an Apollo 12 and if so why I haven't mentioned it, then I would just remind you that I am not writing a textbook here so just look it up yourself. Oh, all right, they went back to the moon and the guys who landed were Charles 'Pete' Conrad and Alan 'Haricot' Bean. And to save you going to Wikipedia again I will admit that I have just made one of those nicknames up. And it's not Pete.

As a kid growing up in the seventies you couldn't help watching developments in space exploration with avid excitement. After all, boys' annuals and comics since the late fifties had been promising that space travel for everyone would be a certainty by this time. We would all be routinely leaving the earth's atmosphere for a family outing on a Sunday in our own rocket ship, a trip that would have been bound to result in frustration for my dad as, whilst building up to escape velocity from the earth's orbit at around eleven kilometres a second or thirty-four times the speed of sound, he would drive up the rear end of an old bloke in a small, brown hatchback spaceship with a Teflon trilby on the parcel shelf, bumbling along at only twenty-eight times the speed of sound before muttering: 'Bloody Sunday drivers,' and then getting into an argument with my mum because he was using bad language and getting aggressive in front of the silver-suited children. At least with pipes and hoses attached to our bottom areas there would have been no need for the interminable toilet stops he found so irksome. Even so, we would still have needed to stop for a snack as I'm pretty sure we would have complained if our lunch only consisted of another tablet. And inevitably when we got to space services we would be unable to find a docking space and once through the airlock would find the place packed with weightless Hell's Angels eating greasy bacon butties in caplet form.

Despite all that, for a kid who wanted to be an astronaut the lack of opportunity to get into the stratosphere is disappointing. It's only now that space tourism is becoming a reality and frankly, it's looking a bit more pricey than I was hoping. Founder of Cirque Du Soleil Guy Laliberté paid, depending on which figures you accept, between 25 and 35 million dollars to go to the International Space Station in 2009. He apparently turned down a space walk for an extra 15 million, which seems a bit daft if, like Guy, you're a billionaire accordionist, which I accept is unlikely as he's the only person ever to have lived to fall into that category. But if you're going all that way you might as well go the whole hog, don't you think? It's like being in Cairo and not wandering past the pyramids or going to St Mark's Square in Venice and not paying far too much for a coffee.

And so my yearning for space travel seems destined to remain unsatisfied. I never even flew in Concorde to experience breaking the sound barrier, which seemed as near to leaving earth orbit as any of us could realistically aspire to. The closest I got to that was waiting with thousands of others at RAF Fairford in Gloucestershire as that graceful albatross of an aircraft was gently lowered onto the tarmac by its test pilot Brian Trubshaw. It's not a great name for a crack test pilot, that, is it? I'm sure he was an absolute gentleman and clearly a first-rate aviator but the man was also practically a superhero. He was Dan Dare, Douglas Bader, the Red Baron, Scott Tracy, and Wilbur and Orville Wright rolled into one. He was a superstar of the skies and his name was Brian Trubshaw. I know he couldn't help his name but they could have changed it to something a bit sexier, surely. How brilliant to report that the British Concorde had impressed onlookers at international air shows as it was put through its supersonic paces by crack test pilot Dan 'Chip' Dangerfield. I know it's just a name but sometimes they matter a great deal. Would 007 have become such a potent presence, and such a winner with the ladies, if when introduced he intoned the sentence: 'The name's Trubshaw. Brian Trubshaw.'

I imagine that if journeys into space were now frequent occurrences for regular people, then the craft we'd be using would be built by car manufacturers, and this would probably have presented its own problems. Would you seriously be happy to trust your ability to withstand re-entry to the company who built the Morris Marina? In 2010 the previously trustworthy and reliable Toyota had to accept there were fundamental problems with the Prius and recall around half a million of them. Apparently, and I am no automotive expert

as I've admitted, there was the chance that the brakes could
fail to engage immediately on uneven surfaces. Now whilst
there are no rocky roads in space as such, you never know
when you're going to encounter some turbulence due to
meteor showers and so the issue is a pertinent one when
related to interplanetary jaunts. On Earth the brake problem
is bad enough as you skid off a farm track into a thicket
hedge. In space there's nothing to stop you. One brake failure and you could find yourself at the Crab Nebula with no
way of getting home, as you'll find the AA pretty reluctant to
cover those sort of distances. However, there is some consolation in knowing that you invested in a hybrid Prius for the
sake of the environment and, as you sit there wasting away,
lost in space with only the Crab Pulsar for company, you can
at least die in the knowledge that your carbon footprint was
looking pretty good.

Sadly, I would have to say that the 1969 launch that had
the most impact on Radcliffe family life was not that of
Apollo 11 but of the Austin Maxi. If you've seen the
'Gourmet Night' episode of *Fawlty Towers* you'll be familiar
with the scene in which Basil thrashes his errant car with a
branch from a nearby tree. So ingrained on the British consciousness was this moment of televisual perfection that
toymakers Corgi produced a boxed set of the car and a
miniature Basil brandishing a miniature branch. That luckless
red car was an Austin 1100 and the Maxi was, not unreasonably, a bigger version of that. It was one of the revolutionary
five-door hatchbacks which left the boot space of a saloon car
open so that you could lean over from the back seats for stuff
and also leave everything you were carrying conveniently on
display for thieves. It was one of a series of memorable Austin
designs from British Leyland during the 70s and 80s, including the optimistically named Allegro, the distinctly
un-Caribbean looking Montego and the jewel in the badly

spot-welded crown, the Princess. Designers must have searched far and wide for the inspiration of the body contours of the Princess before settling on a wedge of cheese. My Uncle Pat had a yellow model with the optional extra of a black vinyl roof, which meant that the car not only looked like a wedge of cheese, but a wedge of cheese that had gone off. The lads at Ferrari must have been deeply worried.

Quite why the Maxi was seen as such a revolutionary vehicle is hard to imagine now, as it was basically an estate car. My parents were inordinately pleased with it, though, and we enjoyed many picnics on Ainsdale Beach near Southport where the food was laid out on the flat surface afforded by the open tailgate. I think what made it really desirable, however, was the colour. It was lime green. Cars up to that point had generally been available in vaguely utilitarian shades, but as this was the seventies the bodywork colour charts started to offer enticing options such as orange, turquoise, purple and lime green. These, with a generous dollop of brown, were the hues of the new *Zeitgeist*. Kitchen tiles, shower curtains, loose cushion covers, carpets, curtains, ponchos and snoods – you name it, it came in orange, brown and lime green swirls. As a nation we were finally breaking away from post-war austerity into a multicoloured future inspired by the set dressing in Swedish pornographic magazines. Everybody wanted their house to resemble a ski-lodge. Walls, where for decades woodchip had hung, became adorned with hessian or tongue-and-groove boarding. Chintz lampshades were replaced with woven raffia to increase not only fashionability but also fire risk. The concept of eating out of doors was gathering momentum, and the regulation yucca and cheese plants got ever larger. This was what defined progress. The garden became more like a house and the house more like a garden. They were exhilarating times, if bewildering for the older generation. My grandpa struggled with the idea that his Sunday tea was going to consist of something called a beefburger and it was going to be not only served outside but cooked outside as well.

'But why, when you've got a lovely fitted kitchen?' he enquired with some justification.

'Because it's a barbecue, George,' said my dad.

'But why cook outside when you've got an eye-level grill and a chip-pan inside?' retorted George with rising exasperation.

'Because it keeps the smells out of the house,' came the patient explanation.

'Well how come you haven't still got an outside toilet, then?'

There wasn't much you could say to that.

The domestic environment was undergoing rapid change and in theory that applied to the world of home entertainment. Many families had invested in what was known as a music centre, which was a single unit incorporating a gramophone, radio and cassette deck, usually housed under a smoked plastic lid. For the first time this enabled you to borrow albums from your mates and tape them onto C30 or C60 cassettes depending on the length of the LP. A C90 would allow you to have a different record on each side. This practice outraged the music industry and would eventually lead to a campaign under the slogan: 'home taping is killing music'. Well, guess what? It didn't. You could argue that it marked the start of a chain of events that would eventually lead to downloading and would kill the profits of many record companies, but that's not quite the same thing.

At 18 Towncroft Lane my father made a substantial, and rare, investment in the hi-fi future. He purchased a stereo sound system in 'separates', as this was what all audio buffs insisted upon. He began to subscribe to *Gramophone* magazine in which even the highest grade music centres would be sneered at. If you were serious about your listening, you had to research the different products and put your chosen combination together yourself, rather like a guitarist endlessy experimenting with different instruments, amplifiers and effects. The buying of these luxury items was such a big deal in our house that I can still remember the brands. There was a Goldring Lenco turntable, Leak amplifier and Wharfedale Super Linton speakers. Wow! We might not have been going to the moon but we were certainly going to get the full benefit of the latest album by pianist Ronnie Aldrich in Phase 4 stereo.

The arrival of this prestigious equipment also meant that our old record player was removed from the lounge and put in the back bedroom I shared with my brother Joe, who was younger than me, cuter than me and much better at football than me. Which wasn't saying much. Behind a hessian curtain in one alcove were stacked our toys and games, behind another in the opposite alcove our Ladybird and home-sewn clothes, and between the beds was placed the formerly precious Pye Black Box. This was, as you've probably guessed, a roughly cube-shaped item with mahogany veneer. You would place the records on a central spindle from which they would drop onto the deck before the Bakelite arm swung across and lowered itself onto the grooves. Because it was in a solid wooden cabinet the sound from this now outmoded and callously rejected unit was actually pretty good, and quite rightly so as it wasn't cheap. My parents had purchased it sometime in the mid-sixties. In a review from the esteemed *Gramophone* magazine from 1964 the price is quoted as forty-one guineas. That's around forty-five pounds at a time when a labourer could be earning around nine or ten quid a week. How many of us now would think of spending a month's pay on a record player?

Alongside the Black Box in our bedroom I had placed my

growing collection of drum and percussion oddments, which I was forever trying to blend into something that looked like a proper kit. At the centre was my sparkly red plastic Ringo Starr snare drum with a caricature of the handsomely hootered mop-top on the skin, so that every time you hit it you would batter the hapless hipster in the face. Around this were old toy drums, ragged cymbals, glockenspiels, xylophones, bongos, maracas and the odd real drum purchased from second-hand shops for birthdays or Christmas. This assembled I would play along to the few records I had access to. I played to an album called *Direct from the Balls Pond Road Cocoa Rooms* by The Temperance Seven purchased from the sale at Boots, a purchase in which I assume cost must have been the deciding factor. I drummed to 'The Pushbike Song' by The Mixtures and Mungo Jerry's 'In The Summertime'. I did not drum to *Sgt. Pepper* as my dad's records were not allowed out of the newly installed shelving downstairs. He maintained that the obsolete and rather heavy arm mechanism of the Black Box scratched his precious discs and he preferred to lower the stylus of the Goldring onto the vinyl himself so he could scratch the records by hand.

A lot of the records I could afford I would buy from market stalls, where you could get bundles of singles that had been played for many years on jukeboxes in pubs and coffee bars. They would accordingly be 'dinked', which is to say they had a larger hole punched through the centre of the label to be playable on the nation's Rock-olas. Once you had the required plastic hub to slot over your home record player spindle you could play these worn artefacts and discover bands you'd never heard of, as the records were sold as a package in which only the ones on the top and bottom were visible. There was always the chance that you were going to have wasted your pocket money on rubbish, but for every 'Young New Mexican Puppeteer' by Tom Jones, there was a 'Let's Work Together' by Canned Heat.

Hard rock was really getting into its stride, and indeed flared strides, by 1970 and this was the year its most effective exponents unleashed *Led Zeppelin III*. It's hard now to imagine how utterly thrilling that music sounded back then, but if you listen to 'The Immigrant Song' played very loud you might begin to feel it. Canned Heat's track may be easier to play along with but the Zep song does the lot in under two and a half minutes. Fantastical lyrics, a monster riff, intricate bass runs, drums like cannons going off and some screaming. If it's hard rock you want, everything you need to know is here.

'Let's Work Together' isn't as good as that. Not many things are, but it will always be a special tune to me. I still have it with the large hole in the centre of the green and turquoise Liberty label. With its gruff vocals, distorted slide guitar and throbbing beat it had a drive and excitement unlike any other tune I'd heard up to that point and I sat by the Black Box thrashing along to it for hours on end, often until my mum told me to stop because Joe was trying to sleep inches from the cacophony. But that was it. I knew that I was addicted to the drums when I played along to that record and would go to bed myself secure in the knowledge that sometime in the future I would be as famous as the drummer in Canned Heat. Whose name escapes me.

1971

SLADE – 'COZ I LUV YOU'

On 15 February 1971 the UK's currency went decimal to coincide with my sister Jaine's eleventh birthday. For weeks building up to this momentous change there had been posters in shops and on buses detailing the new coinage. The old easy-to-understand system of 12d to 1/- was being replaced with a bizarre new system based on units of ten. To make matters even more confusing, L.S.D., the old, logical abbreviation for pounds, shillings and pence, was going to be done away with in favour of N.P., which stood for these weird little new pence.

To make matters more confusing, some of the old coins would still be legal tender, meaning that a bob could be used as five new pence and a florin for ten. Are you following all this? My grandma certainly wasn't and was particularly alarmed by the disappearance of the old ha'penny because the new halfpence piece, worth about two and a half d, was deemed to be as small a denomination as anyone was likely to need. Grandma looked upon this as a surreptitious way of increasing bus fares and prices in general by rounding every-thing up to the nearest np, and she may well have been right. The same low trick was perpetrated in many countries years later with the switch to the euro. In fact, my grandma may even have underestimated the extent of the conspiracy, as the new halfpennies were so ridiculously small, not much bigger than a shirt button, that they were forever getting lost and were done away with altogether in 1984.

For many years they were collected by my grandparents to use as betting chips on Sunday nights at my Aunty Mary's, where feverish and extended bouts of a card game called Newmarket took place. On the occasions of bank or school holidays when we didn't have school on a Monday morning my brother or sister or I would receive the special privilege of staying over on our own and would spend a delicious evening during which not only would you not have to compete for attention with your siblings, but would also enter the high-octane world of gambling. Specifically for these occasions my gran kept a special purse full of half new p's, or 'tiddlers' as she had rechristened them, in the left-hand drawer of the powder blue and cream kitchenette. The purse was made of brown 'wet-look' plastic and had a gold clasp. Funny what you remember in vivid detail, isn't it? I mean, there is absolutely no point in having retained that information, and yet there it is, resurfacing forty years later. I suppose I'm just lucky I've got such a great memory. Now, where was I?...

Errm ...

Give me a minute ...

Right, got it.

Immediately post-decimalisation I bought my first album: *Master of Reality* by Black Sabbath. This was purchased second hand from a school friend called Pete Leatham for the sum of ten shillings or, more accurately, fifty new pence. The Sabbs are a hugely significant band not only for me and the British music scene but in the history of rock as a global phenomenon because if Dave Davies didn't invent the heavy metal riff, then Tony Iommi did. And this with two finger-tips of one hand missing and replaced with the remoulded caps off washing-up liquid bottles. To this day the courtly and Zorro-like Iommi plays his trademark SG with hardened leather caps on those same fingers. If that wasn't amazing enough, there is a supreme irony at the centre of this story. He not only lost those fingertips working with sheet steel in a foundry on machinery he hadn't been trained to use on, get this, the very last shift he was going to fulfil before departing for a career in rock and roll. The tension on the strings of his guitar proved initially problematic until he came up with the idea of tuning down a couple of tones, thereby giving that now all too familiar deep churning sound. If you want to get technical about it, for *Master of Reality* he is riffing in C-sharp. But how amazing that heavy metal should have been created due to a freak accident involving some heavy metal.

The album opens with the riffmeister general coughing his guts up before a trademark grinding motif that feels like it's been dredged up from the primordial deposits at the bottom of the River Severn, which heralds in a sludge-rock classic, and a paean to the joys of the herbal cigarette, 'Sweet Leaf'. It has been said that the opening of their 1970 eponymous debut album with its falling rain, tolling bell and Iommi's gut-wrenching power chords is as close to misery as has been captured on record, though this is a claim made by people who have evidently heard very little of The Stereophonics.

But it is pretty much impossible to overstate the influence of Black Sabbath on rock's dark side and yet, rather wonderfully, they are nothing if not amiable and larky in the flesh. Though Ozzy Osbourne's descent into reality TV caricature hell has perhaps diluted the brand somewhat, their sense of humour has undoubtedly been a factor in keeping the flame alive. The same night I met The Kinks at the UK Music Hall of Fame induction ceremony at Alexandra Palace, I also shared that same room with the original and forever the best line-up of Black Sabbath: Ozzy and Iommi along with drummer Bill

Ward and bassist 'Geezer' Butler. A less Satanic bunch you would struggle to meet and one recent incident they recalled and retold seemed to sum up the mentality within the band. Apparently they'd been playing one of their periodic reunion shows to the enormous delight of hardened fans ecstatic at seeing them together again, shrieking and cavorting over a selection of riffs that ate the Western world. As they stood abreast in a triumphant communal salute to the adoring throng at the end of the show, Ozzy quickly ducked down and with one swift tug pulled Bill's jogging bottoms down below his knees, leaving him facing a crowd of over two hundred thousand in his distinctly non-heavy-metal Y-fronts. All of them, Ward included, evidently found this hilarious and by way of explanation at what had possessed him to do it Osbourne replied simply: 'Well, he's got a big old schlong has Bill.'

This refusal to take yourself too seriously, whilst simultaneously taking your music very seriously indeed, seems to be a characteristic of musicians from the Black Country. Robert Plant is very much like that, as is the largely unacknowledged genius of sixties and seventies Brit-pop Roy Wood of The Move, Wizzard and ELO. And in the recession-hit Britain of the early seventies, with mass unemployment and the country heading for the three-day week, humour and fun were very much in demand. We were instinctively looking for music to raise our spirits, music that was tuned up a tone or two rather than down. Dark times were approaching and we needed shafts of brilliant light to come from somewhere and illuminate our dingiest corners. And the brightest beams of light anywhere radiated from Noddy Holder's hat.

I have very few what you might call 'showbiz' friends but one of them is Noddy Holder. Having spent plenty of time with him over the years I can tell you with some authority that it's great being Nod because everywhere he goes people are so pleased to see him. He has also aged fantastically well, by which I do not mean that he's desperately trying to cling on to his youth, but looks like a cheery, curly-headed, be-whiskered character from *The Pickwick Papers*. He also shares my belief that the mature man needs good footwear and possesses a pair of exquisitely practical and yet dainty lace-up ankle boots in the highest quality leather, which I refer to as his Emmeline Pankhurst shoes, to his characteristic glee.

Like Plant, Wood and The Sabbs, he is not remotely precious. I recently took him to a guitar shop to purchase a Gretsch and a Martin followed by steak-and-ale pie and hand-cut chips at my favourite pub The Spinner and Bergamot. There in the snug bar I urged him to show his new purchases to one of the locals known only as Badger, a keen wood man, as I knew he would appreciate the aged condition of the vintage timbers. Badger lovingly stroked the instruments before asking Nod, 'So, were you ever in a band or anything then?' Nod replied that he wasn't any more, though he had done a few gigs in the seventies.

The first time I saw Slade on television performing 'Coz I Luv You' I really did know it was going to be a hit. You could just tell. It was a great tune sung in an unmistakable voice with a rollicking beat and an uplifting sentiment. It had it all. At least as importantly they looked amazing. Dave Hill was obviously the court jester of glitter rock, with Noddy the cheerleader-in-chief, backed by the unimpressed-in-the-style-of-Charlie-Watts gum-chewing drummer Don Powell, and the serious musician Jim Lea. In fact my lasting memory of seeing them perform the song from those days was not the antics of the more colourful members but the tightness of Jimmy Lea's trousers. As he was playing fiddle at neck height, and stomping fervently to the beat, it was hard even for the nascent heterosexual not to be drawn towards his quivering crown jewels.

Talking to Noddy about their image, he says they were still

a skinhead band when fame seemed like a possibility. In their Doc Martens, Ben Shermans, braces and Crombies they found it easy to get gigs but tended to scare off TV producers. Their manager, ex-Animals bassist and Hendrix head honcho Chas Chandler, was convinced that a rock band could have pop hits and didn't want their threatening image to ruin their chances. Accordingly, says Nod, 'we coloured up', and if you check out his outfits from that period they are pretty much multicoloured versions of the classic skinhead look: the boots are still big, the trousers still ankle length, the braces still in place, though gurning guitarist Dave Hill dived headlong into the satin sartorial stakes, appearing on at least one occasion as a glam nun! Not a look previously popular amongst 'skins' indigenous to the Walsall area.

Nod credits the glittery tear stencilled onto Marc Bolan's cheek as the starting point of glam rock but Slade were very quick to follow. 'We thought we were cool because no one else was doing it,' he told me. 'All the other bands used to laugh at us but a year later, they were all doing it.'

Slade were a fixture of the pop scene right through until the eighties and their appearance never failed to lighten the nation's mood. The most potent symbol of their chart reign, however, remains that hat, the most famous hat in pop. Entranced with a revolving disco ball at some cheesy nightspot, Nod became intrigued by the bullets of light peppering the walls and ceiling, thinking, 'If I could do that on stage it'd look fantastic.' He had also been much taken with a metallic dress worn by Lulu that created a similar effect. The hat itself was subsequently purchased from Kensington Market, where the band often shopped for clothes. One of the stalls they frequented was run by a hyperactive glam-rock aspirant who was never slow to tell Noddy and the boys that he too was going to be a big star like them one day. This they took with a pinch of rock salt and on one occasion, having tired of hearing it yet again, Nod confesses that he said, 'Oh, fuck off, Freddie.' Uncharacteristically caustic though this was, it did not puncture the young market trader's self-belief, which proved to be in plentiful supply when he later changed his surname to Mercury.

Having bought what he calls 'that coachman's hat' Nod then found himself wandering past an interior design emporium which had strings of circular mirrors dangling in the window. Persuading the assistant to take them down from the display and sell them, Nod painstakingly glued them onto his new hat himself, knowing full well that when the spotlight hit on a blacked-out stage the results would be dramatic. As he eloquently describes it: 'When the lights went boom and the spotlight went bang on me hat, bumph, you could hear the crowd gasp.' Indeed you could. History was made and the gloom of the three-day week lifted momentarily.

Remarkably Neville Holder's services to national morale have yet to be rewarded with a knighthood, though he does have an MBE. Because of this oversight by the honours system I, and several others, have enobled him anyway and commonly refer to him as Sir Nod. How odd, then, to be tipped off in the great man's presence during one of the radio shows I present with Stuart Maconie of the 7.35 race at Wolverhampton the next night featuring a runner called Sir Nod at 16–1. Spooky, eh? Following this tip-off many listeners stuck a bet on and delighted in telling us how much they'd won the following week. I myself completely forgot to go to the bookies and so when I saw it had won immediately phoned Nod to congratulate him on yet another success. And guess what? He'd forgotten to back it too. Poor old Sir Nod. Obviously it's not such a big deal for me because I'm all right for cash as you've all bought this book, but spare a thought for Nod and the money that just slipped away. That's the story of his life in many ways. If only he'd written a big Christmas hit or something.

1972

MOTT THE HOOPLE –
'ALL THE YOUNG DUDES'

Despite having spent great swathes of my life searching out
new music, I've never been particularly bothered about the
bragging rights of having played it first. All I've ever wanted
to do is find great new tunes and share them with as many
people as possible, and if some other radio show has got
there before me, well, who cares? The important thing is that
it's getting heard.

When you're young, though, you do like that feeling of
having discovered something very early on before it got really
successful. This I thought I had managed in a big way in the
summer of 1972. My dad was by now working at Manchester
University as their press officer and had managed to get a lec-
turing post at a summer media school at a university in
Ontario. Accordingly my family took up residence for six
weeks in the pleasant college town of Windsor, which despite
being in Canada is actually further south than Detroit just
across the river over the Ambassador Bridge. That summer I
experienced such staples of the American way of life as bowling alleys, shopping malls and burger joints for the first time.
The fast-food culture really was exciting, as the first
McDonald's didn't open in the UK until two years later and
then only down south in a place called Woolwich, which was

apparently a quaint fishing hamlet close to that there London. You could get hamburgers in England but only from Wimpy Bars, which my grandma assured me 'attracted the wrong sort'.

Whether she was right was a moot point but on Saturday afternoons in Bolton I would occasionally consider escorting Hilary Wardle in there for a milk shake before being put off by the cloying stench of grease, the dense tobacco fug and the large numbers of large-booted, large skin and suedeheads who were largeing it up on the undersized leatherette banquettes. Perhaps we missed out on a vital part of youth coffee bar culture, but at least in the café in the small, independent department store Whitakers, a young courting couple in duffel coats from the grammar school could enjoy spaghetti hoops on toast without the underlying threat of violence.

The burger outlets in the states, predominantly McDonald's and Red Barn, were pristine, family friendly places by comparison and were located not only in downtown areas but in huge out-of-town parking lots where you could sit on a high stool in the window and watch the funny big cars with pointy fins cruising around like a scene from *American Graffiti*, which came out the following year, or such James Dean classics as *Rebel Without a Cause* and *The Boy Who Cruised Around In a Funny Big Pointy Fin Car*. You could also prepare for having to get used to the taste of ale in adult life by drinking something called root beer, which seemed to be a cocktail whose ingredients had been found in the cupboard where cleaning products were kept. Bizarrely, these diners were often found next to a chain of fish and chip shops called H. Salt, where meals were served in facsimile pages of 'The Times of London'. We weren't interested in that as we could get chips in newspaper back home, though never in pages of *The Times*. The *Bolton Evening News*, the *Sporting Life* or the *News of the World* maybe, but *The Times*, never.

Another feature of American life that seemed thrilling was the hypermarket. The concept of one shop where you could buy everything from groceries to clothing to electrical items to heavy artillery weapons had yet to be considered in the UK and so when we took family outings to K-Mart, we could be in there for hours as we all made our way to the departments that interested us. My mum and sister would do a bit of food shopping before heading for the clothes, my dad and brother would hit the sports section, whilst I would head straight for the music area. Here you would often find not only records but guitars, drum kits and keyboards as well and I would happily while away several hours there before it was time to head back to our rented house, stopping en route to pick up another burger and large cup of disinfectant.

It was whilst in one of these stores that I purchased the album I knew was going to give me real bragging rights back home. Everywhere you went in Ontario that summer you heard the primal yelp of freedom that was 'School's Out' by a panda-eyed, sword-wielding, heavily perspiring, satin-bodice-split-to-the-waist-wearing, Moral Majority-infuriating zombie who went by the name of Alice Cooper. And he was a bloke! Called Alice. How bonkers was that? Much later we discovered his name was Vince and he'd been in Beatle-esque garage beat groups like The Spiders and The Nazz, but in the summer of '72 he and his impressively long-haired accomplices seemed to symbolise liberty from the constraints of the system. I bought the *School's Out* album right there and then in K-Mart and pored over the sleeve, which was modelled on a graffiti-scarred school desk. This in itself marked it out as the work of rebels. My lasting contribution to the chemistry labs of Bolton School was to have heated up a set of tongs in a Bunsen burner and bored a charred hole through the workbench over the course of an academic year in cahoots with the redoubtable Roger Milne, who would waft away the resulting smoke with an exercise book. You could argue that this might have contributed to both of us failing chemistry O level, but a more important lesson of team work was learned that year and if school does anything useful it should be to teach things that will stand you in good stead in later life. I feel that the understanding in working together that Rog and I developed in those endless double periods has been of far more use to me than $SnO2(s)+2H2(g)->Sn(s)+2H20(g)$, though perhaps I'll be forced to change my opinion if I find myself doing any radio discussions on diatomic gas. After all, science is now the new rock'n'roll.

The early Alice Cooper records still seem to retain that illicit excitement when I hear them today. 'Elected' in particular still makes me tingle and seems to point to the limitless possibilities that you want to imagine are out there when you are a bored, spotty, spoddy teenager. *Love it to Death*, *Killer* and *Billion Dollar Babies* are all worth owning, but it's *School's Out* that will always be the one for me and not only because of the music, which, with tracks such as 'Luney Tune', 'My Stars' and the prescient reworking of the West Side Story gangland setting in 'Gutter Cat vs The Jets', bridles with a snotty unrest that would inspire both the punk and grunge movements years later. However, the other reason this record was extra special was because once you took off the shrink wrap and opened up the desk it revealed a vinyl LP wrapped in a pair of disposable girls' pants, which for boys of my age was as close to a pair of girls' pants as we were likely to get. I still have the record enveloped in those pants today and it's possible even now to relive the seamy rush of excitement they instilled in the fantasising adolescent. Unfortunately, later copies of the album came without the accompanying knickers because apparently they weren't 'flame retardant'. Not that anyone was going to burn them. Why would you? And anyway, isn't all underwear flammable? Certainly when

I was sharing a flat with the respectable building design consultant Phil Walmsley in our student days his lurid briefs caught fire whilst drying over the gas fire, leaving them practically arse-less though still wearable as he was, and is, nothing if not thrifty. In fact he began to extol the virtues of the backside-free underpant as when you went to the bathroom . . . well . . . let's just leave that there.

Returning to England in time to go back to school for the autumn term I was therefore cock and indeed ahoop that I had discovered this radical new rock star who, though nobody knew it yet, was going to change our lives forever and very much for the better. You can imagine, then, my disappointment to find that he was not only establishing a reputation over here but was actually number one in the charts. No cool points scored after all. Bugger.

There were other great records released that year which I forever associate with the first itchings of needing to break out in some way. In June Roxy Music released their debut album with its tantalising blend of glam rock and greasy rock-'n'roll combined with the sonic terrorism of one Brian Eno. Eno has been one of the most significant people to work in rock'n'roll because not only has he made great records of his own and produced aural installations of quality and distinction for countless other artists, notably U2, but he has constantly challenged the notions and possibilities of what rock can be. It is a source of some sadness to me that he and the creative lynchpin of Roxy, Bryan Ferry, couldn't find a way of combining their visions and talents for longer than just the first two albums, Eno leaving the following year after their masterpiece *For Your Pleasure*.

Perhaps, though, a parting was inevitable. In Reykjavik in 1972 Bobby Fischer beat Boris Spassky in perhaps the most keenly observed chess match of all time, and maybe Bobby Ferry would always have been locked in combat with Boris

Eno had they tried to stay in the same band. I once had the chance to ask Brian why he'd left Roxy Music and he said that having achieved what he'd set out to achieve and having created through that success the space and freedom to do whatever he pleased, why then would he choose to go back and do the same thing over again? And it is a perfectly fair question. For him, after *For Your Pleasure* school was indeed out for ever.

I have often thought that Eno bears a striking resemblance to the Mekon out of the Dan Dare strips and in fact his voyages and adventures in sound and ideas would make the basis for a comic book devoted to him, which I'm thinking of christening The B.Eno, but his notions and urgings have actually had an ongoing effect on my life through his Oblique Strategy cards. Developed with the artist Peter Schmidt, they're a box of business cards on which are written enigmatic instructions. The idea is that if you're stuck with something, then a seemingly random pointer can lead you somewhere you wouldn't otherwise have gone. I keep my set, signed by himself, in my desk drawer here and so if I hit writer's block I can just select any card, read 'overtly resist change', and carry on with what I was doing anyway. Genius. Brian himself told me he keeps a set by the front door and picks one up as he goes out so that the mantra might affect and infuse that day. Other cards read: 'abandon normal instruments', 'give way to your worst impulse', 'do we need holes?' (which Roger Milne and I had rather pre-imagined) and, what is perhaps the thought that has stayed with me most, 'honour thy error as a hidden intention'.

That great year of music for the fourteen-year-old me also produced *The Slider* by T. Rex and David Bowie's *Ziggy Stardust*. The effect Bowie had on me, as I have written about extensively in two other books, was positively life-changing.

If I had to select only one album to listen to ever again it would be *Ziggy* followed, quite possibly, by *Hunky Dory*. I'm not a great believer in picking single favourites, but when asked by my kids who my favourite singer is, I always answer Bowie. No one else has had the effect on me that he did and I think we all experience falling in love with music around about that age and, by definition, you can only have a first love once.

Not content with creating that masterpiece, Bowie, who would later collaborate to majestic effect with the similarly relentlessly inquisitive Eno on *Low* and *Heroes*, produced great works for other people that magical year. Lou Reed's *Transformer* catalogued the street life of a faraway place called New York, his songs of neon decadence and ragged comedown set to the sequinned cloaks of sound created by Bowie and his crown prince Mick Ronson.

The record that will forever mark my first blinking emergence into the possibilities of the future, however, was 'All The Young Dudes'. A solid, respected though struggling rock band from Hereford, Mott The Hoople, named as everyone knows after the Willard Manus novel that no one seems to have read, were on the brink of calling it a day before Bowie agreed to donate a song charitably to their cause as the last roll of their collective dice. He first offered them 'Suffragette City' which, displaying a sense of judgement that may well have contributed to the predicament they found themselves in, they rejected. 'All The Young Dudes', though, turned out to be their defining moment and revived a career that ran for many years afterwards.

For myself, I was old enough to be allowed to go up to Will Watson's house and, incredibly, stay out all night. Will's family were pretty well off, being the owners of a steel company, and so had a seriously big house. Across the yard from the main house was a stable block which had been floor-boarded, carpeted, plastered and heated, and it was to this den that we would retire with our drums, guitars, records and cider to get inspired, aroused, plastered and heated. In fact, on one memorable night I was so plastered that I removed my eyebrows and lashes whilst attempting to light the gas eye-level grill to make late-night cheese on toast. Wild times, indeed. School was definitely out. Occasionally my girlfriend Hilary and her mates could be persuaded to lounge around on the scatter cushions and bean bags for a few hours, in which case we might stick 'In A Broken Dream' by Python Lee Jackson on the hi-fi. A truly great track, it featured one of Rod Stewart's finest vocal performances, which is saying something, for which he was paid, legend has it, with a set of stretch-nylon faux leopardskin car seat covers. Whether these were the inspiration for his later leggings is hard to say. Naturally, the girls weren't allowed to stay over and so once they'd gone it was just us lads again with the long night in front of us, and 'All The Young Dudes' would be straight back on the turntable; and whenever I hear Mick Ralph's shimmering guitar intro I hear the chimes of freedom all over again.

1973

PINK FLOYD – 'THE DARK SIDE OF THE MOON'

So you think I've broken my own rule, don't you? For all the other years so far I've picked a single song and this is an album. Well, yes and no, because whilst you're technically right, *Dark Side Of The Moon* was a concept album and so, received wisdom had it, you had to listen to the whole thing in one sitting. Ideally on headphones.

OK, so here's what you need to know. It was released on St Patrick's Day and no doubt there are those who will think that significant, as every detail pertaining to this album is supposed to mean something. It is generally accepted that the 'concept' follows a journey into madness and St Patrick is credited with ridding Ireland of snakes, despite the fact that after the glaciers had been through, there were no snakes in Ireland. Bonkers. D'you see?

Further related mythology claims that you can listen to this album whilst watching *The Wizard of Oz* and it all marries together. This despite the band repeatedly denying there is any connection and engineer Alan Parsons stating that he never once heard that film mentioned by any member of the band. You can probably listen to *Dark Side* whilst watching *Holiday on the Buses* and find that just as 'On The Run' begins, Reg Varney, as larky bus driver Stan Butler, and Bob

Grant, portraying lecherous, buck-toothed conductor Jack Harper, skip away from raging, Hitler-moustached Inspector Blakey, played by Stephen Lewis. Shortly after 'Money' begins, someone is seen paying their bus fare. And when was *Holiday on the Buses* premiered? 1973! Now, that's got to be more than random chance. Or so some people would have you believe. Let me put this to bed once and for all. I have met David Gilmour, Roger Waters and Nick Mason several times and not once did I ever hear one of them mutter, 'I hate you, Butler' or refer in any way to *On the Buses*. Having said that, the TV series was killed off in 1973 too. What does that snatch of speech in the *Dark Side* mix say? 'I am not frightened of dying'. Hmmm.

Some other facts. *Dark Side Of The Moon* stayed on the album charts for 741 weeks from its release right through until 1988. It has sold over 45 million copies and you're reading this a while after I wrote it so it's got to be more than that now. Let's say 45 million and seventeen. In the 1980s a German pressing plant was devoted solely to producing CD copies of it. The first Pizza Hut in England opened in 1973 in Islington. Facts don't lie.

You couldn't really have lived through the seventies and remained unaware of *Dark Side Of The Moon*. Even if you weren't interested in 'that kind of music' you would have seen the famous Hipgnosis cover image of the prism distorting a beam of light (obeying the Huygens principle, science buffs) on posters in any record shop in the UK. Inside the gatefold sleeve the multicoloured strands of light then seem to be visually registering the heartbeat pulse that is a feature of the actual record. It is the perfect cover – memorable, interpretive of the music and just arty enough to let you know this band is 'serious'.

I suppose that's why I will never accept that the album as an art form is dead. I know there are millions of people for whom downloading a track onto their iPod is sufficient and that's absolutely fair enough. I've heard thousands of records on the radio that I enjoyed but didn't feel the need to own. However, you are missing out on the full sensory experience of records if that's the only way you ever consume music. Aged fifteen and lying on my bed in my attic room on Albert Road in Bolton, window flung wide open to let in the night air and uninterrupted views of the stars, with *Dark Side* swirling through my dad's headphones, was sheer blissful escapism. The way the sound shifted with fractured details of noise whipping across the stereo spectrum, those bursts of dialogue that seemed so random but now appear perfectly positioned, and the stately widescreen progress of a band at the peak of their powers. For me, a truly great album brings you something that individual tracks can never do. It takes you into another world where the sequencing of the songs marks some kind of journey.

Now I'm not saying that every concept album has done this successfully. Many are overblown and pompous and we could discuss some of the works of ELP and Yes here, perhaps. Nor am I saying that a great album has to be conceptual. Sometimes there are great LPs which are simply collections of wonderful songs that are entirely unrelated. The starting point for this book, Steely Dan's *Can't Buy A Thrill*, would be a good example as would *Moondance* or *Rubber Soul* or *Marquee Moon* or any number of others. But the order the songs are presented in is crucial. If I hear 'Five Years', the opening track of *Ziggy Stardust*, in isolation I'm still expecting it to slam into 'Moonage Daydream' as it does on the original record. That's one of the hallmarks of a great album, I think. Downloading is clearly a wonderful thing in making music accessible to everyone who wants it, but I'd hate to see it replace the all-embracing immersion in the good old-fashioned album.

Dark Side Of The Moon drew you into its cocoon in all these ways, though ultimately it is a great album because it is full of great music. There are the integral tone poems of 'On The Run' and 'Any Colour You Like' with its colliding clouds of sublime Stratocaster. 'Us And Them', 'Breathe', 'Great Gig In The Sky', 'Money', 'Time', 'Brain Damage' and 'Eclipse' are wonderful songs enriched by the washes of Rick Wright's keyboards and the beautifully melodic, distinctive and genuinely exciting guitar of David Gilmour, who is probably in my top five guitarists of all time along with Wilko Johnson, Tom Verlaine, Nick Drake and another bloke I haven't decided on yet.

I'm always loath to make lists of favourite things because it's always better to just enjoy everything as you encounter it rather than passing something by in favour of your favourite. Funnily enough, 'What is your favourite colour?' was one of the many questions that was asked of members of Floyd's crew, studio technicians, security men and, though they didn't make the final cut or indeed 'The Final Cut', Paul and Linda McCartney. As someone who has conducted many hundreds of interviews, the 'favourite colour' question has often been presented as evidence of the giveaway of the shallow and underprepared disc jockey. Pop mags used to pose just that sort of question to the sniffy disdain of we *NME* and *Melody Maker* readers. And yet, as any psychiatrist will tell you, knowing someone's favourite colour can actually be quite a revealing thing. For what it's worth, I can tell you that mine is purple and that may well confirm or alter what you think about me and, seeing as we're going to be together for a good few pages yet, I will give you an insight into my fascinating psyche so you feel you know me better:

Fave singer: David Bowie
Fave beer: Deuchars IPA

Fave cheese: Lancashire Leigh Toaster
Fave shoes: Church's Grafton brogue (brown)
Fave drums: Gretsch
Fave breed of dog: Cocker Spaniel
Fave poem: 'The Good Morrow' by John Donne
Fave guitar: Fender Telecaster
Fave football team: Manchester City
Fave curry: Lamb Madras
Hi, good to know you.

The other wonderful thing about Pink Floyd was their live show. They were by no means an ugly group, Wright and Gilmour being much admired in particular, and yet they were one of the first bands not to present themselves as pop stars. There was the sense when you saw them that they were an orchestra providing the soundtrack for a complete audiovisual experience. This made them ideal for the arena and stadium circuit. When I saw them in 1974 at the Palace Theatre in Manchester they started with some new as-yet-unrecorded songs, including 'Shine On You Crazy Diamond', before playing *Dark Side* in its entirety and encoring with the epic 'Echoes'. The band would often be spectral figures in the half-light, leading you to concentrate on the images projected onto the circular screen hanging over the stage. It was like a live movie if such a thing is possible. The album had come with posters and stickers which prominently featured the pyramids of the Giza plateau, and though it might sound ridiculous and insinuate hubris, there was the sense that in this music Floyd had created something on a similar scale.

Now I've just returned from seeing those pyramids for myself and I can tell you it is mind-bending. The Great Pyramid of Cheops, or Khafu as we serious Egyptologists who've been on a day trip prefer, consists of two and half million three-tonne limestone blocks, some of which had come from Aswan 500 miles away. I imagine that during the Floyd's shows to promote *The Wall* album, which featured an actual wall being built, there were roadies who felt they could empathise with the hordes who had been involved in the pyramid building that had gone on 4,000 years or so earlier. Clearly no one is suggesting that Roger Waters' creative vision was on a par with that, and anyway twice the length of Rog's wall divided by its height didn't correspond to pi as the Great Pyramid does so, without being competitive about it, Fourth Dynasty of the Old Kingdom 1 – Roger Waters 0.

But when you later saw Floyd at a stadium, as I did at Maine Road, they not only filled that arena with an epic soundtrack but provided a sound and light show, complete with the requisite floating pigs, that seemed to extend out into the whole night sky. 1973 also saw the launch of the first American space station Skylab and there was the sense that, if it had flown over during the show, Pink Floyd had probably put it there.

Another major scientific breakthrough that year was the launch of the food processor, but I prefer to revisit the revolutionary sound processing of *Dark Side Of The Moon* to take me back to those times when the grim reality of the three-day week could be left behind simply by listening to an album. Ideally on headphones. Unless there was a power cut, of course.

1974

GENESIS – 'THE LAMB LIES DOWN ON BROADWAY'

The creation of the disposable plastic razor by Gillette in 1974 has probably had a greater lasting impact on my life than the creation of 'The Lamb Lies Down' by Genesis but it didn't seem that way as a sixteen-year-old with the merest whisp of 'bum fluff' on the acne-peppered chin.

At Bolton School I was now entering the sixth form and as grown-ups in that establishment we obviously prided ourselves on listening to grown-up music and that meant progressive rock. In some ways the genre's name is inappropriate, as many of the bands looked back beyond the start of rock'n'roll to classical music for their influences. 'Prog' bands favoured extended pieces, suites and song cycles with recurring motifs and themes. Yes even credited their theme composers separately to the writers of the song on occasion. The compositions were as complicated as they could be and whilst generally melodic were riddled with shifting time signatures to baffle the young acolyte. The music was also universally grandiose with cathedrals of sound emanating from the increasingly prominent electronic keyboards, in particular the ethereal strains of the mellotron. Fantastical lyrical imagery was never far away, except if there was a twenty-minute drum solo.

Arguments rage as to what is the first progressive rock album, at least they have between me and my friends who don't get out much. The Canterbury-scene stalwarts Caravan and Soft Machine are right there at the start around 1968 although I've never been quite convinced that they are pure 'prog' with their jazz and hippy-dippy leanings and noodlings. Concept albums begin around the same time with the emphatically non-prog *Ogdens' Nut Gone Flake* by The Small Faces and *S.F. Sorrow* by The Rolling Stones' Dartford alumni The Pretty Things. Sneaking in a year earlier and taking the first concept album prize, though, are venerable Brummagens The Moody Blues with *Days Of Future Passed* in 1967. None of these would claim to be 'progressive rock', however, and so in prog year zero 1969 the honour is bestowed on King Crimson with *In The Court Of The Crimson King*, which remains a classic album, or the technically slightly earlier *The Aerosol Gray Machine* by Van der Graaf Generator, which doesn't. Many of the other giants of the scene were functioning around that time but had yet to leave their beat group pupas to become fully fledged prog butterflies. Gentle Giant were still trading as Simon Dupree and The Big Sound, Jethro Tull still too full-on folkie, Barclay James Harvest don't release their first album until 1970, Yes don't become fully proggified until *Fragile* and possibly bits of *The Yes Album* in '71, Emerson, Lake and Palmer can't get started until Greg Lake leaves Crimson and Genesis are still a pastorally polite public school pop group.

By 1974 Yes and Genesis had become the twin colossi of prog. At the back end of the previous year Yes had released *Tales From Topographic Oceans*, which is a double album containing just four pieces linked by a concept inspired by the Shastric scriptures discussed in *Autobiography of a Yogi* by Paramahansa Yogananda. Naturally.

Not to be outdone, Genesis unleashed their rambling

double-album concept piece less than a year later and if the Yes thread appears hard to follow then *The Lamb* is possibly even more impenetrable. Based on a dream-inspired short story which adorns the gatefold sleeve, the plot, such as it is, seems to involve a Puerto Rican bloke called Rael who is swept underground in New York City and encounters all kinds of weird creatures the likes of which you might find popping up in *Doctor Who* such as The Slippermen and The Lamia as he searches for his brother John. Or something like that. Even at the time of its release certain members of the band professed to be mystified at aspects of the saga and this turns out to have been fair enough, as talking to Peter Gabriel recently he cheerfully admitted that he wasn't entirely sure either. And it was his idea.

In contrast to *Tales from Topographic Oceans*, however, *The Lamb* has tons of tracks, twenty-two in fact, and includes some genuinely spine-tingling moments and surprising splashes of quirky pop. This, I think, is what ultimately made me fall in with the Genesis camp. They were the only prog band who were prepared to admit to a sense of humour and didn't shy away from the simple tune. They were also willing to take experimental turns into music concrete and abstract sound, no doubt pushed along by the credited Brian Eno whose touch is somewhere in the audio soup. Eno also had a good year, releasing not only *Taking Tiger Mountain (By Strategy)* but also, in *Here Come The Warm Jets*, one of the very few albums to make the UK charts with a photograph of a lady urinating on the cover.

Genesis were also blessed with a shy yet charismatic frontman in Gabriel and a musical visionary in organist Tony Banks accompanied by the serpentine guitar of Steve Hackett, Mike Rutherford's rumbling Rickenbacker bass and the world-class Phil Collins providing the fire from the drums. Their earlier albums *Nursery Cryme*, *Selling England*

By The Pound and especially *Foxtrot* are as good as prog rock ever got, although it is *The Lamb* that the diehard fans dream of them getting back together to perform. Peter says he hasn't ruled it out, though the others say he's been not ruling it out for a very long time.

I saw Genesis performing *The Lamb Lies Down On Broadway* at the Palace Theatre in Manchester that same year. They played two nights. I went to both. As a live act they were unimaginably imaginative to the impressionable teen and I'd been captivated ever since I saw them the previous year at the Opera House, opening with 'Watcher Of The Skies' with its swathes of ghostly mellotron in complete darkness save for the illuminated white outlines around Peter's blinking eyes.

That night me and my school friends waited around the back to see if we could get some autographs on the photocopied album sleeves we'd brought with us, not wanting to risk our precious real copies in the big-city scrum. Eventually a cheerily dishevelled Phil Collins came out in a sheepskin jacket and obliged. Whilst we were waiting I became absolutely fascinated with the phalanx of roadies who were packing the gear away into a truck so long that it had a small cart on rails that ran the length of the trailer. A couple of burly handlers would load a flight case onto this bogey and then send it on its way into the shadowy depths of the wagon where two similarly burly troglodytes would manhandle it into position before sending the empty cart whizzing back for the mellotron or tubular bells. That was when I became utterly convinced I had to be in a group, as I found the whole backstage operation compelling and strangely seductive.

The first time I got backstage for real was at a concert at the Free Trade Hall in Manchester. Chris Ecob, Andy Wright and myself had taken the bus from Moor Lane terminus in Bolton to go and watch Argent, who had created one of the anthems of those times in 'Hold Your Head Up', which was played at every scout hut disco. After the show we hung around on the narrow part of the balcony overlooking the stage to watch the ballet of the technicians deconstructing the 'rig'. Looking up at us, one of the crew, presumably with a keen pre-Health and Safety regulations eye for slave labour, asked us if we wanted to help. What, us? Three lowly schoolboys from Bolton handling the drum cases of the great Bob Henrit? Wow, it was like *Jim'll Fix It* only better, because Jim'll wasn't there. As we risked slipped teenage discs and adolescent hernias humping a Hammond organ and Leslie speaker out of the backstage doors we really thought we'd arrived. If we hadn't been moving at such a sluggish rate anyway I'm sure we'd have slowed down just in case any rank-and-file 'civilian' ardent Argent admirer hanging around by the trucks wanted our autographs. After we'd finished lugging amps the size of Welsh dressers around, the same roadie gave us four English pounds. Between us. Fantastic. That was enough for fried chicken and chips at the all-night café just off Peter Square before shuffling back across town to catch the night bus. What a night!

Since then I've been backstage many times and it still gives me a real buzz whether at a large gig by a proper band or at a small club where I'm performing with either The Family Mahone or The Big Figures. I was once charged with producing a live Fleetwood Mac concert for Radio 1 and watched as Mick Fleetwood's drum technician Reedo wheeled out a flight case that housed a lathe on which he turned Mick's drumsticks to create grooves to aid the gentleman sticksman's grip. Why this couldn't have been done before they left LA was perhaps a question no one had thought to ask. One extra flight case amongst several hundred wasn't going to make any difference, was it? And so a lathe travelled the world to be used to make ruts in drumsticks for five minutes every other day or so. Mick and John McVie came from the hotel to the gig in a 52-seater coach. Just two old bald fellas in hats on a big old bus. Stevie Nicks and Christine McVie had director's chairs with their names on the back that they sat in while they had their make-up done. Why not, eh?

Rick Wakeman told me that Yes lead singer Jon Anderson used to have a tepee in his dressing room and it seemed all too believable from what I saw backstage at a concert at the Birmingham NEC in the late eighties. Due to one of their regular wrangles, the line-up of Yes that was touring at that time wasn't allowed to call itself Yes because of some legal issues involving absent bass player Chris Squire. Back then there was a television advert for Lloyds TSB which used the slogan 'The bank that likes to say yes', and not just to enriching its own traders. This was rather wonderfully co-opted for an article in Q magazine which ran: 'Anderson, Bruford, Wakeman and Howe – the band that likes to say Yes. Except they can't.'

Before the whole band took to the stage to perform a selection of symphonic greats, each of the four princes of prog performed a solo spot. I became intrigued by a member of the crew standing outside the corridor of separate dressing rooms with a silk dressing gown over his arm. Jon Anderson was out front performing some acoustic balladry, possibly from his solo album *Olias of Sunhillow*, which tells the story of Olias, the architect of the glider Moorglade, which, with help from Ranyart the navigator, is going to help the Sunhillow tribes under the command of QoQuak escape to a new life. Naturally. Shortly before this part of the concert came to an end Yes' spectacularly dextrous and skeletally thin guitarist Steve Howe emerged from the inner sanctum, and the aide-de-camp placed the kimono around the plank-spanking pixie's paltry shoulders. As Anderson basked in the adulation of the crowd he took a bow and announced Steve Howe, at which point the satin-clad elf ascended the ramp to the stage, pausing in the wings just long enough for another roadie to gently remove the dressing gown before he went on. I recalled this incident with the garrulous giant of the baroque keyboards Lord Richard of Wakeman and he roared with laughter, as he often does. He then went on to tell me about the time that Yes were recording an album and there was a split in the ranks, inevitably, about whether to record in London or 'get it together in the country'. A compromise was reached by recording in the city but with several large stuffed farm animals and bales of hay in the studio. You couldn't make it up. Because that would bring a lawsuit.

The Wakemeister is full of such stories, much better tales than you'd find in any topographic ocean. Whilst staging his solo epic *The Myths and Legends of King Arthur and the Knights of the Round Table* on ice, naturally, he recalled how one of the knights had phoned in sick for that evening's show. Sadly it wasn't until the battle scene that the realisation dawned that with an odd number of knights, there was one left over skating round and round with no one to kill him and no visible means of dying, resulting in someone in the audience shouting out, 'Shoot him, Rick.'

He also cheerfully confirmed what I'd assumed to be a rock myth. Apparently, whilst playing in Manchester at the hoary old Free Trade Hall, home of the Hallé Orchestra, a peckish Rick had despatched his assistant the three miles down the road to Rusholme and its celebrated 'curry mile', where neon-lit Indian restaurants competed for the student and prog rock pound. Returning with the requisite biryani banquet the roadie nipped back onto the side of the stage and gleefully brandished the carrier bags at the famished keyboard wizard. Conveniently underemployed at that moment, due to another Jon Anderson interlude, Rick beckoned the bemused chap on and proceeded to demolish the grub whilst ducking down behind the bank of Minimoogs. Anderson, his concentration threatened by a sudden infusion of aromatic aromas, was understandably less than amused.

It's easy to laugh at the pomposity of some of these records now but *The Lamb Lies Down on Broadway* still holds thrills driven not only by nostalgia but by genuine appreciation of the ambition and scale of the thing. Not only that, but the vinyl copy I still own was the first album bought for me by my paternal grandma Doris. When I tore open the gift paper at Christmas she was so nervous that she'd bought the wrong record that she'd wrapped it in the carrier bag from the shop in case I wanted to take it back. Bless. At first, as it was a concept album, I assumed that the carrier bag was part of the official packaging, which was by no means an impossibilty.

These then were the musical scenes that were forming the backdrop of my last years as a schoolboy. But life was about to change. University was beckoning and across the Atlantic the New York Dolls were already at work destroying everything we had come to hold sacred.

1975

BOB MARLEY –
'TRENCHTOWN ROCK (LIVE)'

Of all the venues in which to have seen the biggest reggae star the world has ever known an ice rink must be easily the least appropriate. Ideally you would want to have witnessed The Wailers on a balmy, herbally infused Kingston evening overlooking the Palisadoes with a smoky haze resting on the distant Blue Mountains. The sound of sporadic gunfire may have added to the piquancy of the heady atmosphere. Thankfully, there were no firearms incidents at Deeside Leisure Centre that night in July 1980 when I went to see His Bobness, a name also used to refer to Dylan, who released the classic *Blood On The Tracks* this year, but rarely, if ever, Monkhouse.

I had been besotted by Marley since hearing the album *Catch a Fire*, which came in a sleeve that was a facsimile of a Zippo cigarette lighter complete with a flip-top opening, and seeing them perform on television on *The Old Grey Whistle Test*. On screen they appeared not so much laid-back as asleep. They made Little Feat look like The Ramones. At the time I put their somnambulant state, if that's not a little unfair on somnambulists who can at least summon the energy to walk, down to jet lag, little understanding the effects of sustained infusion of the kind of 'herb' that didn't appear to have a place on my mum's spice-rack.

In some ways this lack of effort or indeed consciousness was compelling. I'd never seen a band before who didn't want to jump around, gurn at the audience or at least pull pained facial expressions to make it look like what they were doing was more difficult than it really was. But if the band appeared to have been exhumed shortly before the cameras rolled, the music and the passion in the voice had me hooked from the very beginning. Even to the extent that it translated across the damp sheeting spread across the disintegrating surface of an ice rink in North Wales. Heaven knows what Marley, the Barrett brothers, Al Anderson, Tyrone Downie and The I Threes made of it – even if they had liberally ingested some herbal aperitifs, they must still have been aware that it was a bit parky. I would later return to the same venue to spend a couple of hours shivering whilst The Police patrolled their cod reggae beat.

Neither of these gigs, though, felt as cold as Happy Mondays at Whitley Bay ice rink. If Scott of the Antarctic's stoic companion Lawrence Oates had been there he may well have turned to the hardy captain during 'Kinky Afro' and said, 'I am just going outside and I may be some time because it has got to be warmer out there in the car park.' Although the wind that bit hard as it rampaged in off the North Sea that night made that questionable. The Stone Roses, Oasis, The Jam and The Cure also took to the stage at Whitley Bay ice rink, as did the sweaty, heaving Speedo-clad buttocks of the millionaire knuckleheads of the World Wrestling Federation, who were presumably the warmest people ever to have performed there. Heavens, it was cold that night. No wonder Pope Nicholas IV got so much enthusiasm from the Bay area when he was looking for Crusaders. A few months in the Holy Land would have been a welcome break from those kind of icy conditions, I would imagine. In fact, the town does seem to have yearned for

warmer climes, as its long-gone permanent funfair, and setting for the Dire Straits' 'Tunnel Of Love', was called The
Spanish City.

The Happy Mondays, possibly having chemically shielded
themselves against hypothermia, probably put in a reasonable
performance that night, although I was so numb it was hard to
concentrate. Adding to the evening's sense of the bizarre was
the fact that the support act was bucolic star-gazing balladeer
Donovan. At the time he had not one, but two daughters
romantically entwined with members of the Mondays. One
can only imagine that tested his hippy, live-and-let-live ideals
to the full. I mean, to lose one child to a Ryder brother looks
careless, but to lose two? What was going through Donovan
Leitch's head as he faced a crowd of hoodied urchins swashing
round an ice rink is hard to imagine, though he may well have
wondered if he hadn't fallen asleep and woken up in *The Lord
of the Rings* struggling to recall the exact scene where the
Hobbits started skating. Or perhaps it was all a spectacular
pageant staged by Rick Wakeman.

Knowing Donovan, as I don't, really, though I have met
him twice, he probably took it all in his stride. After all, if
you've led the life he's led involving communes and the
swinging sixties and being regarded by Dylan as his British
counterpart, you're probably beyond being surprised by anything. However, he may still be moderately nonplussed by
my claiming here and now that I once played lead guitar for
him. It was in the bar at The Master Builder's House Hotel
in Bucklers Hard, Hampshire, where some of the ships of
Nelson's fleet were constructed and launched into the
Beaulieu River. I was down there producing some programmes for Radio 1 with my long-time cohort 'Fish' John
Leonard. During the day we staged a full-on, tight white
tennis shorts, satin bomber jacket, Smiley Miley roadshow
with guests including, would you believe, Jason Donovan. In

the evening, from the bar of the sumptuous hotel, we broadcast a specialist music show titled 'The Mike Read Collection'. Mike was an alarmingly tall, charmingly mulletted disc jockey who was a passionate collector of vinyl records, making him something of a rarity amongst the mainstream presenters of that time.

That night we had invited Donovan to appear on the show and ended up sitting round the bar, late into the night, strumming the guitars that Mike and 'Fish' John always had with them. Being a drummer and not knowing the chords but not wanting to be left out I accordingly joined in as best I could by plinking and plonking random notes and trying to look as though I knew what I was doing for the assembled crowd of locals and work colleagues. I more or less got away with it by obeying the simple rules that The Wailers so casually eschewed – by screwing my face up to make it look demanding and by playing any horrible bum-note a second time to make it look like I meant it. What did Brian Eno say about 'honour thy mistake as a hidden intention'? That was my modus operandi. It might have sounded awful but it was what I had intended. Except when it wasn't.

Eventually, as the day I met Donovan and Jason Donovan melted into the night, I noticed that the man himself had vanished.

'Has Donovan gone to bed?' I enquired of his manager.

'Donovan doesn't go to bed,' came the reply, 'Donovan crashes.'

In 1975 Margaret Thatcher became leader of the Conservative Party, inflation was running at 25 per cent, *Fawlty Towers* began and Paul McCartney, who evidently shared some of Bob Marley's recreational enthusiasms, was fined for growing this marijuana stuff. Of far greater significance to me personally was the fact that I passed my driving test at the second attempt and was now officially a 'boyfriend who could drive', which would enable me to hang on to Zoe Thompson for a while longer. Several mates of mine had suffered ignoble terminations of relationships due to the absence of a full licence. Poor Colin Seddon had ridden round to girlfriend Kathy Rowlinson's house to show off his new drop-handlebar push-bike with derailleur gears, as opposed to *Disraeli Gears*, which is an album by Cream. Though no doubt a more impressive machine than the one ridden by my granddad, concealed during wet weather by a large yellow cape that covered both him and the bike, leaving only his flat-capped head exposed to the elements, it was still no match for the powder blue Triumph Dolomite Sprint she was whisked away in by Barry Atkinson, who was one of the leaders at the Venture Scouts. The flash bastard.

I didn't have my own car until I was twenty-one but I was allowed to borrow my parents' Citroën GS by prior arrangement and so was able to chauffeur the fragrant Zoe out to Bolton and stand her dinner at the Berni Inn on Churchgate. Whether I remember the exact details of the bill because it was the first time I ever bought a woman a meal, or because I'm a tightwad who checks these things copiously, I couldn't really say, but I know we had chicken and chips and gammon and chips with half a bottle of Mateus Rosé and it came to £2.75, which might not sound a lot but that's a thousand pounds in today's money.

The atmosphere between us I'm sure would have been relaxed though slightly heightened by nervousness at how to behave like real adults. Fascinating company though I am, it's probably fair to say that there was a more charged atmosphere at the London Lyceum in July 1975 when The Wailers did their stuff. The LP recording of the gigs is one of those rarest of things, a live album you'd want to hear over and over again and with versions of the tracks that are, if anything, better than the studio versions. In particular the opening 'Trenchtown Rock' seems to be an uplifting invitation to a whole other world. At least, that's how it sounded to me. I was seventeen and fully aware that the following year I would be leaving home and there would have to be a new sound-track to accompany this new life. Walking down Oxford Road in Manchester, having spent the afternoon rummaging around in the back rooms and bargain buckets of the music shops and heading for my dad's office at the university to get a lift home, I wandered into the record shop in the student precinct and bought *Bob Marley and The Wailers Live at the Lyceum*. Surrounded by the hustle and excitement of the undergraduate hoards, in strolling distance of art galleries, theatres, good pubs, guitar shops, ethnic takeaways and rock-'n'roll venues, that purchase seemed to signify that life was going to change beyond all recognition. I had yet to dis-cover Patti Smith, who released the seminal *Horses* that year; Dr Feelgood put out *Down By The Jetty*, which would have a long-lasting influence and was much discussed in my last book; and Led Zeppelin unveiled *Physical Graffiti*, which though another of those rarest of things, a double album that wouldn't actually have made a better single album, signified the past and not the future in my expanding mind. Reggae was something I hadn't really absorbed before and in fact it would become a regular accompaniment to the punk gigs we would start to frequent the following year, as the DJs couldn't play punk records before the bands came on because there weren't any. Accordingly the reggae sound systems forged the new counterculture along with the snotty white guitar bands, and the first step into this new wonderland came when I heard 'Trenchtown Rock'.

1976

THE DAMNED – 'NEW ROSE'

With the possible exception of the birth of rock'n'roll in the late fifties there can't have been a better time to be eighteen than 1976. Leaving home and moving into a hall of residence in Manchester may have taken me only a dozen miles or so from where I'd grown up but it was like visiting a promised land, such were the opportunities and experiences that presented themselves from the very first day. You met people who had never been to Bolton, or even heard of it, and saw the world in an entirely different way. There were exciting bands on in numerous sweaty dives, combined with the prospect of an occasional sweaty dive onto a willowy female undergraduate in cheesecloth rooming in the next hall. And there was the blissful freedom of coming and going as you pleased without anyone saying, 'What time do you call this, then?'

The sound of punk perfectly encapsulated this new sense of year zero, when everything I had known before accounted for nothing. The punk bands declared war on Genesis and Yes and I signed up for national service, rejecting the flared trouser and the prog rock concept in the name of progress.

The Damned have the honour of being credited with releasing the first punk single when 'New Rose' came out in November 1976 a couple of weeks ahead of The Sex Pistols'

'Anarchy In The UK'. Buzzcocks followed relatively quickly with the 'Spiral Scratch' EP in January the following year with the tardy Clash bringing up the rear in March with 'White Riot'. The Ramones had, of course, beaten everyone to it by releasing their stupendous eponymous debut album in July '76.

The Ramones are a truly seminal group in the history of pop music in that they were at the forefront of a gritty revolution that stripped away all the fluff and excess of music that had gone before and yet simultaneously revered the finer points of classic pop. Later they would work with Phil Spector, proving that their prime influence was not the Velvet Underground but The Ronettes.

The Damned wittily echoed this by kicking off 'New Rose' with a nod to 'Leader Of The Pack' by The Shangri-Las before the punk Keith Moon Rat Scabies' drum tsunami swept all before it. It was such an energising and empowering sound that it just made you feel glad to be alive. Especially if you were eighteen and living away from home for the first time.

With punk rock everything changed. A record company wasn't necessarily a glass-fronted office block with heavy security somewhere in a leafy square in that there London. New Hormones, run by Richard Boon for his charges Buzzcocks, was through a grubby shop doorway on Newton Street, just near the one-room Virgin record shop in Manchester city centre. If you were in a band it was scintillating to know that other bands were releasing era-defining records without having to go flat cap in hand to lofty London labels to be given permission. Musicianship also became gratifyingly less prized. Most of the great bands have started off as bunches of mates who made a wonderful racket together, not musical protégés hand-picked from the local conservatoire. Everything suddenly became so much more attainable.

The Damned live were also an inspiring spectacle. The aforementioned Rat Scabies was a whirlwind on the drums and energy, and therefore youth, were prized elements of the punk sound. They also had a suspiciously adept rock guitarist in Brian James, a lovably cartoon punk bassist going by the name of Captain Sensible and a vampire on lead vocals called Dave 'Transyl' Vanian.

The best band I saw in that era was Johnny Thunders and The Heartbreakers, who had honed their trade for years with The New York Dolls posse. Viewed in the celebrated Eric's club in Liverpool they seemed like a bomb going off. This, I think, is something that everyone needs to see at some point in their life. Part of you will always be missing if you haven't experienced that utterly absorbing, physical thrill of standing too close to the overloud speakers of a young, impassioned, stick-thin group of hucksters who are literally exploding on stage. The Damned certainly had an incendiary presence and 'New Rose' became such a moment in my life that I chose it as the first record I played on my first show on Radio 1 many years later.

One of the characters from the punk era I found particularly engaging was the self-styled punk poet John Cooper Clarke. A laconically loquacious, lanky Lancastrian, he was working as the clerk in the technical stores department of Salford College of Technology and resembled a cruelly underfed Bob Dylan. He is without doubt the thinnest man I have ever met, with spindly legs that are no wider than my not especially beefy arms. He began to be a regular figure on the punk circuit, often as support act, confronting braying, seething masses of mucus-spraying spods with only a microphone and his rapid-fire poems. He would later tour as opening act to art rockers Be-Bop Deluxe, no doubt under the express instruction of Be-Bop's mischievous and inquisitive reluctant guitar hero leader Bill Nelson, and also with Dave Edmunds and Nick Lowe's Rockpile in America. What they made of him in Coal Scuttle, North Dakota, or Urinal, Idaho, heaven only knows.

I have seen John perform many times and never been less than entranced by his implausible combination of such classic poems as 'I Married A Monster From Outer Space' and 'Beasley Street', delivered from what ought to be an impossibly addled memory given the lifestyle choices he's made along the way, along with straight gags, rambling anecdotes, half-realised flights of surreal fancy and uncanny impressions of Jimmy Savile. Why it works I'll never know, but that was punk for you. Everything you know is worthless and the only rules are the ones you set yourself.

I have come to know John reasonably well and not that long ago hired him for one of my radio shows with the mixed portfolio of fashion and doo-wop correspondent. He is a dapper guy in his own inimitable way, as a man with such an odd build and need of made-to-measure tailoring has to be, and we have had many conversations on such burning issues as the Tootal scarf and the definitive brogue. He is also a gentleman with impeccable manners, something I witnessed when he phoned my house. We wandered in from the garden with some friends to find my youngest daughter Rose, then aged around two, chatting away on the phone. She was at that age when kids want to talk but haven't yet mastered actual words and so just rattle out streams of gibberish.

'Ah, look,' said the indulgent father, 'she's having one of her pretend conversations.'

No doubt our guests managed a wan smile with a raising of the eyes when my back was turned as we let this scene play out for several minutes.

'What's really amazing,' I continued, 'is that she leaves gaps in the conversation for the imaginary person on the other end of the line.'

We then viewed this spectacle that only a parent could really be interested in for some time before I realised that there actually was someone on the other end of the line. I took the receiver from Rose and put it to my ear.

'Hello.'

'Hiya, Mark, Johnny Clarke here. Just been having a chat with one of your kids.'

Typical John. He hadn't hung up or complained about being kept on the line for ages without any discernible sense having been spoken. He had just cheerfully enjoyed a phone encounter with a toddler he had never met standing in a kitchen two hundred miles away.

John was the first performance poet I had ever encountered. I was a real poetry fan, having been encouraged by the inspirational teacher Charles Winder to appreciate the works of Gerard Manley Hopkins, and then going through a major Metaphysical period at university, although that may have been in a doomed attempt to impress the intimidatingly bright, Titian-haired girl in the brocade trench coat who I sat next to in tutorials who'd professed great admiration for the sumptuous stanzas of George Herbert. But aside from Pam Ayres and that boss-eyed bloke on *That's Life* and the occasional appearance of Roger McGough or Adrian Henri on the regional arts programmes, poetry was something that was very much of the page. Cooper Clarke changed all that and without him there would have been no ongoing oral culture and therefore no rap. (I'm not sure I really believe this to be honest. I've just introduced it as a topic for discussion for when this book appears on the reading list at the University of Bourton-on-the-Water (Lower Slaughter campus) for the degree course in Poetic Licence and Creative Graffiti. You may find some useful points here to counter your lecturer's claim that if Andrew Marvell was alive today he'd be Jay-Z.)

Like many teenagers, I wrote my own verse in my suitably lofty garret bedroom at the family home on Albert Road in Bolton and having expressed a love of poetry I thought I would use this point to publish exclusively for the first time some of my seminal early poetic works. Obviously it would be inappropriate for me to comment on these marvels, if not perhaps quite Marvells, as my assessment of my own genius may not be completely objective. I have therefore enlisted the help of Simon Armitage, who is a friend of mine and considered by some to be the finest poet of his generation, although those same people haven't seen my works until now. It is my heartfelt wish that Simon becomes the next poet laureate. With all due respect to Carol Ann Duffy, I think he should have had it when Andrew Motion left the post, and I can only hope that the discovery of my selected verses, written precociously at the age of fifteen and sixteen, doesn't derail Simon's claim on the post.

The first one is called 'The Machine Stops':

My clock is ticking on my bedroom shelf
It is controlling my mind an inner self
No longer have I got a will of my own
All things I have done the clock face has shown
Each tick gives me a new piece of knowledge
I'll never have the need to go to a college
All day long in my room with nothing to do but sit
Clock controls my life but something's wrong with it
Now it's slowly stopping, knowledge from me is flying
Then I knew just what it meant, the earth was truly
    dying.

Well, either that or it needed a new battery. And to be perfectly fair I wasn't often in my room all day with 'nothing to do but sit' as I could play records, cross the landing to bash the drums, nip to my brother's bedroom to play table football, watch telly or go out on my bike. It is also true that I did eventually go to college and whether my career would have turned out quite the same way if I had restricted my studies to a clock face is doubtful. However, those caveats aside, it is still marvellously evocative of teenage disenfranchisement and really says everything that Holden Caulfield took a whole book to whinge about. Simon's view is slightly different:

> Shades of Bowie in the last line and the piece has a very seventies prog rock feel to it mixed with a bit of Dali and the college/knowledge rhyme that even Jarvis Cocker couldn't breathe life into so many years later. Advice: get out more.

Hmmm. Admittedly this work was from my pre–punk canon and perhaps I should have sent him some of my more 'new wave' works such as 'Breakfast In Bondage' or 'Alpine Woman, Mountain Bullock'. So, moving on, the next one is called 'Future Death':

> Life is one great cycle, it goes round and round
> And with atom bombs and warfare
> Man can't keep his feet on the ground
> This is the true story I have found
>
> Technology builds our world with man power employed
> They build us an ideal society but the end is only being
>   decoyed
> We don't know that in future war
> We will all be destroyed

It continues cycling on and on again
Killing, polluting it races on killing another race of men
Where will it all end you ask
I don't know it could be now or then

OK, I'll admit that I always meant to go back and tweak that
'end is only being decoyed' bit, but I do think it is elegiacally
prescient about the wars that have raged in the intervening
years and owes more than a little to Robert Frost, Alfred
Lord Tennyson and Geezer 'Lord' Butler of Black Sabbath.
The rather unnecessarily scathing Armitage shows scant
regard for the inherent poignancy of the poem however:

This is one of Adrian Mole's at his most pubescent, surely?
It's very depressing so on that front it's certainly a poem. I
like the shrug of the shoulders at the end. The apocalypse?
Oh well, I'll just have my tea first.

Yes, well, it's all very well for 'poets' who've got nothing
better to do than swan around the hills and dales in a chiffon
scarf and floppy hat, isn't it? Some of us had to fit writing
poetry in with homework, and lying on Zoe Thompson's
bed and watching *Midweek Sports Special.*

Still, let's push on, as I know how much you, dear reader,
will be enjoying these verses in spite of the cynicism expressed
by Mr Cocky Armitage-Fotherington-Thomas.

This one is called 'Silver Decanter Labels' and it goes like
this:

Silver decanter labels hang round the necks
Of their tall cut glass sentinels
Containing brandy and port
Standing on silver trays, not touched for days and days
Dust is gathering, surrounding

One book lies on the shelf
One book all by itself
Pages are yellow and fading
Metal binder always creaks
Not touched for weeks and weeks
Dust is gathering, surrounding

Sorrowful inscriptions of graves and epitaphs
Overgrown and forgotten
Memories of sorrow tears
Not touched for years and years
Nobody cares in this society we live in
Nobody wants to know
People come and people go
. . . are you sure?

Well, quite sure as it happens, but we'll let that go. There may be some critics who will take the fact that the decanters remained untouched for days on end as creditable evidence of my parents' moderation when it came to drinking and that if I had enough time to wander around the house making observations about the gathering grime whilst they were at work then I could have just got a duster and helped out a bit more. But if I'd spent my time on domestic chores then I wouldn't have had time to compose and the world would have been deprived of these profundities. Reading the line about the book with 'yellow and fading' pages I'm actually wondering if this was Yellow Pages, but that's part of my gift, I think. To take the everyday and make it universal somehow. Let's see what smarty-pants Simon says:

This is more like it.

Well, whoop-de-doo! Finally he starts to see sense.

Focus on detail is always useful in a poem. The small noun objects of the everyday. Things by which we measure our lives. Unfortunately . . .

Here we go.

Unfortunately it then descends into a list of airbrushed abstractions and unsupported concepts that are always the preserve of the novice. So, nothing to suggest a T.S. Eliot in the making I'm afraid.

Bloody philistine. I'm beginning to think they were right to give it to Carol Ann after all. And anyway, Simon, if T.S. Eliot was alive today he'd be Dizzee Rascal. Discuss.

1977

KRAFTWERK – 'EUROPE ENDLESS'

'So they're a pop group with machines instead of guitars, then, Dad?'

This was the question posed by my eleven-year-old daughter Mia on hearing Kraftwerk for the first time. She and her younger sister Rose have been exposed to many different styles of music on the school run, as have I with their regular insistence on the paternally approved Black Eyed Peas and the less easy on the 52-year-old ear Hannah Montana. I love playing them records they've never heard before as they respond in such an intuitive way, free of any pigeon-holing or prejudice, just open-mindedly absorbing new sounds. Amongst the artists they have come to love are Led Zeppelin, with 'Immigrant Song' a particular favourite, Dr Feelgood, Creedence Clearwater Revival, Hank Williams, The Sensational Alex Harvey Band (not 'Next' for reasons of parental guidance), Ry Cooder, Fleet Foxes, The Rolling Stones, Chuck Berry and Supertramp. Going down less well have been Bruce Springsteen, who has been deemed 'too shouty', and Bob Dylan of whom they have independently posed the perennial question, 'But is that really singing?' Captain Beefheart's *Trout Mask Replica* they found intriguing but unsettling like a Tim Burton film and decided they 'didn't really understand what was going on', which is fair enough as I don't either and I've been listening to it for thirty-five years.

Kraftwerk they took to instantly, which didn't surprise me as their music not only has a nursery rhyme simplicity in the melody lines but is also immediately accessible in terms of subject matter. In contrast to *Trout Mask Replica* even a cursory listen to 'Trans-Europe Express', 'Autobahn', 'The Robots' or 'Tour De France' will be enough to fully 'understand what's going on'.

Nineteen seventy-seven was an interesting year for music in that punk was well established and some of the most fascinating records of that era appeared that took the liberating energy rush of the new wave somewhere more artistically intriguing. Talking Heads, Elvis Costello and XTC debuted, and Television unveiled what I consider to be one of the greatest albums of all time in *Marquee Moon*. Even now I'm not quite sure how they did it. Listening to 'Venus' it is as if both guitars, the bass and the drums are all playing lead parts, and not necessarily of the same song. And yet, like a string quartet with Fenders, it all melds together beautifully.

To further confirm that a new age of musical republicanism had arrived, the King toppled from his jewel-encrusted 'throne' when Elvis died on 16 August. I was on a camping trip in France when I heard the news and will always have a vivid memory of the newspaper hoardings proclaiming '*Elvis est mort*'. In the interests of historical accuracy, which hasn't overtly troubled me thus far, I'd better admit that this republicanistic fervour was somewhat compromised by celebrations for the Queen's Silver Jubilee. I may even have attended a street party myself but in drainpipe trousers and spiky hair with my fingers crossed behind my back.

Kraftwerk I had known principally through their unlikely global hit single 'Autobahn' and had tried to lock on to their early albums without really 'understanding what was going on'. Their initial art-rock noodlings gradually began to refine through the *Autobahn* and *Radio-Activity* albums before they perfected the template on the essential and wondrous *Trans-Europe Express*. Released this year, it was quickly followed in 1978 by their other masterpiece *The Man Machine*, which would spawn another unlikely global hit single: 'The Model'.

Trans-Europe Express is a perfectly realised sonic ride on that defunct line. The opening track 'Europe Endless' in particular combines their trademark pure beats with a tune that seems to have existed forever. The rhythm of the album is generated by an electronic facsimile of the rattle and crunch of rolling stock on rail with melodies of stately elegance floating gracefully above like sedate, decadent passengers admiring the passing views from the cocoon of the dining car. The band themselves appeared to be people just like that. They looked nothing like a rock band. They were formally dressed with neat, militaristic haircuts and seemed to be playing with the notions of Germanic formality and inscrutability. They even, without the slightest suggestion that they were politically that way inclined, appeared to be toying with the idealised, air-brushed 'master race' ideas that lay at the heart of the Nazi ethos. Of course, as personalities they were impenetrable and so we assumed that they were lampooning such notions given their artistic background, though we had no way of knowing for sure, which gave them a sinister air of intangibility. To some extent they have succeeded in concealing all traces of humour throughout their career though the lighter moments are best captured by their estranged percussionist Wolfgang Flür's memoir *I Was A Robot*. I won't attempt to condense his engaging book into a few lines but suffice to say it contains a picture taken backstage of the famous band members' doppelgänger robots in which leader Ralf Hütter is snogging Wolfgang whilst his drumming accomplice Karl Bartos gooses Hütter in the anal crevice. Such antics were not hallmarks of a Kraftwerk show under normal circumstances.

Normally a complete lack of humour would put me off a band, but with Kraftwerk it's hard to see how it could be accommodated. At the heart of their work lies an exploration of the relationship between man and machine, and the possible subjugation of individualism that many feared as technology marched ever onwards. Whether any similar notions occurred to Steve Jobs, who had founded Apple Computers the previous year, is hard to say, but Kraftwerk reflected a world that was changing. Strangely, their work ethic seemed quaintly old-fashioned. Their Kling Klang studio in Düsseldorf was where they clocked on daily, working intently at their stations without fear of distraction as the premises famously had no phone. With this kind of work rate then you would have to question their productivity. Since the creatively rich period from 1975 through to *Electric Cafe* in 1986, new material has been thin on the ground. In fact, recent releases seem to have been restricted primarily to variations on the theme of their 1983 single 'Tour De France'.

Somehow, though, this only adds to the Kraftwerk conundrum and forces us to return again to the glory of the major extant works. Perhaps having achieved perfection, it's hard to know where to go next. Not that they would admit that. Well, I say 'they', though these days Kraftwerk appears to be primarily 'he'. The classic line-up remains the foursome of Flür and Bartos on electronic percussion centre stage, with leader and vocalist Ralf Hütter on the left bookended by the other founder member, the professorial Florian Schneider at the other side of the stage wrestling with his array of gadgetry. Drummers have come and gone but the central pairing, the Lennon and McCartney of electro, the Simon and Garfunkel of synth, The Krankies of Krautrock, were ever present. Imagine, then, the shockwaves caused by the announcement in 2009 that Florian had left the band. The unthinkable had happened. The timing in particular seemed odd. Why had he left a band that hadn't released any new records for years? There can't have been musical differences because there wasn't really any music to have differences over. Had they simply fallen out as friends? Or lovers? Rumours abounded and so it was with great interest that I met fanatical cyclist Ralf Hütter backstage at the Manchester Velodrome that same summer where they were staging a concert which would also feature the multi-medal-winning British Olympic cycling team. How wonderful to be able to ask him myself what had happened to Florian.

Being ushered into a standard backstage arena gig dressing room, with anonymous grey sofas and a large table bearing tea and coffee in steel flasks and a plate of Kit-Kats, I waited for him to arrive. I wasn't nervous. I'd met them before several years earlier when I'd followed them on tour from the Manchester Free Trade Hall to the Liverpool Empire and then to the London Lyceum, scene of those euphoric Bob Marley concerts. Working for local radio I had managed to get an interview with them in the bowels of the Empire where they proved polite and not overly reserved and cheerfully signed my copy of *Trans-Europe Express*. Ralf also wrote a little note on the sleeve which reads: '*Für unseren radio freund Mark aus den Englischen wellen vom funk*', which roughly translates as 'For the best mate we have ever had in England and you are better than Tony Blackburn on the radio with funk', or words to that effect.

In Manchester I was also treated by the record company to a high-end Italian meal at Cesare's with the talkative Ralf and the urbane Wolfgang. Karl was presumably elsewhere throwing pocket calculators out of hotel windows. Florian wasn't there either, though I did bump into him the following morning in Piccadilly Gardens, where he cheerfully showed me what toiletries he had just purchased from Boots. Mouthwash was involved, as I recall.

Ralf walked casually, though stopping short of sauntering, into the room at the velodrome, shook hands and sat down. He was wearing his greying hair in a side parting, a dark striped shirt, black trousers and, incongruously, Converse sneakers. I thought it might be indelicate to ask about Florian straight away and so began by enquiring what all Kraftwerk fans wanted to know. Was there any new stuff set for imminent release?

'Yes,' he replied with visible glee. This, it had to be said, was thrilling news. There hadn't been the slightest hint that anything was on the horizon so this was quite an exclusive. Could he expand at all?

'The immediate future will see the release of "The Catalogue", which is all the eight albums in original artwork for the first time.'

Ah, right. That's wonderful but not exactly what I meant. When I had asked about 'new stuff' I meant new 'new stuff' not new 'old stuff', welcome though that was. I probed further.

'New ideas are coming, we are composing always.'

He then went on to explain that it was he who had invented the concept of the 168-hour working week where 'there's no separation between work and free time as there is a continuous process of making music, finding ideas, staying in shape, travelling, being home, regeneration, activities, sleep'.

OK. This is an enticing theory and one that, if you work in a job where you charge by the hour, an extremely profitable one, however it's hard to envisage customers cheerfully coughing up large amounts of cash to plumbers and landscape gardeners who have happened upon waste disposal and shrubbery solutions in their dreams.

He maintained that they are constantly working on new music, which must mean that their work rate is painfully slow or their quality control formidably rigorous – quite possibly both.

'The best music comes like automatic,' he said, 'and when it is finished, we know. The *Tour De France* album was sleeping with me for twenty years.'

Finally I decided the time was right to confront the elephant in the room, as there was a travelling circus in town that same night.

So no Florian, then.

'No.'

A pause. I wondered if he could explain why.

'We continue working. He's working on other projects at the university. We just continue working.'

'Are you still friends?'

A longer pause.

'I don't know.'

'So it needs a little time, does it?'

An even longer pause.

'I can't say.'

At the time I came away thinking that we'd had an engaging and productive conversation and in some ways we had, though on listening to it again I'm struck by the calm and polite way he answers all my questions without really telling me anything I didn't already know. Perhaps this is down to my ineptitude as an interviewer, but in a way I was glad it had turned out that way. Kraftwerk were always a mystery and an enigma and some mysteries are better left unsolved, some enigmas forever unlocked.

1978

PATTI SMITH – 'BECAUSE THE NIGHT'

In 1978 a lot of the confusion about hydrogen ions, which had certainly been keeping me awake at nights, was put to bed when Peter Mitchell was awarded the Nobel prize for chemistry due to his contribution to the uncertainty of biological energy transfer through the formulation of the chemiosmotic theory, narrowly taking the title ahead of Bolton-based wunderkinds Radcliffe and Milne, who had made a major contribution to the certainty of hole boring in a lab bench through the formulation of the tong–Bunsen theory.

Since being overlooked in such a condescending way by the Nobel Foundation I have, of course, been quite rightly garlanded with a plethora of awards for my pioneering radio work, the certificates for which I proudly display in the baronial hall of my DJ castle along with one I received earlier in life for ten lengths and a dive. Nevertheless, the snub still smarts. It seems to me that the categories in the Nobel pantheon are hugely biased towards scientific swots. Admittedly there are awards for literature and peace, which seems an odd one given that old Alfie Nobel was the originator of dynamite, but the others are for stuff like physics, chemistry, physiology and medicine. That's ridiculously biased in favour of white-coated boffins in jam-jar-bottom spectacles shuffling round laboratories scratching their testicles.

Weirdly, as the system seems to have been set up to reward geeks, there is no Nobel prize for sums, or mathematics as they prefer to call it. There is, however, a gong for economics, which is more or less the same as it's all numbers. Unless it's those really advanced spod sums which seem to have letters in them. What's that all about, then? Letters should be the exclusive domain of towering literary giants like myself and Jackie Collins. Why are these supposed bright sparks invading our territory? Have they run out of numbers? They can't have been as clever as they thought they were if they've allowed that to happen. I'm on the twenty-first chapter of this book and I haven't run out of letters and suddenly had to resort to a sentence like: 'I have always loved Patti Smith because 34%->7836 minus the square on the hypotenuse = 137', have I? Keep the numbers where they belong, mathletes, and leave the letters in the hands of us expurts.

But why aren't there more Nobel prizes for those of us unconnected with the world of science? Why no Nobel prize for architecture or painting or painting and decorating? Apart from the welcome recognition on the world stage, these prizes come with a hefty cheque for more than a million dollars. Laurence Llewelyn-Bowen aside, what painter and decorator couldn't use that?

Of course, I'm not suggesting that science doesn't play a vital role in our lives and shouldn't be publicly rewarded. Nineteen seventy-eight saw not only the birth of the world's first test-tube baby, Louise Brown, but also the advent of the mobile phone and the introduction of the Space Invaders computer game.

Space Invaders marked the great leap forward for computer technology, as if it hadn't been for this innovation by the Taito corporation of Japan we would still be playing that 'blip-blop' table tennis game with a little line for a bat. So a scientific advance like that would have to be rewarded with a

Nobel prize for physics, right? Wrong. That year it went to Pyotr Leonidovich Kapitsa for his work in low-temperature physics. Big deal. So he worked in a laboratory where the central heating had packed up in the Russian winter, but did he produce a game that kept thousands of people entertained at home and in pubs? No, he didn't.

Personally, I wasn't surprised that the mobile phone guys got overlooked as they still had some way to go before they could really justify the 'mobile' tag. The first 'mobile' phones came with a battery the size of a chest freezer, which the canny British government responded to by introducing the Motability scheme this year to provide disabled people with cars so they would be able to carry their 'mobile' phones about.

My first experience of a portable cell phone came a decade later when in 1988 I produced Bon Jovi in concert for Radio 1 from the Milton Keynes Bowl. My principal memory of this day is of sitting in the recording truck after the show whilst erstwhile bassist Alec John Such, a cheery pomp-rock pixie of a man in white high-heeled boots, replaced the bass line on the opening song having played all the wrong notes on stage, whilst the rest of the band waited testily in a nearby idling helicopter. It was also a memorable occasion because I was entrusted with one of the BBC's precious mobile phones. By this time technology had moved at such a pace that the handset, now as miraculously small as a carton of 200 duty-free cigarettes, was accompanied by one of the new lightweight charger packs, which was almost as light as a mere car battery. The equipment worked fairly well although if you walked out onto the site without the back-up battery the charge dropped rapidly resulting in very low call volume, which at least gave you a good excuse to get as far away from Bon Jovi as possible.

★

There is also no Nobel prize for music, which if there had been in 1978 would almost certainly have gone to The Bee Gees, at least one of whom does look like a lab technician, for their sterling work in soundtrack advancement and research through the 'Saturday Night Fever/Grease' theory. But here's a thing. Even if you win a Nobel prize as a team of people, it can't be awarded to more than two of you. In 2002 an award was made for the development of mass spectrometry in protein chemistry. Fair enough. No argument there. Quite rightly John Fenn and, if I had to choose probably my favourite mass spectromatist, Koichi Tanaka were enNobeled. But poor old Franz Hillenkamp and Michael Karas got nothing and presumably consoled each other over several subsidised pints of scrumpy in the union bar at the University of Frankfurt. That would have meant that one of The Bee Gees, and I'm thinking Robin, would not only have missed out but would have had to have gone for a drink on his own whilst his brothers took all the credit. The heartless sods.

Other contenders for the 1978 Nobel prize for pop would have been Fleetwood Mac for their advancement of middle-of-the-road marriage-guidance music research through the 'Rumours' theory, or the suitably scientific Kraftwerk for breakthroughs in the world of electro-robotic-ambient-disco research commonly known as 'The Man Machine' theory.

Controversially, or at least as controversially as the arbitrary awarding of a prize that doesn't exist can be, I've decided to bestow the honour on Patti Smith.

I have always loved Patti Smith because 34%->7836 minus the square on the hypotenuse = 137. More than this, though, she was undoubtedly one of the key voices in the founding of the punk movement despite creating music that complied to very few of the basic punk rules. Her music could be abrasive, certainly, but it was never a simple thrash. She seemed to be combining a background in the arts, and performance poetry particularly, working from a musical palette that broke new ground and discarded old ways, but refused to be confined by the restrictive tenets of the new-wave template. Her piano player, the late Richard Sohl, was an unashamedly adept tousle-haired cherub with classical training. She was also a hugely important role model for women, and I was led to fully embrace Patti by my girlfriend of the time, Carole, who was a devoted fan.

Smith had her own distinctive look, captured perfectly forever by Robert Mapplethorpe in one of only twelve polaroids he took of her for the cover of her 1975 debut album *Horses*. It is a simple portrait of a frail figure in a plain white shirt with a black jacket thrown casually over one shoulder and yet it brims with presence and attitude. There is a touch of androgyny about her and yet the confidence of a woman in control shines through. If you get the chance to read her book *Just Kids* about her life as an impoverished book store clerk in New York and her relationship with Mapplethorpe, you'll discover an outcast in cast-offs feeding less on food than on the bohemian buzz of that great city, and yet you will be struck by her absolute sureness that they would both be artists the world would have to take note of. That conviction is there for all to see on the cover of *Horses*. Here is someone who is where she always knew she would be, where she always felt she deserved to be, and woe betide anyone who told her otherwise.

There were other female icons in punk, of course. Debbie Harry fronted Blondie, and should not be underestimated as a songwriter and musical force in her own right, as her looks made it all too easy to recall her past as a Bunny Girl. But her band was called Blondie. Patti's was called The Patti Smith Group. England had Poly Styrene of X-Ray Spex, Pauline Murray fronting Penetration and all-female band The Slits.

Tina Weymouth and Gaye Advert were bass players for Talking Heads and The Adverts. But no other woman in the public eye in 1978 seemed to be as sure-footed as Patti Smith, with the possible exception of Anna Ford, who became the first female newsreader for ITN that same year. Oh, and Margaret Thatcher.

I have met and interviewed Patti Smith several times and it has been wonderful to discover what a charming and erudite person she is. She is one of those rarest of interviewees, someone who is not only fascinating but fascinated. When she visited me at the studios of the BBC on Oxford Road in Manchester she had an old-fashioned Polaroid camera with her. She took a solitary frame of the tower cranes in the Mancunian gloom on the construction site on the opposite side of the street. I have it here now. 'Cranes in Manchester' she has written on the back and signed it. I always said that one day I would use it as the cover photo to a book or a record because it is a highly evocative picture of the town I know and love and its seemingly continuous regeneration, but also just so I could have a credit that reads 'cover photograph by Patti Smith'. She also signed the sleeve of my original vinyl copy of *Horses* making it one of the personalised vinyl artefacts I treasure the most, along with *Ziggy* signed by Bowie, *Down By The Jetty* scrawled upon by the three remaining original members of Dr Feelgood, that Kraftwerk LP and *The White Album* inscribed by Paul McCartney. Patti's message is generous and positive: 'To Mark, wonderful to meet you. People have the power.'

In 1978 Patti Smith released perhaps her most elegiac album, *Easter*. One of the tracks was a real surprise. It was co-written by Patti with that shouty Bruce Springsteen. Initially this seemed a strange collaboration, as Patti was the queen of the underground, Bruce the boss of the blue-collar big beat. The contact came about due to producer and engineer

Jimmy Iovine, who was working simultaneously on *Easter* and *Darkness On The Edge Of Town*, which was being recorded in the studio next door. Bruce recorded but did not release his version of the song at the time, so Patti reworked the lyrics to give it a female perspective and made it entirely her own. And 'Because The Night' became a huge hit on both sides of the Atlantic. Robert Mapplethorpe, hearing the ubiquitous song emanating from a dozen stores in downtown New York, turned to Patti, as she recalls in *Just Kids*, and grins, saying, 'What do you know? You got famous before me.'

Her new-found success Carole and I, and legions of other ardent admirers, found inevitably bittersweet. A world where Patti Smith could have hits was obviously a better place to be than it had been before. And yet, though we knew she deserved it, and though it was great that the word was spreading, she wasn't our secret any more.

JOY DIVISION – 'TRANSMISSION'

In 1979 I was twenty-one and for my birthday was given my first car. I know that sounds terribly grand and privileged and all that and I suppose it was, though you didn't see the car in question. It was an aged Renault 6 L which, if you search online for a picture, is a model that looked like it had been produced and designed in an Eastern Bloc country where style and comfort were viewed as capitalist indulgences. Utilitarian might be the word to describe it. I think it's fair to say that it's not what I would have chosen if choice had come into it. It didn't, as it was passed on to me from the previous careful lady owner: my mum.

I was still highly chuffed to have my own transport, of course, and enthusiastically embraced the peculiar layout of the car's interior. The front seat was, like the rear, one long bench running the width of the car like a cut-price vinyl couch from a budget furniture warehouse in Gdansk. The gear stick was accordingly situated in the middle of the dashboard and resembled the handle from a lady's umbrella. Pushing and pulling it to select a gear would therefore have been a complicated game of chance at the best of times for the inexperienced driver and the apparent lack of any synchromesh just added to the sense of adventure.

Petrolheads will want to know about the performance, of

course, and though I'm not very good with statistics of this kind I can tell you that it wasn't the speediest car on the road. In fact on the frequent journeys Carole and I made over the M62 to visit her family in Bingley it appeared to be the least speedy car on the road. I vividly recall struggling over Saddleworth Moor in a snowstorm and having to drive on the hard shoulder just so irate HGV drivers could sprint on at speeds of up to thirty-five miles an hour in the inside lane. The engine size of the early Renault 6 I now see was a mighty 845 cc, which may have had something to do with it.

You could probably have achieved higher speeds on certain models of ride-on lawnmower, which reminds me of Shirley, the wife of country music legend George Jones, being phoned by local law enforcement officers to come and retrieve her drunk husband from a bar in Beaumont, Texas, around eight miles from the Jones homestead. The long-suffering Southern-fried spouse was not only furious but also bemused as she'd hidden the keys to all the couple's cars and so was curious how he'd managed to get there. What her reaction was when she was told that he'd driven there on his lawnmower we can only surmise. Incidentally, if you're thinking of buying one of these machines, George's was apparently a John Deere. I'm not on commission or anything but it does seem to be a pretty good recommendation. Whether the company signed Georgie boy up for an advertising campaign with a slogan along the lines of 'get the grass cut whilst being half-cut' I couldn't say, but if they didn't, they missed a trick.

My Renault 6 L was finished in an attractive combination of cream with what looked like burnt orange detail over the wheel arches, which closer inspection would reveal as rust. This necessitated me spending several weeks in the garage with paints, primers and fillers of which I knew little. I am to car maintenance what Alex Ferguson is to cordiality. Someone who would have made a far better job of it was

Peter Hook of Joy Division. I remember Factory Records supremo Tony Wilson telling me how he was looking out of the window of their modest headquarters on Palatine Road and saw Hooky lying on the oil-stained driveway tinkering with something on the underside of another vehicle that had seen better days. Tony said he found it almost impossible to equate this burly, bearded figure who was cursing and grappling with a monkey wrench with the man who composed and played those majestic soaring bass lines.

There were many important records released in 1979 including albums by The Specials, Madness and, not least, *London Calling* by The Clash. But if you lived in Manchester, and were 'that way inclined', the music of Joy Division cast some kind of spell over the city. Manchester is a place I love, having visited it regularly as a kid growing up in Bolton and then moving there to go to college in 1976. I've lived in it, or on the southern outskirts of it, for all but two of the intervening years but in 1979 it was a hard place to love. Photographs of me and my friends taken at that time with the concrete walkways of the Hulme housing projects in the background, trudging towards the squat, rendered building known as the Russell Club in our long raincoats with haircuts by the council, make it look like East Berlin just after the war.

What is now the pristine conference and exhibition centre formerly known as G-Mex was the dark decaying shell of Manchester Central Station, its abandoned clock frozen in time on its abandoned facade – a symbol of a once proud city that had suffered decades of decline. For those of us who had grown up in a town in the shadow of this great Northern metropolis – and Manchester was by no means unique in this respect – the decay and neglect was hard to understand. Further evidence of the blight was visible at the crumbling docks and if anything this was even more depressing. After all,

hadn't we pulled off one of the sneakiest tricks ever perpetrated by one city over another in stealing the sea from nearby
Liverpool? Wealthy and powerful Mancunian industrialists,
jealous of the seaport status of our Merseyside neighbour,
decided that we would have a port, too, despite the minor
inconvenience of being landlocked. So it was that in 1887
Lord Egerton cut the first turf to commence construction of
the Manchester Ship Canal, a project that would employ
16,000 navvies. This, combined with our mighty Freddie and
The Dreamers stealing the thunder of The Beatles, probably
explains the bitter rivalry between the two cities to this day.
Most fans of Manchester United reserve their most vitriolic
bile for Liverpool FC rather than Manchester City. This may
be because Liverpool proved peskily persistent in running off
with silverware for many years, something that we gentlemen
of the blue persuasion could never be accused of.

'The FA Cup? No, please, after you.'

Both red clubs have gleefully maintained this long-stand-
ing battle and, though it hurts to admit it, I have to
acknowledge the achievements of United. Alex Ferguson has
skilfully assembled a squad of individuals who are not only
marvellous players but also impossible to like if you don't support the club. Look at Gary Neville. Has he ever smiled
d'you think? If you were ever to meet a giant wasp face to
face and that wasp had had a shave, his face would look very
like that of Gary Neville. His brother Phil, on the other
hand, looks like giant of American song Burt Bacharach.
With his mouth open.

Walking the city streets of Manchester in 1979 you would
have heard the music of Joy Division in your head even if
they hadn't invented it. Their records seemed to draw
together an industrial heritage and epic grandeur with that
sense of disenfranchisement, of dereliction, of melancholy.

There was also a real sense of mystery about them. Their photographs never appeared on their covers. Their names were never mentioned. Eventually we would see them live many times and start to understand them as personalities. Much later I would get to know three of them personally and come to realise that they were ordinary guys who just happened to have made extraordinary music. Sadly, Ian Curtis was someone I never got the chance to know.

The music of Joy Division, made in Manchester and released on the inspirational Factory Records under the auspices of the Lord Manc Mayor Tony Wilson, did seem to embody the pulse of the city at that time. Working at Piccadilly Radio I managed to convince the benevolent bosses that there really ought to be one show a week reflecting the burgeoning indie music scene both nationally and, in particular, locally. When they agreed I named the first radio programme I would ever present *Transmission* after the flawlessly euphonious Joy Division single.

I recently rummaged through several boxes of gubbins in my loft before finding an old cassette on which is a recording of the last *Transmission* dated 2 September 1982. The show begins with eerie organ theme music which I explain at length is titled 'Rue Fortune' and is by Hans-Joachim Roedelius of the band Cluster from an album called *Jardin Au Feu* on the Sky label. And this on commercial radio. It's hard to imagine a young producer being indulged with that sort of freedom now. I then proceed to give a rundown of some of the bands that are going to be featured in the programme, which include: The Mothmen, Associates, The Enthusiasts, Syncopation, Weekend, Echo and The Bunnymen, Sandie Shaw, Bauhaus, A Certain Ratio, The Pale Fountains, Blue Zoo, The Higsons, Leisure Process, Paul Haig, Some Detergents, Dr Filth, Mick Karn, Agency Music, Scritti Politti, ABC, Ben Watt, Dexy's Midnight Runners, Orange Juice, Kevin Harrison, Ministry,

Elli and Jacno, The Clash, Robyn Hitchcock, Elvis Costello, New Order and of course Joy Division. Several things struck me on hearing my 24-year-old self go through this list, most notably that at least half of these artists I still feature on radio programmes to this day. Of course there are those who have faded into obscurity but then that was always going to be the way of things with a show like that and, anyway, I've never been able to spot a hit to save my life. At one point on the tape I predict a great future for The Wild Swans, who sound rather like a Liverpool take on Joy Division, and speculate that U2 may struggle to get much recognition in the UK having concentrated too much effort on the American market. With that uncanny ability to foresee the musical future it is perhaps surprising that my radio career has lasted as long as it has. Oddly, I seem preoccupied with the failure of most of the records I championed to break into the national charts and in some ways, whilst smiling at my own naivety and blind idealism, this is something that pains me even now. Every week I heard and still hear what I came to christen the 'hit parade of a parallel universe' as some of the greatest records ever made, in my opinion, failed and fail to capture the imagination of the wider public.

The other thing that was really striking is how quietly I was speaking. Evidently influenced massively by John Peel, I sound like a flat-lining manic depressive who has lost the ability to feel or convey the slightest evidence of enthusiasm or excitement. I'm sure that this was an intentional ploy to distance myself from the standard hyperventilation of the standard disc jockey but, goodness, it's not easy to listen to. I wanted to shake myself vigorously by the shoulders and tell myself to wake up.

That year saw the launch of Trivial Pursuit and the Sony Walkman, Village People proclaim the delights of life at the YMCA and the opening of the first designated nudist beach at Brighton, so you would have to conclude that fun was happening somewhere. It didn't appear to be happening on my radio show, however, and you may be struck by the thought that nothing much has changed.

1980

JOY DIVISION – 'ATMOSPHERE'

John Lennon got shot.
Ian Curtis committed suicide.
Margaret Thatcher was 'not for turning'.
Radio Caroline sank.
Blimey. Perhaps I should have picked 'Atmosphere' by Russ Abbot.*

* I know it wasn't released until 1984 but you know what I'm saying

1981

THE HUMAN LEAGUE – 'LOVE ACTION'

In some ways the record that is the most apposite reminder of 1981 is The Specials' 'Ghost Town'. As hordes of the disaffected and dispossessed took to the city streets the ominous, mournful and yet reflective voice of Terry Hall oozed from radios everywhere. As one commentator of popular culture put it: '"Ghost Town", with its backdrop of disembodied sirens and slack ska menace, and released as inner city riots swept the nation, remains as much a snapshot of those times as any news footage.' I couldn't have put it better myself. In fact I did put it myself. That is a quote from my first major foray into the literary world – *Showbusiness: Diary of a Rock'n'Roll Nobody* – and if you think I've got a bit of a cheek padding this book out with extracts from earlier ones then try and look on it as environmentally friendly recycling. After all, the new words I haven't used to illustrate this point will now be left behind for my granddaughter and, to introduce an original thought that may not have occurred to anyone at all, I believe that the children are our future.

The concept of reusability gathered momentum in 1981, not least because the space shuttle Columbia blasted off and then came back again. This gave me hope that my much desired trip into space might become a reality, as the ticket prices had to drop substantially once you didn't need a brand-new Saturn 5 every time you send someone up there. I mean, second-hand vehicles are much cheaper, aren't they? My S-reg Honda CRV was £16,000 when I bought it and is now worth about £700 so that's a depreciation of around 95 per cent and so if ticket prices to the moon were reduced in line with that, and I can see no good reason why they shouldn't be, then 5 per cent of what that accordionist in a clown suit from Cirque Du Soleil paid would be around £1,250,000. Now that begins to look more affordable. All I'd need to do would be to sell everything I own, borrow against everything I'm ever likely to earn and condemn my family to a life of poverty and I'll be there.

In fact, there's a strong argument for bringing fares down even more. My Honda has done around 139,000 miles. The average distance from earth to the moon is 238,857 miles, therefore their mileage is higher, ergo more wear and tear on the shuttle or whatever we're going to the moon in. That should really mean that the price of an off-peak lunar saver should be lower still. Interestingly, you could buy Post-It notes in the UK from this year and enough of these sticky blighters have now been sold that if you stuck them all together they would stretch to the moon and back, which is amazing as I had no idea that the adhesive was that strong. Now, I have yet to confirm when I'm off to the Sea of Tranquility but I do have a packet of Post-It notes on my desk here and so I feel, as I gaze forever starwards, that I have got one foot on that rocket ship. Which proportionally is about what I'll be able to afford.

Technological advances were gathering speed in other areas of life too. The Chinese managed to clone a beautiful golden carp, which was marvellous news. Especially when paired with some cloned chips and eaten out of newspaper in Tiananmen Square. The British aristocracy had managed to clone a beautiful Sloane Ranger, which was also marvellous news. Especially when paired with a cloned Prince they'd made earlier. They got married at a big church in super-posh clothes and created the year's second most eagerly anticipated conjoining of two people in a public place after Simon and Garfunkel fell into each other's arms again in New York's Central Park.

The decade's major musical developments came in the launch that year of MTV and the release of The Human League's album *Dare*. Sheffield's Human League are one of this country's most significant pop groups as they not only made new technology absolutely key to their sound and style, but embraced the DIY punk ethic whilst also respecting the rules of classic pop. They wanted to innovate and to alter the perception of what a pop group could be, but they also wanted to create hummable tunes that would stand alongside The Beatles, Abba and the Tamla Motown catalogue forever more.

Originally they were a four-piece of badly dressed, occasionally moustachioed and inadvisably coiffured blokes. Frontman Phil Oakey appeared to be wearing the halves of two different hairstyles on his head at the same time. It was as if he was a hairy biker who had gone to the barber for a respectable cut prior to a job interview and changed his mind halfway through. Ian Craig Marsh and Martyn Ware looked like a bank clerk and prop forward respectively as they stared down at their electronic consoles. Adrian Wright, the Ringo of the quartet, projected slides onto the wall behind them. This was not as easy as it sounds, as my dad would have to testify. In the seventies it became *de rigueur* to shoot your family holiday snaps on colour transparencies. These would then need to be perused on a battery-powered viewer which would illuminate the beach at Ilfracombe from behind. The obvious disadvantage to this arrangement was that you couldn't stick these things in an album, or if you did, the glue would prevent that lustrous glow ever returning to the Swanage skyline when that slide was next inserted into the temperamental viewing device. Undeterred, my dad borrowed a rotary projector from the audiovisual department at the university and patiently stacked the carousel with dozens of slides in order to mount a major son et lumière experience in the front room when my godparents Derek and Joan came round. So it was that the whole family, and guests, jostled for seats as my father aimed the beam of light at the wall and proceeded to give us a running commentary on the history of Corfe Castle as the visual spectacle unfolded. I have often felt that time appeared to stand still when I was in the Regal cinema, Northwich, watching Madonna and Jimmy Nail in *Evita*, however that was a positively 'Avatar-esque' white-knuckle experience compared to my dad's epic Devon presentation. At one point there was a series of images purporting to show a hang-glider over Babbacombe Beach, though the object was so far in the distance it was hard to distinguish it from passing seagulls. My Uncle Derek, wiping tears from his eyes and working his way through a crate of Double Diamond, asked whether this airborne novelty wasn't in fact just a nobble on the woodchip wallpaper.

Fortunately for The Human League, Adrian Wright had honed his act to a greater degree than my dad and gave their live shows a visual dimension that singled them out from the vast majority of bands. Their gigs were more like audiovisual presentations and in fact they had earlier considered using flip charts and flow charts to further confound the audience.

Their early records, like 'Being Boiled' and 'Empire State Human', are quirky synthetic pop gems, though a certain menace and darkness, perhaps best demonstrated in 'Circus of Death', is never far away. They made two albums and then, in what appeared a possibly terminally catastrophic move, Marsh and Ware left to form the British Electric Foundation and

Heaven 17. This left The Human League as a two-piece with the unusually limiting line-up of singer and slide projectionist. Faced with their evident musical shortcomings they did the obvious thing – they hired two girls who had never been in a band or sung in public before who they saw dancing at the Crazy Daisy nightclub (where Sean Bean was also a regular) in Sheffield city centre. Inspired. Now they had three singers to go with the projector.

Shortly afterwards, however, Phil, Adrian, Joanne Catherall and Susan Ann Sulley were joined by some people who could actually play some instruments in bassist Ian Burden and guitarist Jo Callis, who had created some classic power pop singles with The Rezillos. All of them played synthesizer at some point, as that had become more about reading the instruction booklet than musicianship, a phenomenon that condemned classically trained keyboard players to poorly paid bookings in wine bars and hotel lobbies in perpetuity whilst guys who could just about turn the keyboard on and play with one finger headlined at Wembley.

The other key man in the *Dare* enterprise was producer Martin Rushent who, like a technocrat Phil Spector, was simply the best person in the world at that point to make a record sound absolutely of its time. The combination of his pristine sound and the League's brilliantly accessible songs was irresistible. It proved successful commercially as 'Don't You Want Me?' that enduring story of fatal cocktail bar attraction, became a number one hit. Classic though that record is, 'Love Action' is even better. It is melodically and lyrically simple and infectious, sonically pristine and yet emotionally vulnerable. This, I think, gets to the heart of the band. They had great songs and great studios and great producers but at the heart was a band who couldn't really play. A band who were . . . well . . . human.

The Human League is one of the great band names and it's

always easier to love a band with a great name. I know there have been terrific groups with dodgy names, although not many, but it takes more to convince you of their greatness if you've got to overcome a shocking monicker. Once on our Radio 1 afternoon show Marc Riley and I asked listeners to vote on the worst name for a band of all time. The winners were Grab Grab The Haddock. They were worthy winners, although I'm not sure they'd retain their title if we held the vote again now. The Cribs, now featuring Johnny Marr and a group I like a lot, did an *NME* tour with three bands on the supporting bill. I don't claim to be an expert on these groups, though I have subsequently enjoyed singles by one of them, but it must surely go down in history as the package tour with the duffest-named bands: The Ting Tings, Joe Lean & The Jing Jang Jong, and Does It Offend You Yeah? I mean, that last one is barely even a sentence let alone a band name. They may well be brilliant but so repelled have I been by their name (and long names never work) that I've never really bothered to investigate. A good band name should give you a clue what kind of music you're going to hear whilst also adding a little lustre, glamour and intrigue to the equation.

So, some good band names:

Metallica
The Rolling Stones
Aerosmith
Roxy Music
Wu-Tang Clan
AC/DC
Pink Floyd
Dr Feelgood
Radiohead
Peter, Paul and Mary

And some bad ones:

The Police
Does It Offend You Yeah?
Yes
Does It Offend You Yeah?
Spandau Ballet
Does It Offend You Yeah?
Dave Dee, Dozy, Beaky, Mick & Tich
Does It Offend You Yeah?
4 Non Blondes
Does It Offend You Yeah?
Counting Crows
Does It Offend You Yeah?
Emerson, Lake & Palmer
Does It Offend You Yeah?
The Beatles

The Human League. Good band. Good name.
Does It Offend You Yeah? I'll be honest with you, lads.
Yes. It does.

1982

PRINCE – '1999'

I met Prince once. We didn't actually speak but I nodded to him as I waited to introduce him on the Channel 4 music show *The White Room*. I was wearing a very sharply tailored suit, he was wearing a swathe of veil over his face. I think the introduction might have made some reference to bee-keeping. This may have been why he didn't seem especially eager to chat in the bar afterwards, although it was hard to know for sure as he wasn't in the bar afterwards. Perhaps he'd gone home to check on how the honey was coming on.

The first time I became aware of Prince was when I saw his picture on the cover of his 1980 album *For You*. Dressed in a pair of skimpy black underpants, neckerchief and flapping trench coat he resembled a male stripper halfway through a raunchy pirate routine. He looked like a character invented by Sacha Baron Cohen. I naturally assumed it wasn't going to be my kind of thing as I've never been particularly attracted to men in their Y-fronts, whether musicians or any other kind of artisans. Call me old-fashioned, but I feel more comfortable in the company of a man in trousers. I'm a huge Bowie fan as you know, and respect the way he pushed the boundaries of male dressing, but I still felt more at home with him in the old Oxford bags than the flimsy Oriental-print leotard which looked liable to reveal his glam rock liver and bacon at every stride. Bowie alumnus Iggy Pop is another sinewy gentleman who is prone to appearing on stage underdressed and, in fact, appeared on that same TV show sporting a pair of transparent plastic slacks which, but for the zip on the fly, would have rendered the shrink-wrapped Osterberg privates public. It's not what you want, is it? I mean, even the most enthusiastic lover of sausages doesn't want to see them uncooked.

Mercifully, by the time '1999' was released Prince had made enough money to afford several decent pairs of strides, which he might well have saved money on by buying from a children's range as, from where I was standing on that studio stage, his inside leg measurement looked to be around sixteen inches. With him suitably clad I was now free to absorb the music without thinking of his purple pubis every time I put the disc on.

On first hearing it was clear that '1999' was a very special record. It had an irresistible synth riff and remains one of the very few records that instil the urge to play air keyboards. It was also unfashionably sparse. At a time when big hair and big production were all the rage, Prince began to reduce tracks to their essential components. I'm told that when Clint Eastwood gets a film script he goes through it crossing out huge chunks of dialogue and reducing it down to the bare bones knowing that one look, one twitch of a nostril, can sometimes say more than several paragraphs. Prince seemed to share the same philosophy. If you go back and listen to 'Kiss' or 'When Doves Cry' now it's astonishing how little appears to be going on. And yet it all sounds perfect. Just the right things are in just the right places.

He was also an incredibly exciting guitarist and seemed to have infused some of the Hendrix fire to put those of us approaching from a rock background a little more at ease. When seeing him perform live, as I subsequently did on several occasions but most notably on the *Lovesexy* tour, any reservations that may have lingered evaporated immediately. His shows were electrifying spectacles with glamorous trappings and imaginative staging with a real, live pulsating rock band and bona fide rock star at the centre of it. In trousers. The more revealing attire of his drummer Sheila E, playing in high heels and chaps, and dancer Cat, prancing in a very short skirt, I found to be less of a problem than their leader's earlier tanga brief encounters.

Sartorially those were interesting times. Michael Jackson unveiled *Thriller* which, with sales of over 110 million copies, remains the bestselling album of all time. That the first compact disc players went on sale in Japan this year probably helped. On the cover Jacko, no doubt keen to avoid any Prince-like under-cracker faux pas, opts for a smartly casual pale suit and yet his enduring stylistic ciphers are the shiny glove, the half-mast trouser and the white sock. None of these have attained what you might call 'design classic' status outside of the police force.

The dunderheaded Duran Duran were seen in documentary footage ploughing through the ocean on what used to be known as a yacht, but is probably now what Roman Abramovich thinks of as a dinghy, in pastel-coloured suits. Now, I know Le Bon and his assorted Taylors were married to glamour, and they always kept their trews on, I'll give them that, but clothing of that style and fabric was always going to be wholly impractical for seafaring. Just think of the unsightly saltwater stains on a salmon-pink silk suit. I began to wonder whether the whole thing hadn't been staged just for the cameras and that they weren't real sailors at all. For a start, not one of them was wearing a flotation garment. This flagrant disregard for health and safety set a very poor example to impressionable youth, as did their music, and you'd have thought there were enough of them in the group for someone to have been in charge of that kind of thing. Nick Rhodes in particular seemed to be standing behind keyboards on stage rather than actually playing them, so surely with all that kind of computer equipment available to him he could have done something useful and ordered some life jackets online. Admittedly, he would have had to have beaten Tim Berners-Lee to the creation of the World Wide Web and, as Rhodes was only one-fifth responsible for the creation of 'Rio', this was always going to be unlikely. Nevertheless, I'm sure those synths were programmed to play themselves at shows, leaving Nick plenty of time to tour outdoor-activity superstores to make sure that the next time they were filmed on a boat they weren't all trussed up in their wedding suits. At least Prince in his pants would have been easier to wipe down.

Martin Fry and ABC, who released the exquisitely glossy *The Lexicon of Love* this year, were parading around in gold lamé suits but were wisely forgoing any kind of waterborne pastimes. The debonair Bryan Ferry and Roxy Music avoided any maritime missions whilst recording 'Avalon'. Really, and it's all too easy to say this with the benefit of hindsight, it might have been better to have left any boating and related maintenance to Dexy's Midnight Runners. The *Too-Rye-Ay* album, also released in 1982, was a brilliantly conceived and executed blend of a Celtic folk band playing with the passion and urgency of a Stax soul review and yielded two colossal hits in 'Jackie Wilson Said' and 'Come On Eileen'. Runner-in-chief Kevin Rowland had kitted the band out in rustic plaid shirts, moth-eaten espadrilles, dis-tressed dungarees and flea-bitten bandannas, lending them the air of a troupe of Romany bargees and therefore ideally attired to take on the boatyard and chandlery duties that Duran were so patently unsuited to. A grubby and noticeably less shouty Bruce Springsteen, holed up in a cabin recording *Nebraska* on a 4-track Portastudio wearing a sweaty singlet and ripe denim jeans, could probably have helped out with the bilge pumps.

All of the above acts were huge concert attractions, though the biggest gigs of that year were by a solo performer whose style of dress is still very much in evidence today. Pope John Paul II was a cheerful-looking little Polish chap in a white dress who bore an uncanny resemblance to the then manager of the England football team Ron Greenwood. In fact, rumours persist that they were one and the same person. Let's look at the evidence. That year there was a World Cup being held in Spain. The Pontiff arrived in the UK in late May right at the end of the domestic football season. He then appeared to countless millions at open-air gigs, doing all the crowd-pleasers like ordinations, baptisms and anointings and stuff, at Wembley, Cardiff, Coventry, York and Manchester, plus a few arena dates in cathedrals and the like. I saw him at the Manchester show as I was there not only for the performance but all the previous night with his fans broadcasting live for Piccadilly Radio. I'm not really what you might call one of his biggest followers, and have never owned any of his albums, but his loyal supporters, and there were over a million of them there that day, displayed an even higher level of devotion than Springsteen's crowd. If anyone deserved to be known as 'The Boss' in 1982 it was Karol Wojtyła. And how is a football manager commonly addressed by his squad? As 'Boss', that's how.

Now you can dismiss this as rampant conspiracy theorising if you like, but when you consider that the Papal visit coincided with the England World Cup squad assembling at their training camp and that Ron Greenwood was not seen at any of the Pope's masses, you begin to wonder. His Holiness, that's the Pope, not Greenwood, departed these shores on 2 June. The tournament kicked off on 13 June. And where is the Holy Father doing his stuff for the bulk of July when he appears to be in the England dug-out? Here's the thing. There are no tour dates for the whole of July. Coincidence? Well, that's for you to decide.

As regards the football, England proceeded through the first round but Kevin Keegan was injured and didn't play much. It was therefore left to the likes of Peter Shilton, Mick Mills, Terry Butcher, Ray Wilkins, Bryan Robson and Trevor Francis to go out in the second round after scoring a grand total of no goals against the hosts and West Germany.

The final took place on 11 July between Italy and West Germany. Two days beforehand Michael Fagan stunned the world by turning up sitting on the end of the Queen's divan in Buckingham Palace, but if it's bedroom stories you're looking for, get this: I watched the 1982 World Cup final lying on a hotel bed with Marianne Faithfull. No, really. My friend Tony was working for Island Records and Marianne was on a promotional jaunt. After I interviewed her for the radio station we all went out for a couple of drinks and a bowl of the old carbonara before having a discussion about where to watch the game. Obviously you couldn't just go and stand in a pub with your actual Marianne Faithfull. Tony's house was considered but dismissed because it was twenty miles away. My house was considered but dismissed because it was a shit-hole. A conveniently close shit-hole, admittedly, but a shit-hole nonetheless, and not somewhere I'd anticipated taking one of Mick Jagger's exes back to. So it was that the elegantly husky Ms Faithfull graciously granted us reclining rights to her queen-size at The Sandpiper in order to witness the Azzurri triumph 3–1. Result. We didn't want the Germans to win, did we? Suitably elated, we partied like it was 1999.

1983

TALKING HEADS – 'BURNING DOWN THE HOUSE'

In 1983 I moved down to that there London to start work at Radio 1 as one of the new breed of thrusting young bucks employed to bring some fresh ideas to what was deemed to have become a rather staid gentlemen's club. In point of fact, and this I discussed at length in my previous book *Thank You for the Days*, the station was anything but staid, it was just that all the creativity and energy seemed to be directed at social activities rather than broadcasting ones. It took me a while to catch on to this and I imagine I was seen as something of a swot by senior production staff, or at least the ones who noticed I was there at all. My problem was, and I've still yet to overcome this, I really liked doing the work.

I was the same at university. I really liked reading the books. That was why I'd gone there. It made no sense to me to be given access to the world's best literature in a historic library and to reject it all in favour of ten-pence-a-shot whisky. I did have my fair share of ten-pence-a-shot whisky, but it never held such an allure that it could compete with *The Mill on the Floss*.

I felt the same way at Radio 1. I had access to the BBC studios and archives and the ear of the music business and threw myself wholeheartedly into the work. It wasn't real work, anyway. It was listening to records and sorting out live bands and interviews and then turning up to make sure it all happened in the right order before going to The Stag's Head for draught Kronenbourg.

My taste for lager is a problem I've been much more successful in overcoming, having seen the real ale light after many years dipping into the folk circuit with my band The Family Mahone. How strange it would have been to have passed by all those micro breweries and free houses only to sup the same old pint of Carling. If you are one of those people then you are no better than those reluctant travellers who take Tetley tea bags and Branston Pickle with them wherever they go. People who look for an English pub serving an English breakfast in Goa. Why? You don't go looking for somewhere serving Indian food and beer if you're out and about in Birmingham, do you? Oh no, hang on, you do. I need to have a pint while I work this one out. Let's see if there are any cans of Fosters ... errmm, I mean bottles of Black Sheep left in the fridge.

Nineteen eighty-three was a year of great change in the media as full English breakfast television was launched. ITV's TV-AM launched with a stellar cast of household names known as the 'famous five': Anna Ford, Angela Rippon, Michael Parkinson, David Frost and Robert Kee. No, me neither. He must have been famous at the time, though, or they'd have been the 'famous four'. And the other one.

The BBC's illustrious team featured Frank Bough, Selina Scott and a bloke who presented the weather in the style of Douglas Fairbanks Jnr called Francis Wilson. That the central pairing differed wildly in terms of their looks fuelled an argument that still goes on now. Selina Scott was elegant, sexy, poised and beautiful. Frank Bough wasn't. This combination of mature male host coupled with young, attractive female has become all too familiar in television and is hugely demeaning. To men. I mean, there are many millions of us chaps who are drop-dead gorgeous, so why put balding lumps with grey hair growing out of their ears next to these goddesses? It's just not fair. Men deserve to be respected for their looks as well, you know. It's terribly condescending to perpetuate the myth that the only clever bloke is an ugly bloke. Things on television are supposed to look good. Smart beautiful women like Katie Derham, Fiona Bruce, Julia Somerville, Penny Smith and Kirsty Young are allowed to read the news, so why not get a bit of beefcake on there to even things up a bit? Huw Edwards is probably a very nice bloke but he's hardly going to set the nation's female pulse racing, is he? You might ask whether that matters. He's there to read the news and sound authoritative, not to look handsome. Rubbish. I repeat. Things on television are supposed to look good. We've got radio for unremarkable-looking people, or you can get your news fix from a newspaper with no personalities to get in the way. But if you're on telly, you need to brighten our day. Poor old Frank Bough never stood a chance. No wonder he was later exposed as a regular visitor to brothels. The man's self-respect had been eroded after years of appearing on TV looking like a manure-encrusted estate labourer forced to perch on a sofa next to the lady of the manor. He was never going to get off with anybody ever again in everyday life, was he? And then the papers had a go at him because he'd put his hand in his pocket and paid for it. That's called persecution. Oh no, sorry, prostitution. I always get those two mixed up.

Elsewhere on television, the last episode of *M*A*S*H* was transmitted to an estimated audience of 125 million. It remains the most watched single episode of a series in TV history. There have been bigger television audiences of course. The moon landing of Apollo 11 drew upwards of 600 million, with Elvis's 1973 special 'Aloha from Hawaii' topping a billion. Bizarrely, the most-watched television broadcasts of all time are reckoned to be football matches from the full English Premier League, which are regularly beamed to over one and a quarter billion homes worldwide with an audience in the region of two billion. Strange to think, then, that more people could be watching Stoke City versus Sunderland than saw Neil Armstrong step out onto the moon, and it's worth pondering also how far a Rory Delap throw-in would travel in zero gravity.

These figures can partially be explained by acknowledging that not everyone had a television set back then, whereas the only people who don't these days have made that decision for a reason. Either they don't want to pay their licence fee, consider there's nothing much on, prefer radio or just really hate Alan Titchmarsh. All perfectly good reasons for not owning a TV and, after all, any information role that television used to fulfil has been superseded by the internet. I know there are those who eschew this as well, but this I find harder to understand. Fair enough if you can't afford your own computer or feel too old to get to grips with the technology, but why as a point of principle would you decide not to subscribe to something that contains all the knowledge in the world?

Of course, what any of us does with that knowledge is the really interesting thing. If we all have access to the same reservoir of information then the connections and progressions we make become the really valuable commodity. A fact becomes hugely less important than a thought. There are people, usually dullards in turtleneck sweaters on pub quiz teams, who would have us believe that the world is a less well-educated place if we don't all know that the monarch who immediately preceded Canute was Svein Forkbeard. But this is the point, eggheads, we do all know it. We can

Google it. No doubt these same individuals can do lightning mental arithmetic, but so can the rest of us. With a calculator. If the tools have been invented to do a job more efficiently, then why not use them? At school, calculators were of course forbidden in maths lessons and exams because they made things too easy. But isn't that one of the main points of education? You're supposed to be learning how to do things more efficiently and expertly, not how to make it harder and get it wrong more often. It's easier in a woodwork class to knock in a nail with a hammer than it is to 'nut' it in with your forehead, so why forgo the calculator in favour of doing it in your head? Tools have been invented for a purpose and we should always remember that. Kids should be able to use a calculator just as they are expected to eat their meals with cutlery even if, as polite society has dictated, it means trying to consume peas off the curved back of a fork.

Interestingly, it also became law in 1983 that you had to wear a seatbelt. This is a rule I have never agreed with as it still seems to me to be an infringement of our personal freedom. I wear a seatbelt myself at all times but if I choose not to, preferring in the event of a collision to stave my head in on the windscreen, then it seems to me that I should be allowed to make that decision. It's my forehead and my windscreen and my stupidity and shouldn't involve or affect anyone else. You can't make stupidity illegal, can you? What would happen to *The Jeremy Kyle Show*?

Talking Heads were a band I had always loved from hearing their debut single 'Love Goes To Buildings On Fire' in 1977 before witnessing them open for The Ramones at the Manchester Electric Circus. They'd become lumped in with the punk movement, being very much a key band in the New York new-wave scene, but they seemed to be cut from a very different cloth. Aertex, possibly. At least, that's what their polo shirts appeared to be made of as they stood on stage at the Circus before a somewhat bemused safety-pinned and spittle-spattered crowd. A lot of punk rock was based on primal yelps of snotty rebellion, but Talking Heads made no effort to disguise their college background, having met in Providence at the Rhode Island College of Design. Their twitchy, literate take on pop, combined with a quintessential preppy look, is a blueprint you still see followed to this day by bands like Vampire Weekend. Perhaps, as a vaguely swotty, occasionally spotty and accordingly low on totty college kid from a middle-class grammar school background, I knew deep down that I was never going to really be a true punk rocker living in a rundown squat and raging against alien-ation and deprivation. I hadn't suffered any deprivation or alienation except when my sister wasn't talking to me. In Talking Heads I saw that you could be part of the exciting new world but come at it from a more studiedly artistic, quirky direction and without needing to have holes in your pants.

I saw them play live many times. At the student's union in Manchester I paid £1.20 to attend their concert and was quite intrigued by the guitar playing demonstrated by the bloke fronting the unknown support band Dire Straits. I saw them at the Manchester Free Trade Hall where local lads A Certain Ratio opened. I also saw them at the Hammersmith Palais where I was engaged in explaining to my old university pal Annie that I'd got free tickets and that relationships that had thus far been platonic didn't have to be that way forever, and therefore failed to pay much attention to that night's special guests U2. The Talking Heads were never less than enthralling and if you never got the chance to see them I can only point you in the direction of the Jonathan Demme live concert film *Stop Making Sense*, where you will begin to understand how inventive, clever and funny a 'rock' band can be.

Sitting in my new ten-foot-square office at Radio 1 that day, and slightly nervous about having to go out and walk through the large outer office where all the secretaries sat, I was concerned about how I was going to fill my time. I had no one to talk to (though I did have my very own phone and called my mum for a bit of a chat), no real work to do and no records to listen to. It occurred to me that Talking Heads were about to release their new album *Speaking In Tongues* and I could kill an hour or two listening through it. I considered walking down to Oxford Street and buying it as I was, after all, pretty well off having been employed by the BBC on a whopping £13,000 a year. However, as the album wasn't actually released until the following week, it hadn't reached the shops yet. Tentatively I decided to phone the record company and ask if I could have a review copy.

Working up North in local radio this was always something of a hit-and-miss approach. A representative of each company might pass through the radio station occasionally but would be loath to give freebies to oiks who only had one show a week, and that was if they had actually heard of the records you were asking for. Nevertheless, I was astonished to learn from the promotions department in question that they not only had copies of *Speaking In Tongues* in stock and would let me have one for nothing, they would also bike it over right away. Amazing. I had it within twenty minutes. The first record I ever received in a packet with my name on it and it had been sent immediately by despatch rider. As if it was important or something.

I asked my new PA Sue if she wouldn't mind making me a cup of tea and once she'd cheerfully obliged sat down to listen to the new Talking Heads LP. Sipping Earl Grey, I eased into the opening track 'Burning Down The House' as I looked over the heating ducts towards Broadcasting House, a flaming image of which would later adorn the cover when that same track was released as a single, and waif astray though I was, decided that being a member of this peculiar gentlemen's club might come to suit me perfectly well.

1984

THE SMITHS – 'HEAVEN KNOWS I'M MISERABLE NOW'

The miners' strike began that March and misery was going to be readily available for the next twelve months. Even for the vast majority of us who weren't directly involved, who would suffer none of the angst and deprivation of those fighting for their very existence, it was a conflict that cast a long shadow over the country for those grinding months. I will never begin to know how it felt to work down a mine and then to see the forces of law and order lining up against you to take away your way of life. I'm not even making a political point here, and wouldn't pretend to have enough knowledge or insight to bring anything new to the understanding of what went on. Perhaps changes needed to be made, but there had to be a better way of sorting it out than that. It's almost impossible to believe that the Battle of Orgreave actually happened. It seems more like a film, a work of gritty Northern fiction, than a real-life event. But it was real life. And real lives changed forever. Communities and families were ripped apart, wounds inflicted that will never heal.

In some ways the music of The Smiths seems to chime perfectly with those times. They were emphatically Northern and were prepared to admit, to resort to cliché, that it could be grim at times. In 1984, for many thousands of people, it had never seemed grimmer. The Smiths were a pop group, but one that seemed to have absorbed classic Northern influences that strayed beyond just music. Echoes of *Coronation Street*, Walter Greenwood, Shelagh Delaney, Stan Barstow, L.S. Lowry, Ken Loach, Alan Bleasdale, Willy Russell and Bill Naughton could be detected in their songs.

Their brilliantly conceived sleeve portraits included Delaney, writer of *A Taste Of Honey*, brassy 'spend, spend, spend' pools winner Viv Nicholson and hatchet-faced back-street battleaxes Ena Sharples and Elsie Tanner, played indelibly by Violet Carson and Pat Phoenix. Often, grimy terraced streets would form the backdrop. They would release an album immortalising Manchester's prison in *Strangeways Here We Come*. The Moors Murders would get the Morrissey treatment. They would write songs like 'Cemetery Gates', the portal to the sprawling Southern Cemetery where Princess Parkway meets Barlow Moor Road, and 'Rusholme Ruffians', set on the now neon-garlanded strip known as curry mile. It was darker back then. Everything was darker back then.

The genius of The Smiths, however, is that though they never shied away from a particularly Northern brand of misery, their records were anything but miserable. There was an element of no-nonsense Northernism about them. They were called The Smiths for a start, which placed them at the far end of the pretension spectrum from soft Southerners Spandau Ballet, who probably could have battered Morrissey and friends in a fight, but you know what I mean. And anyway, the Spandau Ballet gang, numbering five, had numerical advantage. That's just the kind of trick you'd expect from that shower. But The Smiths were clearly proud of their roots and seemed to understand that to love somewhere, and indeed someone, you have to accept and embrace the faults and failings. But having accepted that a dash of grimness was always going to form part of their cocktail, more uplifting, sweeping and romantic ingredients would be added.

In this they were hugely fortunate to have a genuine musical genius in Johnny Marr as well as the often overlooked poetic bass of Andy Rourke, demonstrated most deftly perhaps on 'This Charming Man'. Think of that record without that bass line and, though still good, it would fall short of greatness. If Morrissey and Marr were Lennon and McCartney, then Rourke was very much the Harrison of the organisation. And Mike Joyce was definitely the best drummer in The Smiths. But in Johnny the band was blessed with one of the greatest British guitarists there has ever been. The records simply drip with melodic and heartbreaking motifs emanating, seemingly effortlessly, from his fretboard. Listen to the largely instrumental playout from 'The Boy With The Thorn In His Side' and tell me that you don't feel a little misty-eyed and perhaps slightly weak in the presence of beauty. I last saw Johnny in central Manchester where we were both having trousers altered at the same backstreet tailors, and as he stood there, making sure his jeans were cut to just the right width, it was easy to see how his attention to detail had given those records that grandeur. And yet his guitar playing never seems overwrought or flashy. 'How Soon Is Now' has more tracks of guitar on it than even he can remember but you're not particularly conscious of it as they have all been crafted and melded into this one big wonderful, irresistible thing. The records of The Smiths soar because of Marr's attacks and even though we are connected to the shadowy Northern cityscape when we listen to The Smiths, we are holding hands with Johnny and flying above it like pallid, provincial Peter Pans.

This undoubtedly helped to give the band a real sense of glamour. Their music shimmered in a way that could have seemed at odds with some of the lyrics in less skilled hands. But they were nothing if not figures of desire. Some of their other cover stars were Terence Stamp and James Dean and Alain Delon. The members themselves were not without their legions of admirers. Johnny Marr was a very pretty boy, every inch the gamine guitar god. Drummer Mike Joyce and bassist Andy Rourke looked perfectly presentable. They appeared to be the kind of guys you could share a cheery pint with then take home for a nightcap whilst they got off with your sister. They looked just the right side of roguish.

Morrissey's appeal was harder to fathom. A handsome devil, his sexuality was ambivalent. He had many female admirers but seemed from the very beginning to attract the passionate worship of young male disciples, many of whom were quite possibly trying to understand those kind of feelings for a man for the first time. The band, like all great bands, looked like they belonged together. They weren't in a uniform, but matched without looking as if they'd tried to. They all had vaguely the same rockabilly haircut though, in a twist on the old communist adage that would hint at the true relationships within the group, everyone had a quiff but some quiffs were bigger than others. Back in '84 they seemed the perfect band. They were all individuals, but four quarters of the same whole. They were the other-end-of-the-ship-canal Beatles for a whole new generation.

Their clothes were, for the most part, low key. Stephen Wright's iconic picture of them outside Salford Lads Club, now quite rightly in the collection of the National Portrait Gallery, sees them in relaxed garb. Morrissey's chemise seems to have some brocade detail, Johnny's shirt may be daringly floral, but for the most part their apparel is unremarkable. Mike Joyce is in a black suit smoking a fag. Andy Rourke, appearing vaguely amused by the whole thing, is wearing a suede blouson jacket and a pair of snug denims. When asked about this picture, and if he would have dressed any differently if he'd known how many times it was going to be reprinted, he did comment that he would probably have gone for a less tight pair of jeans and, looking again, it's easy to get Rourke's drift.

But part of The Smiths' appeal was that they didn't seem to be trying too hard, unlike Spandau Ballet in their kilts and tablecloths. Johnny's looks notwithstanding, they would have looked like a standard indie quartet were it not for Morrissey and the quirks he introduced. Yes, he was dressed in baggy jeans and a generous shirt, but he would often have bunches of flowers, predominantly gladioli, sprouting from his back pocket. That let you know that though he was dealing with dark matters, he was not afraid to proclaim a love of beauty. He may well have absorbed the poetry of the Liverpool scene and John Cooper Clarke, but he had definitely wandered lonely as a cloud on occasion as well. He also often wore then unfashionable thick-framed glasses. And a hearing aid. With these gestures he was saying that he had no truck with fashion, poking fun at what constituted accessories, whilst simultaneously glamorising those deemed society's misfits. He opened his arms to the disenfranchised and the avowedly uncool and they came to pay homage in their droves. Look, I'm not saying he was bigger than Jesus or anything, but The Smiths quickly became a quasi-religion and if Moz wasn't the godhead then he was certainly an archbishop. He remains the missing link between Elvis and Alan Bennett.

Another thing The Smiths had was a sense of humour. This remains an all too rare commodity for rock'n'roll bands, as the very nature of the beast is to take yourselves too seriously. You are surrounded by people telling you how great you are and spend your time indulgently bound together as tortured souls creating 'your art'. That The Smiths did all these things was not in question but their songs were often very funny. Spandau Ballet's were too, but not intentionally. The Smiths' Northern references seemed to acknowledge George Formby and Frank Randle and Les Dawson. The unfortunate Andy Rourke, who sank into a drug addiction that saw him removed from the group, is rumoured to have been sacked when he found a Post-It note giving him the bad news stuck to his car windscreen. There is some dispute over how true it is, but that doesn't matter. The fact that it seems possible is part of what is so wonderful and unique about them. You might also think it rather a cruel way to deal with someone's misfortune and you'd be right but, rather like hearing on the news that Janette Krankie had been injured falling out of a beanstalk, you can't deny that it's funny too. Humour, wit, looks, romanticism, power, musical prowess, style, mystery, tight trousers – The Smiths had it all and even when we were 'miserable now' we were also lifted up by the records they made.

They fell out, of course, as all the best groups do.

They'll never get back together.

Some rifts are too deep.

Just ask the miners.

1985

DIRE STRAITS – 'BROTHERS IN ARMS'

Dear Kate,

I feel that it's only fair to let you know that I have let you down and I only hope that after reading this you will come to understand, if not forgive, this betrayal. You know how highly I regard you. I am one of your biggest fans and think you are one of the most talented women this country has ever produced. You were also really nice to me that day I came round for cheese pie. One day I hope to be able to repay your kindness and hospitality by buying you a cheese and onion pasty from Greggs. D'you know, the other day on the radio someone was telling us about her father-in-law who bought pies and pasties from Greggs and then kept them wrapped up to eat at home, twenty minutes away. What's all that about then, eh, Kate? You want to eat something like that straight away, don't you? When you and I get the chance to have pasties together, rest assured that we will stroll down the street eating them immediately out of the bags and wondering why the filling has always been heated in a nuclear reactor.

Anyway, Kate, I'm writing this book at the moment called *Reelin' In The Years* in which I'm choosing one song from each year of my life and I've reached 1985. You probably remember it well. It was a good year for you and so many amazing things happened. The first mobile phone call was made by Ernie Wise! I know, weird, isn't it? What was it about that amiable, dubiously thatched hoofer that made Vodaphone think, now there's the man who symbolises the new era of telecommunications? Mind you, it's no stranger than the fact that the Automated Teller Machine was launched in 1967 at Barclays in Enfield – which wouldn't have been far for you from Bexleyheath if you got on the North Circular at Woolwich – and was first used by Reg Varney. Yes, off *On the Buses*. I think that's something worth knowing as it's bound to come up in a quiz at the pub or WI or something and when you hear the host pose the question, 'Who was the first person to use a cash machine in the UK?' you will have me to thank for knowing the answer. Perhaps that will help you to look on me a little more charitably.

So, what else happened that year? *EastEnders* started on BBC1 with someone being found dead in a bedsit. Well, that was a cheery tonic after the miners' strike, wasn't it? Clive Sinclair launched that funny little half a bike and half a car thing called the C5 and withdrew it again after seven months having only sold 17,000 of them. Did you buy one? I didn't, though a friend of mine swears blind she saw Paul Daniels driving one round Shepherd's Bush Green. We made up a funny joke about it which went something like this:

'I saw that Paul Daniels in a C5 the other day.'

'Really?'

'Yes, funny little bulbous thing with no covering on top.'

'Right. And what about the C5?'

Well, perhaps you had to be there. Poor old Paul Daniels, eh? I mean, I know that if you're in the public eye you have to accept a bit of piss-taking like you did when Pamela Stephenson did 'Oh, England, My Leotard' on *Not The Nine O'Clock News*, but that was affectionate, wasn't it? Poor old Paul just gets a load of flak and he's never done anything more harmful than being very annoying has he? Unless he's stuck his sword into the wrong bit of Debbie McGee, but I suppose they'd keep that private, wouldn't they? Did you see that advert in *Viz*? There was a tour doing the rounds called 'The Best of British Variety Tour 2008', which featured Cannon and Ball, Frank Carson, Jimmy Cricket, Peters and Lee, The Krankies, Brotherhood of Man and Paul Daniels. I know. Sounds like a long night, doesn't it? But *Viz* subtly altered it to become 'The Best of British Shite Tour 2008', featuring Cannon and Shite, Frank Shite, Jimmy Shite, Peters and Shite, The Shitties, Brotherhood of Shite and ... Paul Daniels. That's not nice, is it, Kate? Funny though, eh? I've got the comic in question here if you want to have a look. The piece in question is on page 11 just across from an advert for a wetdreamcatcher.

Oh, talking of variety shows, Live Aid happened in 1985 as well, didn't it? I liked Status Quo kicking it off and thought Queen were pretty good, even though I've never quite got them really. Bowie was on top form but I could have lived without that down-on-one-knee Lord's Prayer stuff, couldn't you? It would have been better if you'd been on, possibly with your mate Pete, who might have been tied up with that *Birdy* soundtrack. His old mate Phil the drummer was on, though. In fact he played over here and then nipped over there to do a bit of the old tub-thumping for Led Zeppelin. Wasn't all that good, was it, Kate? Mind you, he did have a very good year 'cos that album of his called *No Jacket Required* did really well for him. Did you think his head looked like a baked bean on the cover? I did. Another big album that year was *Cupid and Psyche* by Scritti Politti. The songs and production on that were fantastic, eh? I love Green Gartside's voice so much. He had his hair quite long and flicked with highlights in it at that time and in some photos he looked a bit like Princess Diana I thought. Did you like that 'Take The Skinheads Bowling' by Camper Van Beethoven? I adored that but perhaps it's not quite your sort of thing. The Pogues did *Rum, Sodomy & The Lash* too and, knowing how much you like to dance, I could see you having a tot or two and rolling back the hearth rug to do a jig to 'Sally MacLennane'.

So I could have picked any of those records to represent 1985 but I've chosen Dire Straits and I'll tell you why in the hope that you will understand. For one thing, it was the first album I ever owned on CD. It was the third album ever released on compact disc after *The Visitors* by Abba and something or other by Billy Joel. I still have that original *Brothers in Arms* today and as it's a pre-release copy without any details on the disc I believe it's worth quite a bit now.

When it came out I produced a programme for Radio 1 featuring tracks from this new LP and interviews with Mark Knopfler and d'you know what? I only went and left some edits in the bloody thing. There I was sitting at my mother-in-law's in Harrogate over the Easter weekend listening to it going out only to hear all kinds of tape whirring noises, as we had a few attempts at getting the chat to finish just as the vocals started. What an idiot. My chocolate bunny tasted a lot less sweet after that, I can tell you. I expected a real bollocking but it never happened. I don't imagine anyone from management was listening what with it being Easter and everything.

CDs were very exciting though, weren't they? Some albums really benefited from not having to be broken up into two sides like the old vinyl LPs, I reckon. *The Dark Side Of The Moon* springs to mind. Oh, what did you think of that court case where the judge decided that your old mucker Dave and the rest of Pink Floyd were well within their legal and artistic rights to insist that their tracks shouldn't be available for download individually? I know what they mean, but it seems a bit unrealistic, doesn't it? You haven't always got time to listen to a whole album and, anyway, their tunes have been played separately not only on the radio but at their own concerts for years. I wonder if they aren't shooting themselves in the foot a little bit. If you're a kid who is coming to the band for the first time and fancy checking out 'Echoes' without wanting to pay the full whack for the whole of *Meddle* you might go and get it for free from an illegal site instead, mightn't you?

Don't get me wrong, I love the Floyd and have often listened to their albums from beginning to end, and I think it's important that we protect the album as an art form. Some LPs are really made to be heard in one sitting and the half of your double set *Aerial* called 'Sky Of Honey' with all the songs linked by birdsong is a case in point. Would you be happy for people just to download 'Nocturne' and not bother with the rest? I suppose it's up to them but it would be a shame, wouldn't it?

For a long time, Kate, I sort of pretended that I didn't really like Dire Straits as I was probably bound up in some misplaced notion of being cool. As if. Things are different now. That's one of the great things about being in our fifties, isn't it? We don't have to pretend to be or to like anything we don't want to. I'm still not keen on that track with Sting and 'Walk Of Life' remains a bit cheesy, but the title track is really great, isn't it? Now, admittedly, it's no better than 'Cloudbusting' or 'Hounds Of Love', the title track of your album that same year. It's certainly nowhere near as good as 'Running Up That Hill (A Deal With God)', which still sounds groundbreaking and wonderfully, oddly grandiose when you hear it now. But it wasn't the first CD I ever owned, so that's why I've done what I've done and, if it's any consolation, when our interview about *Aerial* went out on Radio 2 I at least made sure all the editing had been done.

So, I'll sign off because Toto is wanting to go out for his walk down to Dutton Locks and then I have to pick the girls up from school. Love to the family and hope to hear from you soon. You do understand, don't you? I really hope so.

Cheers, Mark.

1986

PETER GABRIEL – 'DON'T GIVE UP'

There were over 3 million people on the dole in 1986. This despite the unemployed having been presented with the admirable cycling option by Norman Tebbit, once dubbed 'a semi-house-trained polecat' by Michael Foot, who told them to 'get on your bikes and look for work'. Except he didn't, apparently. When interviewed in the aftermath of the inner city riots of 1981 and reacting to the suggestion that it's nat-ural to take to civil disorder when deprived of basic rights and opportunities he talked of his father's experiences during the depression of the 1930s when 'he got on his bike and looked for work and he kept looking until he found it'.

The implication was clearly similar, but there were several problems with what he was suggesting. For a start there were plenty of people who couldn't afford a bike. Perhaps the government of the time should have had the foresight to introduce a plan similar to the white bicycle scheme that was tried in Amsterdam in the mid-sixties. Here a fleet of cycles, all painted uniformly white, were left on the streets for all to use free of charge. This egalitarian notion was hatched by the radical Provo movement and seemed to per-fectly encapsulate the liberal Amsterdam psyche and epitomise the counterculture's ability to improve mainstream life. Except that within weeks those with a less liberal

Amsterdam psyche had nicked most of the bikes and thrown
a great many of them into the canals, thereby blighting two
of the city's boasts at once.

Why they would do this is not clear. Why would you steal
something that is in plentiful supply for free? I can understand stealing out of need, out of hunger, out of desperation.
I can understand stealing for the sheer thrill of it, which is
how I got those pint glasses from The Blundell Arms in 1976
and also, and I'm confessing this here for the first time, several extra black jacks, fruit salads and flying saucers from the
penny tray at Pickersgill's in the late 1960s. I can even imagine why you would steal out of jealousy if you see something
you can't ever dream of affording but want to know how it
feels to have it. But what is the point of pinching something
that you can have any time without paying? It would be like
stealing grass or something.

Of course, there are different kinds of grass and certain
types which I'm led to believe can be smoked, if you can
believe such a thing, tend to be very popular in Amsterdam.
This particular 'grass', which can also be known as marijuana,
dope, weed, teapot, popcorn, omelette, coal scuttle and Sue
Barker mad head candy, apparently makes you a bit dizzy and
compelled to take to the streets looking for confectionery.
This could explain the disappearance of the white bikes.
Perhaps these 'potheads' or 'coal scuttle wigouts', as my
source tells me they're known, were dashing across the city
late at night to the all-night petrol station to buy Lindt
chocolate balls only to come out and find some other 'grass-
bandit' had ridden off into the night leaving them stranded.
This would only have to happen a few times before you kept
one of the bikes hidden in your back passage. What's more, if
the effects of this smokable leaf, or 'clog-turnip' to give it the
accepted Dutch slang, really are disorientating then it seems
entirely likely that many of these addled mounted 'Gouda

gurners' could have simply lost their balance on those narrow
bridges and tumbled, bike and all, into the canal.

The other main problem with Tebbit's suggestion is one of
distance. I have recently taken delivery of a bicycle myself. It
is a Dawes Consulate, which I really have to say is an absolute
steal at just over two hundred quid, which is not to imply
that I swiped it. It has seven gears, a basket on the front for
your newspaper and a saddle that actually seems to have been
designed to sit on rather than cause piles. In fact, other
cyclists I encounter not only have to suffer the indignity of
having been sent out in ridiculous bright clothing by their
mums, but also have saddles that are so uncomfortable they
spend most of their time riding with their backsides in the
air. Their bikes are also so poorly made that they don't even
have mudguards, meaning that when they get home they
have a big stripe of muck up the back of their mustard-
yellow jerkins. You shouldn't laugh really, but it's hard not to
feel smug as I make my stately progress along the lanes with
the dog running alongside, only occasionally causing BMW
X5s to swerve into the ditch, which wouldn't have happened
anyway if they'd been driving a little slower, as the police
officer who wanted tickets for Bon Jovi in the BBC Radio
Theatre said at the time.

Nevertheless my stylish appliance and also my bike means
I only cover distances of a few miles a day and the employment possibilities within that sort of range of my house are
limited to dung shovelling and bar work. Having managed to
avoid manual labour thus far in life I don't feel much drawn
towards either. Sorry, Norman. The second would seem to
be the preferred option as bar work involves beer and it's
always nice to work with something you love. Then again, a
few pints and a bike ride home along the canal late at night
and the fate of one of those Amsterdam 'bong-water-chest-
nut-heads' awaits.

This was obviously one of the real drawbacks of the Tebbit plan. Even the lucky ones who had bikes had limited job prospects, especially if someone had already got the local French onion-selling market sewn up. No wonder the plan to build a Channel Tunnel was announced this year, coinciding with the completion of the M25. Neither of these have cycle lanes, of course, which is just another example of the lack of 'joined-up' thinking in transport policy.

In terms of employment 1986 will always be remembered for the clashes between the print unions and the police outside the News International plant in Wapping, as the 'old ways' of Fleet Street newspaper production were dismantled. *Today*, the first national daily to be produced using offset printing, was launched in March. In colour. The political editor was Alastair Campbell.

In some ways those events seem like a long time ago, although in other ways it feels like nothing much has changed. As I write this British Airways are locked in a bitter struggle with the Unite union and Bob Crow's RMT are preparing for industrial action. Recently Kraft have taken over Cadbury's and despite having said before the buyout that they would keep the Somerdale factory in Keynsham near Bristol open, once the deal had been done, they announced plans to close it. Evidently there was a spanking new plant in Poland ready to come on stream, though you can't help thinking that they must have known that already.

Look, I'm not clever or qualified enough to comment on the nature of global corporate finance and production, but that just shouldn't be allowed to happen, should it? These were the jobs of 400 people who may not even have bikes. The now deposed Secretary of State for Business, Innovation and Skills Peter Mandelson professed himself 'disappointed'. Well, that was all right, then. Interestingly, and history will be sure to note this, Mandelson held that key position in the Labour Government without actually having been elected, which would seem to suggest that he took the innovation part of his brief very seriously. It doesn't make a lot of sense to me. You can apparently buy a massively successful Premiership football club with debt. Donal MacIntyre has appeared on *Dancing on Ice*, *Celebrity Come Dine With Me* and *Celebrity Family Fortunes* and is an undercover reporter. You can say you're going to keep a factory workforce employed if you're allowed to buy the company and then just change your mind. These are things I do not understand.

Having close connections to the West Country, his Real World studios being located in Box, Wiltshire, the Kraft/Cadbury situation will not have escaped the attention of Peter Gabriel. As a humanitarian campaigner, world music patron and sometime donor to the Labour Party we can imagine what his thoughts on Mandelson's 'disappointment' might be. Disappointment might well be too mild a word.

In 1986 Gabriel released the album *So*. It was his first solo record not to be eponymous at the behest of his record company, as evidently the idea of calling every release simply *Peter Gabriel* was causing some confusion in the US where they were having to give them titles to make sure people knew which record they were buying. Despite the covers and all the songs being different. Some of the American kids who weren't sure which LP they were buying are probably now working in the boardroom at Kraft.

There were other important albums released that year. Paul Simon may have had to deal with some accusations of cultural imperialism in the way he used African musicians in the process of making *Graceland* but he, or they, created something of lasting beauty and it doesn't seem to have hurt Ladysmith Black Mambazo's career. The slick soul of Anita Baker's *Rapture* was heard everywhere, which was fine, and

the Cocteau Twins' equally lush *Victorialand* wasn't, which
was a shame. Talk Talk began redrawing the blueprint of
what a band could be with *The Colour Of Spring*.

The same year also heralded the arrival of three noisy
blokes shouting a lot when The Beastie Boys released *Licensed
to Ill*, giving them the massive hits of 'No Sleep Till
Brooklyn' and one of the great hedonistic anthems in '(You
Gotta) Fight For Your Right (To Party!)'. I went to see The
Beastie Boys on their first UK tour with Run DMC and
found them thrilling and hilarious at the same time.
Obviously, as someone brought up on, and steeped in, rock
bands I had to overcome my initial prejudice that they
weren't a 'proper' band because they weren't playing any
instruments. Eventually we would learn that they could play
pretty much anything between the three of them, which
probably explains why they are still making fascinating
records to this day. Back then I watched with a certain child-
like glee as 'Fight For Your Right' exploded out of the
speakers accompanied by blinding stage lights, a huge logo
painted on the floor and some girls dancing in cages.

OK, I know the point you want to raise. Who paints a
logo on the floor, right? Isn't it going to stick to the soles of
your shoes? Possibly. But that was the whole point in many
ways. They revived the spirit of punk in utterly disrespecting
the accepted mores of a concert. They appeared to be a tri-
umvirate of snotty brats from some college frat house who
happened to be having a party in front of an audience of several thousand. It was as if three John Belushi fans had
watched *Animal House* too many times and decided to form
a band. The main constituents of their act seemed to be
shouting and spraying the floor with Budweiser so they could
skid on it. Because they seemed so at odds with the massive
production it seemed brilliantly deconstructivist. For about
ten minutes. Then it got a bit boring and we went to the bar.

As a musical moment from that year it couldn't be further away in timbre from Peter Gabriel's 'Don't Give Up'. Gabriel's voice is one of the most affectingly melancholic in rock and when wedded to this, one of his most spectrally beautiful melodies, it is the stuff of heartbreak even before you start to assimilate the words. Here Peter takes on the role of an unemployed worker shuffling from town to town with thousands of others searching for that elusive job, getting on his bike and looking for work. Though bleak it is beautiful and not without hope. The song is a duet between the battered jobseeker and his loving, protective, faithful, embattled wife. In essence, as the title suggests, she says that things might look grim but whatever happens, they'll be together. There is a touching video with one long, lingering sequence of the desperate downtrodden pair hanging on to the only thing they have left, each other. Perhaps, just months ago, somewhere near Keynsham a husband and wife were doing just the same. Oh, and the woman in the video and on the record? Kate Bush, of course.

There, Kate, you made the cut after all.

1987

U2 – 'WHERE THE STREETS HAVE NO NAME'

Funny old Christmas, that one. We had the chance of there being the greatest seasonal number one hit of all time, with all due respect to Sir Nodward, Duke of Holdershire, and those pesky Pet Shop Boys went and spoiled it all. 'Always On My Mind' is perfectly nice but it's no 'Fairytale Of New York' is it, lads? The least they could have done, like a considerate caravanner on manoeuvres, was to pull over and let higher life forms, and The Pogues, through.

Don't get me wrong, I have nothing against the Pet Shop Boys. I've met them a couple of times and they are as bright, witty, literate and pithy as their perfectly executed electronica suggests. I once asked Chris Lowe if, behind that somewhat grumpy onstage demeanour, there was an excited hyperactive elf struggling to get out. He cheerfully admitted that there wasn't and that he rarely felt excited onstage even at the biggest concerts. In fact, Neil Tennant remarked that Chris could come off stage having played to a rabid crowd of a hundred thousand and then go straight to bed and, what's more, go straight to sleep. Presumably, as there are only two of them, this left Neil to have a schooner of sweet sherry in the hotel bar on his own. They are an endearingly odd pair and are probably the Gilbert and George of technopop, the Frasier and Niles of the synth.

They still spoiled Christmas that year, though, as if things weren't bad enough already with Hilda Ogden bowing out of *Coronation Street*. Lester Piggott was doing three years for tax evasion, of course, so there were some things that cheered you up, but 'Fairytale' at number two? Ridiculous. Even more so than Ultravox's 'Vienna' being held off the top spot by Joe Dolce with 'Shaddap You Face' although, personally, I've never considered that an injustice.

There were other huge records that year. I feel slightly uneasy that New Order's 'True Faith' doesn't head this chapter. A glorious sweep of technologically fuelled wonder, it may be the most euphoric record about drug addiction ever made. It was also the record I chose to open my first show with when I joined Radio 2 in 1994. What a way to begin. It's all been downhill since, but at least we got off to a bright start.

One of the biggest bands in the world at that point were Guns N' Roses who released *Appetite For Destruction* and who seemed to be a rock band put together by cartoonists. It was either extraordinarly good planning, which seemed unlikely, or an amazing stroke of luck that every rock star cliché could be covered by those five guys. Top hats, sunglasses, bandannas, leathers, denims, distressed T-shirts, big hair, scarves, Les Pauls, fags, bottles of Jack Daniel's, drugs, no discernible buttocks – you name it, they had it covered. If there had been an Action Man Rock'n'Roll Star he would have looked like Slash. He certainly wouldn't have looked like lead singer Axl Rose, who was a ginger-headed bloke in skimpy white shorts, which is something you can see at any badminton club. Axl Rose got his name by rearranging the letters of oral sex, though he could just as easily have been T.S. Rose by rearranging the letters of tosser. By contrast Slash's name was given to him by a childhood friend because he was always rushing everywhere, often on his BMX, and not because he had bladder-control issues, which was more than you could say for his co-guitarist Izzy Stradlin.

Stradlin, whose real name is Jeffrey, was once arrested at Phoenix airport after disembarking from a flight during which he had urinated in the galley. And he was supposed to be 'the quiet one'. He was certainly the coolest one, having lifted his image from Keith Richards in contrast to the other four who had stolen their look from a combination of Iggy Pop, Barbie and a stick of candy floss. Evidently miffed at having to wait to use the toilet, Izzy, no doubt needing to pay an urgent call having imbibed a couple of cans whilst wearing overtight trousers, simply hosed down the duty-free trolley with the casual élan of John Terry in an Essex nightspot. His publicist later said that 'relieving himself in the galley was just his way of expressing himself'. In that case he might have been better masturbating.

But rock bands were supposed to behave badly and Guns N' Roses cheerfully obliged. At a gig at Manchester City's Maine Road football ground, the theatre of dreams, the support band finished and Slash and Axl were still in the hotel. In London. They were the bad lads of stadium rock. After all, it was hard to imagine a member of U2 having a pee in the kitchen – and if they did, you feel sure they would have washed their hands afterwards.

Nineteen eighty-seven saw U2 become a true global proposition when they released *The Joshua Tree*, which opens with their finest moment 'Where The Streets Have No Name'. It has become rather fashionable to sneer at U2 not only for their massive success but also because of the proselytising of St Bono. What you cannot deny, though, is that this is one of the greatest openings to an album ever created. The evocative cover photographs by Anton Corbijn show the band looking mean, chiselled and grainy amidst the epic, dusty, brooding landscape of Zabriskie Point in the Death Valley National Park. Before you even put the record on you are being encouraged to expect something of awe-inspiring proportions. You are not going to be disappointed. The album opens with swirling clouds of treated keyboards approaching like a dust storm rolling over the mountains. This sounds powerfully organic rather than pompous. And then you detect the first tingling notes of The Edge's guitar just audible on the sonic horizon. If you've ever seen *Lawrence of Arabia* you'll recall the appearance of Omar Sharif playing Sherif Ali. Dressed in black and riding a camel, he first appears as a smudge, a mirage, distorted by the haze somewhere across the desert. Gradually, the long, long shot beautifully enhanced by the music of Maurice Jarre, he materialises centre stage. The guitar entry on this song is equally compelling. The perfectly enmeshed rumble of the bass and drums is the penultimate ingredient to be added before Bono's impassioned voice completes the perfectly painted picture. It's a great song, and might well have sounded great however it was recorded, but the presence of Brian Eno, and his studio cohort Daniel Lanois, is undoubtedly a major factor in having realised the concept so fully.

In 2005 I first got the chance to speak to Brian Peter George St John le Baptiste de la Salle Eno. I had always assumed that with a name like that he must have been from an aristocratic background but he confirmed that he was from a long line of Suffolk postmen and that his extended nomenclature was the result of his family's Catholicism, which gave you 'guilt, perversion and long names'. And shorter years. 1987 was actually shortened by one whole second in order to keep it running on the Gregorian Calendar, which was introduced in 1582 by the 'Inter Gravissimas' papal bull of Gregory XIII. Who I'm pretty sure was a Catholic.

Eno is conceivably the most important sonic manipulator of our generation as his experimentation has not only informed and infused the left field but has massively influenced the mainstream. 'The studio,' he explained, 'is a place where you make music and not just where you record it.' None of this was conclusive proof for his mother that he wouldn't at some point need to get a proper job. She was sure there would be openings at the Royal Mail given the family connections, his father, grandfather and great-grandfather having run the gauntlet of Suffolk's dog population for many years previously. However, Eno's grandfather also built and repaired mechanical musical instruments, which Brian described as 'the synthesizers of the late nineteenth century'. This redoubtable musical explorer also built a 600-pipe organ in his converted chapel home so that the fabric of the building shook during any recital.

This must have had an effect on young Brian, who would later be dubbed 'the architect of ambient music'. This, Brian told me, had come about when he was ill and found himself listening to a record that was on at low volume. Bedridden, he was unable to walk across the room to turn up the volume and so was forced to listen to the record despite it being obscured by the sound of the falling rain. He immediately became intrigued by the concept of 'listening as part of the landscape and not something stamped on top of it'. And perhaps it was here that the original blueprint for 'Where The Streets Have No Name' was drawn, many years before Larry Mullen Jnr pinned up the notice at school in Dublin to see if anyone wanted to form a band. They did form a band, of course, but Brian's soundscapes made them much more than that. 'I wasn't just hearing four people in a room,' he said, 'I was hearing the landscape.'

Operation Deepspan spent over a million pounds in 1987 looking for conclusive proof of the existence of the Loch

Ness Monster. Brian would surely have approved of the ambition of the sweep. 'I wanted to think,' he recalled, 'that the music was going on right to the horizon and beyond. I wanted to make music that sounded like it was a world. Not a band, but a world.'

Nessie hunters still haven't found what they're looking for but, for Eno at least, it was mission accomplished.

1988

TALK TALK – 'SPIRIT OF EDEN'

Brian Eno would surely approve of *Spirit Of Eden* as it is a record that seems to exist entirely in its own world. Talk Talk had actually had some chart success as a vaguely New Romantic synth pop band and so their transformation into experimental post-rock pioneers was all the more surprising given their initial mainstream sound and success.

With the exceptions of Dylan, Springsteen, Leonard Cohen and Keith Richards I have been lucky enough to meet and interview pretty much everyone whose records have fascinated me down the years, but I've never managed to arrange an audience or a pint with Talk Talk's lynchpin Mark Hollis. When he first appeared on *Top of the Pops* he seemed an unlikely frontman with his FA Cup handle ears and gloomy demeanour. Those first hits are pleasant if unremarkable and it was only when 'It's My Life' was released in 1984 and Hollis began his career-defining collaboration with producer Tim Friese-Greene that you began to suspect this serious and intense-looking young man was going to take to uncharted waters.

One of the original quartet left and bassist Paul Webb and drummer Lee Harris had to accept that the concept of the band they'd formed had been replaced with an ever-changing collective, assembled to create the sounds that Hollis heard inside his head. Like Brian said, the studio was somewhere you went to create music not just to record it.

Spirit Of Eden was assembled from hours of improvised sessions, painstakingly edited, mixed and blended by Hollis and Friese-Greene until the bones of the skeletal songs emerged. It is such a deeply strange and alien record it seems possible that it had been encountered in a different galaxy by the Hubble space telescope, which was launched this year, and yet it's also welcoming and warm somehow even at its most disconcerting. Vocals are rarely more than a whisper, lyrics minimal, rhythms hypnotically simple, melodies hauntingly beautiful. There are no pictures of the band on the sleeve, just a stylised painting of a puffin and some seashells dangling from the branches of a weary tree. What can any of it mean? It's rumoured to have something to do with Luke Reinhardt's book *The Dice Man*, but having tried and failed to get through that cult classic, I can shed no light on that theory. What fuelled it we will never know. Magic mushrooms? All-day drinking? The first Red Nose Day? These were all features of 1988 but none seem to connect with the music recorded here.

Naturally, I think it's an album that everyone should hear as it's more or less impossible for me to convey in words what it sounds like. For those of a certain age parts of it seem to echo the musical accompaniment to the adventures of *Noggin the Nog*. Produced by the genuine potting shed genii Peter Firmin and Oliver Postgate, the saga-based adventures of the genial Norseman formed part of the immortal Smallfilms canon which also boasted *Ivor the Engine*, *Pogles' Wood*, *Bagpuss* and *The Clangers*. Like Talk Talk and Brian Eno, Postgate and Firmin were intent on creating worlds. Their worlds may not have involved landscapes as widescreen as Death Valley but, for children of that generation, they were wholly engaging magical lands to which we would escape. *Noggin* was a fixture of British tele-vison from 1959 to 1965, and how eagerly I awaited the next instalment of the tale. Based on a chess set with a Viking theme, the stories revolve around the eponymous Noggin, son of Knut, King of the Nogs. Other principal characters are the Eskimo princess Nooka, the hapless inventor Olaf the Lofty, captain of the guard Thor Nogson, arch-villain Nogbad the Bad and, naturally, a large green talking bird named Graculus. It's charming, its primitive animation techniques adding to the appeal somehow, and yet also very strange. It's never frightening, just gently out of kilter with the world we know, and you could say the same about *Spirit Of Eden*.

Musically, there are undeniable similarities due to the pres-ence of that most trusted rock'n'roll instrument the bassoon. 'Woodwind instruments in rock' is not a subject that need detain us long. We'll exclude the saxophone, as most bands wisely do, as it isn't a proper woodwind on account of being made out of brass. There has been a bit of rocking flute action thanks principally to the efforts of Jethro Tull main-man Ian Anderson, but it's worth remembering that this is a man who also considered the codpiece an essential folk-rock constituent. There have been other notable rock flautists including Thijs van Leer of Focus who also sang and played organ, and Ray Thomas of The Moody Blues who also played tambourine and looked like a wine waiter in a Spanish restaurant. 'Oboists in rock' is an even smaller club, having just one member in Andy Mackay of Roxy Music. I'm a huge admirer of the early Roxy albums and Mackay's spo-radic interjections are a vital ingredient, but when considering the oboe it's hard to get beyond Eddie Izzard's observation that it looks and sounds like 'someone blowing into a weasel'. The clarinet is a vital component of the Klezmer sound but rarely cuts it as an implement to rock out with. Cor anglais? Cor blimey, don't think so. Let's face it, woodwinds are just not sexy. Do you think that the world's lascivious womenfolk would have found the Presley thrusting so sexually potent if the camera had pulled back and revealed he was holding a piccolo?

It follows, then, that there are no famous bassoonists in rock, although this primitive form of plumbing masquerading as a musical instrument does feature prominently in the immortal 'Tears Of A Clown' by Smokey Robinson and The Miracles. The bassoon, however, is the key instrument in the musical accompaniments to Noggin's outings, having been composed and performed by esteemed British composer, conductor and bassoonist Vernon Elliott. By turns spooky, quirky and comical, it seems the ideal choice to bring to life the land of the Nogs. Quite why Mark Hollis thought it would be an ideal component of *Spirit Of Eden*, where it's played by Andrew Stowell, is hard to say but he is in intriguing company. Nigel Kennedy is the violinist, undisputed guv'nor of the double bass Danny Thompson is in the house, and there is also a rare session booking for Christopher Hooker, who must be in a very small section of the Yellow Pages as cor anglais-ists for hire. The Chelmsford Cathedral Choir are also brought in to enrich the sonic stew.

There's also a namecheck for a man called Hugh Davies, who is credited with 'shozygs'. I assumed this was a percussion instrument made out of a clay pot or an obscure Balkan sousaphone or something, but it is in fact far more interesting and esoteric than that. Hugh Davies was a Devonian musical explorer who spent many years advancing the cause of electronic music. At the age of twenty-one he convinced Karlheinz Stockhausen to take him on in Cologne as his assistant. He also designed and constructed his own musical instruments and the 'shozygs' is one of these. Even after looking into it at some length I've been unable to work out exactly what it does or what sounds it makes but I do know that its name comes from an encyclopedia which was part of a set and contained items beginning with the prefix 'sho' running through to those starting with 'zygs'. Whatever the instrument was, the component parts were housed inside this hollowed-out volume. Amazing. This thing, whatever it is, would seem to symbolise the enigma of Talk Talk.

Mark Hollis went on to make a further Talk Talk album called *Laughing Stock* which makes *Spirit Of Eden* sound like *Motown Chartbusters Volume 5*. Which has some bassoon on it, thanks to the presence of that Smokey classic. Hollis then released a solitary solo album in 1998 which made *Laughing Stock* seem like Jive Bunny. And since then, nothing. Well, there have been occasional 'guest' appearances on avant-garde jazz records and the like, but that's it. All interview requests are politely refused. No public sightings ever reported. We are told he has retired from music.

People like that I find fascinating. Mike Scott of The Waterboys released *Fisherman's Blues* this same year, demonstrating that rather than being the next Bono, which with his 'big music' he could quite easily have been, he chose to hole up in a country house in Spiddal, County Galway, to embark on the traditional music experiment that would forever divide his audience. The Canadian singer-songwriter Mary Margaret O'Hara unveiled her *Miss America* album, featuring the wonderful 'Anew Day', to rapturous acclaim before retreating from view and releasing just one EP since. In an era that seems obsessed with fame it is the select few who attain it and then reject it who beguile. Of course, most of us will never have the luxury of stopping work as we need to continue to earn money. Mark Hollis may well be working on something other than music. I don't know. But though he was probably comfortably off (there was talk of a rectory in Suffolk), he could have enriched himself a great deal more by carrying on. He didn't, though. How wonderful, and bold, to admit that you have said all you came to say.

1989

THE STONE ROSES – 'MADE OF STONE'

If you should ever find yourself in France in the midst of a crowd that the authorities are attempting to disperse with tear gas, which at time of writing seems eminently feasible, it's as well to have a lemon with you. Apparently breathing through a scarf, or perhaps a bandanna if you're a proper revolutionary, soaked in lemon juice helps a lot. It was a technique used by rioting students and other libertarian factions in the Paris uprisings of 1968 and inspired both The Stone Roses' song and debut album cover painting 'Bye Bye Badman'. That's why there are slices of lemon on there, not because John Squire had some left over from his gin and tonic.

That period of French history is seen by people cleverer, and indeed French-er, than me as a watershed in the country's development. Those few weeks of street fighting in Paris are deemed to mark the transformation from the old Conservative ways to a new golden age of liberalism. In theory anyway. As one piece of graffiti of the time put it: 'In a society that has abolished every kind of adventure, the only adventure left is to abolish society.' Which must have taken quite a lot of aerosol paint.

The potent atmosphere in the city during that tempestuous period profoundly affected anyone who was present at the time, including the ursine Greek keyboard conjuror

Vangelis who was there recording an album with his band Aphrodite's Child, featuring the bewilderingly castrato vocals of the bovine Demis Roussos. Having lived through such events and created memorable musical works including *Chariots of Fire*, *Blade Runner* and international hits with Jon Anderson of Yes, Evangelos Odysseus Papathanassiou was probably justifiably convinced of his own reputation. What he made of events when he arrived at a Liverpool radio station to be interviewed by a disc jockey of my acquaintance we can only speculate. The story has it that the Apollonian polyphonic Hagrid breezed into reception wearing a fur coat and with a woman on each arm. Perhaps these details have been added to enrich the scenario, although it all seems plausible. Given his build it would have been eminently possible for him to have turned up in a fur coat with a woman under each arm. What is not in dispute is that the Scouse jobsworth of a security guard manning the desk asked this Grecian Goliath who he was.

'Vangelis,' came the not unreasonable reply.

'Phil,' crackled the voice on the studio intercom, 'there's a Frank Ellis here to see you.'

I first saw The Stone Roses at a wonderful Manchester club called the International, which is on Anson Road and is no longer a music venue but has kept its international flavour by becoming a supermarket with multicultural produce. The Roses were a five-piece then with second guitarist Andy Couzens and bassist 'Mad' Pete Garner in the ranks. They were an utterly electrifying whirlwind of a live band driven by the most stupendous of drummers in Reni and the crackling guitar of John Squire. Crouching and bobbing like a young Ricky Hatton, Ian Brown was a confident and charismatic frontman. When Garner and Couzens departed, the effervescent and ever-amiable Mani was recruited on bass and the classic line-up was in place. Their distinctive sound was matched by the Jackson Pollock-influenced paintwork of Squire, which extended beyond the record sleeves onto the instruments and famously the offices and cars of their record company Silvertone.

I'm never quite sure that I completely 'get' Jackson Pollock, as it's just spilling paint when all's said and done, isn't it? I don't say I don't find it interesting and curiously beautiful to look at, and I have felt some kind of emotional response when gazing at *Summertime* which is a more profound reaction than I've ever had to Mark Rothko, but I can never quite get past the feeling that anyone could do it. Of course, that doesn't really matter. It's having the idea to do it in the first place that's important, and yet for admiration to be unreserved I have to feel it's something I could never do. And there are several billion things that fall into that category.

John Squire seems to have conceived the band, its music and its visuals as equal parts of the same artistic enterprise. It's a shame, then, that he didn't pay more attention to the clothes. It was, of course, the height of chic to wear baggy garments at that time. But looking at video footage now, the Roses seem to be draped in the voluminous sweatshirts and wide-legged jeans of older siblings. It's as if they've been taken shopping by their mums who have insisted on buying clothes they will 'grow into', or are four contenders for young weight-loss champion of the year posing in the obligatory big trousers they used to wear before they stopped eating chips.

Musically, though, they had it all and seemed, whether by accident or design, to have combined some of the crucial elements of popular music in a whole new way. They had rock lead guitar, thunderous reggae bass and furious yet funky drumming. The vocals of Ian Brown have been the subject of much discussion, though listening to those first records now they sound plaintive and rather endearing. If Squire was a 'non-macho' guitar hero then Brown was his similarly non-histrionic vocal foil. Mystifyingly, Ian's vocals seemed to deteriorate the longer the band went on and so let's just say that if The Stone Roses were a revolutionary force in music, breaking down barriers and ignoring the old rules, then Ian ingeniously undermined the commonly held belief that 'practice makes perfect'. For a moment there in 1989, however, The Stone Roses were perfect and the soaring chorus of 'Made Of Stone' perhaps the most perfect moment of all.

Another piece of 1968 Parisian graffiti promised 'underneath the paving stones, the beach'. Appropriated by Brown on his debut solo album *Unfinished Monkey Business*, these words were the result of the mob pulling up paving on the Left Bank (to hurl at the police presumably) and finding sand underneath. Perhaps it was this desire to combine revolutionary fervour with a waterside setting that led to The Stone Roses staging one of the major 'happenings' of the Madchester era: the concert at Spike Island.

Spike Island is an area of around ten hectares near Widnes. Now a splendid country park, it had originally been home to petro-chemical plants and was located where the Sankey Canal opened onto the River Mersey. If you're struggling to work out just how big 'ten hectares' is then let me make it easy by saying it's about the size of ten or eleven football pitches. I know it's old-fashioned but I do tend to stick to the old imperial units of area measurement which, as you'll remember from school, go fag packet, foot, cubit, chain, furlong, double-decker bus, football pitch, Nelson's Column, Wales. Funny what you remember, isn't it? These are the classic units of measurement those of us of a certain age will always fall back on. The cubit is very rarely used these days and in fact was largely dying out even during my school days, as it was only really employed during the construction of pyramids and most of our experts in this field left the UK for Egypt in the great brain drain of 2500 BC.

Wales is often used to illustrate the extent of, for example, the area of rainforest lost in a given period. I have even heard it suggested that Wales doesn't actually exist except as a unit of meausurement, although I seem to remember leaving Chester and driving through something before reaching Anglesey.

Double-decker buses remain the simplest way of conveying size and weight. Interestingly enough, scientists have confirmed recently that the world's strongest animal, in terms of size and tonnage shifted, is the dung beetle, which can pull the equivalent of six fully laden double-decker buses. With such extraordinary natural gifts it seems a shame that it has restricted itself to pushing excrement about, but that's strongmen for you. All that impressive ability and what do they do with it? Lift up even heavier things and blow up hot-water bottles. Brilliant. How very useful. Perhaps that's why you don't get door-to-door strongmen. Door-to-door brush salesmen and gardeners and milkmen and rag-and-bone men and chimney sweeps and God-botherers and even insurance agents were a fixture of suburban life not that long ago. Unlike strongmen, they could actually do something practical and useful when they'd got you to the front door. Your itinerant strongman would just shuffle about on the doorstep in a skimpy leotard before asking if you'd got any hot-water bottles you wanted blowing up. I mean, why would you? That's why they've pretty much died out. Check your Yellow Pages if you don't believe me. Mine goes straight from street furniture to structural engineers.

On 27 May 1990 around 30,000 devotees descended on Spike Island, which is around a hundred and eighty-nine thousandth of a Wales, to attend an event dubbed by one national newspaper 'the Woodstock of the North'. Well, yes, except that there was only one band on and nowhere near the same number of people. It did, however, resemble the 1969 event in that it was outside, was very difficult to get to, had dreadful sound and the beer ran out. On the plus side Ian Brown had a big globe and some bongos and there was a liberal supply of drugs. It was very easy that day in 1995 to be 'sorted for E's and wizz', which we'll come back to later.

Carping aside, and it is easy to accentuate the negative given the organisational failings of the event, it does seem now like the high-water mark of the prevailing youth movement of that time. Certainly there were other great records released at that time, notably by The Pixies and De La Soul. Other cultural developments included *The Simpsons* making its debut as a 'stand-alone' TV show mirroring the dysfunctional aspects of family life that we all knew so well. Certainly growing up with a mother with blue hair and a father who had a cavalier attitude to nuclear safety when given access to the Manchester University laboratories where Rutherford split the atom, it all seemed very close to home. *Baywatch* started too. That seemed less like the life I knew. Sky TV came on stream and the Game Boy appeared in the shops, but The Stone Roses epitomised all that was invigorating and new. Who knows whether Aerosmith, who had a big album in *Pump* this year, looked over their shoulders and saw Nirvana waving copies of *Bleach*. Whether they did or they didn't, it felt like something was happening.

The late Tony Wilson had a theory that musical revolution happened every thirteen years. In 1950 you got trad jazz, 1963 The Beatles and the beat boom, in 1976 it was punk, and therefore in 1989 it was the tipping point for acid house, rave culture and the baggy bands that absorbed those influences. OK, you can probably pick holes in the

theory but in 1989 when you heard 'Made Of Stone'
another revolutionary graffiti slogan found on a wall in 1968
Paris seemed to ring true: 'Run comrade, the old world is
behind you'.

1990

THE CHARLATANS – 'THE ONLY ONE I KNOW'

'Good morning and welcome to Radio 5,' said Andrew Kelly aged, appropriately enough, five. On an August morning towards the end of the last century the BBC launched a new network for the first time since 1967 when Tony Blackburn had spake the immortal words '. . . and good morning everyone! Welcome to the exciting new world of Radio 1.' And lo, there was light.

Nineteen ninety was a torrid year. Margaret Thatcher had resigned as the poll tax battles raged in the city streets. In Manchester disgruntled prisoners took to the roof of the prison. I was present for that extended incident having come out of the Royal Exchange Theatre, where I'd been somnambulantly wafted by the gossamer strains of the Cowboy Junkies. Emerging into St Anne's Square to find helicopters and searchlights peppering the night sky therefore came as a bit of a shock. Gradually gleaning the information that something major was going on at the clink, it was 'Strangeways, here we come' before you could say voyeuristic busybody. We were not alone. By the third night there were so many gawpers turning up to watch these renegades chucking roof tiles into the compound that there were hot-dog sellers on the pavements. Within a week, you could buy a souvenir T-shirt.

In Italy the Leaning Tower of Pisa had to be closed because it was in danger of becoming the Fallen Over Tower of Pisa if any more tourists went up there. If those pumped-up strongmen we were talking about had had anything about them they would have nipped round there and held it up, but no doubt they were tied up bursting their gonads in Lycra body stockings whilst hoisting something the weight of a Mini Metro above their heads. Worst of all, and this did reverberate throughout the world, Milli Vanilli were revealed not to have sung on their own records.

The populace was obviously in need of a pick-me-up and so quite obviously that was where Marc Riley and I came in. Marc had been a member of The Fall and had gone on to front his own band The Creepers, for whom I produced their seminal 'Creeping At Maida Vale' EP. As usual, my interpretation of the word 'production' was to make sure everyone had turned up with some instruments and then ensure they knew where the tea bar was before heading off to the nearest boozer. Marc and his cohorts seemed amiable enough and apparently it was 'supposed to sound ram-shackle'. Happy that they weren't going to set off the fire extinguishers or steal the regulation BBC studio hat stand, I left them to it.

When I moved back to Manchester Marc was working for the *Viz*-inspired comic *Oink* before becoming a record plug-ger. Strangely, though our friends in the North included many of the same people in the deeply glamorous Mancunian media enclave, like Tony the Greek and 'Scally' Pat Gally and other legends of that stature, we had rarely come into contact with each other. That was about to change in a big way. The Midland Hotel on Peter Square was where Mr Rolls first met Mr Royce and history was made. I can't remember a his-toric first meeting for Marc and me, which is a shame because it was plainly just as significant. Or perhaps even more so. I know that sounds bigheaded, but ask yourself this: how many of you reading this own a Rolls-Royce? Not many. Now put your hand up if you've ever had the misfortune to hear one of our radio shows. You see?

Radio 5 was a bit hard to define as an entity as it was basically a radio network broadcasting all the bits of stuff the other channels couldn't really be bothered with. Former and much missed matriarch of BBC radio Jenny Abramsky once described it as: 'The sports output from Radio 2 medium wave, all the Schools and Continuing Education programmes from Radio 4 FM, the Open University programmes from Radios 3 and 4 FM and programmes for children and young people from Radio 4 and some World Service output. This was a network with no audience focus, born out of expediency.'

As a public service station, I've got to say that that looks OK to me and as 'listen again' and online technology have advanced and listeners have become more adept and selective at finding what they want, listening to it at a time that suits them, the idea of the old Radio 5 as a home for these disparate strands seems a perfectly reasonable concept. Of course, what that template was missing was a bit of good old rock'n'roll glamour, which is why they turned to me and Marc. What are you laughing at?

Manchester was at that time the hippest musical place in the UK by a country mile, even though it was a city. The Stone Roses and Happy Mondays were the fashionable names to drop and the word 'Madchester' appeared in the national media on a daily basis. *Newsweek* labelled The Hacienda 'the most famous nightclub in the world'. Everywhere you went, and this was one of the comparatively rare periods of my life when I did go out at night, the new soundtrack boomed out majestically. The Charlatans released 'The Only One I Know', which effortlessly combined vintage beat-era organ with a contemporary drive. All right, it was a bit like 'Hush' by Deep Purple, but they gave it a whole new effervescence. It was exciting, danceable, brash, melodic, and if you want to know how it felt to be 'mad for it' in Madchester then put that record on and you will know.

The grandees of Radio 5 decided they would have an evening programme reflecting 'youth culture' broadcast from a different part of the UK every night. This again seemed to me a perfectly reasonable proposition. And still does. As someone who has spent pretty much their entire career broadcasting from Manchester, you'd expect me to say that, but quite clearly if the entire nation funds the BBC then the BBC should serve and reflect the entire nation and that is not best done by the vast majority of programmes emanating from the West End of that there London. Naturally there was going to have to be a show coming from Manchester and so began the search for a likely presenter.

The man charged with making this vital appointment was a self-confident boffinish chap called Quentin Cooper. After sounding out some significant Manchester luminaries like Tony the Greek and 'Scally' Pat Gally, he decided the only man for the job was Marc Riley. No wonder he had to give up producing after displaying judgement like that. He would later turn up as a presenter himself, notably hosting the Radio 4 science programme *The Material World*, having discovered as I had that compared to producing, presenting is not only better paid but much, much easier. Thankfully the ever cordial and canny Riley said that he didn't really want the job but suggested that 'Radcliffe's your man'.

Our programme *Hit the North* took to the air on 28 August. I occupied the presenter's chair with Marc employed as gossip columnist bringing the all-important tittle and indeed tattle concerning the city's nightspots, fleshpots and tosspots. I'm pretty certain that our intention was to make this a genuine music-news item but after a couple of weeks it became apparent that if anyone was going to know what was going on then it wasn't Marc Riley. A typical anecdote might involve him having seen Dermo, lead singer of Northside, ordering a kebab in Levenshulme.

It was around this time that Marc acquired the nickname of 'Lard'. Whilst riding in the goods lift together he had grabbed his own beer belly and said, 'I must get rid of some of this lard.' This he eventually did, becoming something of a noted Adonis in the Northwest and doing quite a lot of modelling work for various catalogues, often holding a model aeroplane whilst staring into the middle distance in a pair of Y-fronts. Exasperated by his lack of 'gossip' one week, I concluded the piece by shouting, 'Shamble off, Lardy Boy,' and the poor bugger was stuck with it for the next ten years. Quite rightly he has shaken the tag off now and trades as Marc Riley The Artist Formerly Known as Lard on the nation's favourite 6 Music.

Hit the North was pretty much the mixture of live sessions, good records and mindless banter that later listeners to our Radio 1 shows would come to expect. We were nothing if not enthusiastic and ambitious in terms of what we thought you could do with a programme like that. One Christmas special had us travelling to a fancy dress party dressed as liver and bacon. Look, I have no idea, OK? To give ourselves time off to attend this fictitious party we had recorded a bogus edition of *Hit the North*. We then fictitiously travelled round Manchester dressed as offal, listening to ourselves in fictitious off-licences and chip shops and the like. And this for a music show. It took us ages to do it but that didn't matter. We had our own show on the BBC and access to unlimited studio time and it didn't matter if it took us all night.

Not all our concepts were so grandiose. My particular favourite item from that show was a spot called 'Chutney of the Week' in which Lard ... well, you're probably ahead of me here.

Radio 5 had several programming success stories. *They Think It's All Over* and *Room 101* both started there. *Hit the North* is by no means of equal note, though we can boast that we gave Oasis their first ever radio session. I didn't rate them all that highly and so they appeared when I was on holiday and Peter Hook was hosting the show. Doh! At the same time down South, Blur were putting the finishing touches to their first record and Brit-pop appeared as a dot on the horizon.

In 1991 Operation Desert Storm raged in Kuwait and the BBC's commitment to rolling news would lead to the arrival of 5 Live. The old Radio 5's short life was over, but as I sit here and think about it now it strikes me that if Marc had said yes when Quentin asked him the question in the Lass O'Gowrie boozer that day, I may never have had the chance to take to the national airwaves and, while there may be many hundreds of thousands of people who wish that had been the case, I have to say that I owe it all to Marc Riley. Cheers, mate. Did I ever buy you that pint?

R.E.M. – 'SHINY HAPPY PEOPLE'

As a direct result of being on Radio 5 the gaffers at Radio 1, where I was working as a producer based in Manchester, asked me if I'd like to present a music show for them. Incredible. All those years of growing up listening to John Peel, Annie Nightingale and Johnny Walker and here I was being given the opportunity to follow them. I can hardly describe how unbelievable it was. For sure I was going to carry on with the day job in production, but once a week I would have a little sideline hobby radio show where I could play records and talk nonsense. All that knowledge accumulated through decades of being a musical trainspotter and all that garbage previously spouted in the pub could finally be put to constructive use. And I got paid. Being on the BBC staff I was able to claim, and I realise that this is a sensitive subject these days, what was dubbed a 'staff contribution fee'. There were all sorts of archaic allowances back then, including 'staff appearance fee', which meant that if you were working in a studio and some filming took place during which you were caught on camera, you could invoice the Beeb for some dosh. I have a feeling it was around £2.85. You'd be perhaps unsurprised by the number of people who claimed it. For my first programme on Radio 1 I was paid £60 which, as I was on £13,000 a year, was a pretty useful bonus. Naturally, if they'd have asked me, I'd have done it for nothing.

The slot I was given was nine until ten on Monday evenings. As usual in my experience, the management took a fairly laissez-faire attitude to what would form the content. One of the executive producers, Chris Lycett, a real gent, phoned and said they'd thought that it could be a 'sort of acoustic-y, Del Amitri-ish kind of thing'. Well, I wasn't the biggest Del Amitri fan in the world but it was a plausible suggestion. I thought about it for about ten seconds and then said off the top of my head that I was thinking more of a 'psychedelic-y, punky-ish kind of thing'. Chris thought about it for about five seconds and said he thought that would be fine. And that was all the planning we ever did.

Nineteen ninety-one was a momentous year for music. Nirvana released *Nevermind*, which was undoubtedly the landmark record of those times. Rather in the way Human League's *Dare* had been released at the very start of the eighties and defined the decade of music that followed, so Nirvana got in early and moulded the soundtrack of the nineties. Other significant works came from Massive Attack with *Blue Lines*, *Loveless* by My Bloody Valentine, Primal Scream's *Screamadelica*, and The Orb's *Adventures Beyond The Ultraworld*. Blur's first album *Leisure* came out, too, as did *Achtung Baby* by U2 and *Bandwagonesque* from Teenage Fanclub. Oh, and of course British splatter death metal grindcore pioneers Carcass unveiled their *Necroticism – Descanting the Insalubrious* meisterwork, which I'm sure you're all aware of.

R.E.M. released *Out Of Time* as well, which was to spawn their reluctant global anthem 'Shiny Happy People'. If you had encountered the band in their earliest days, as I had, they seemed unlikely contenders for stadium status. They weren't poster boys, didn't dress well, didn't do big guitar solos and had vocals you could barely hear. That they would

come to appear slightly embarrassed by their cheery international hit therefore came as no surprise, though they would
eventually come to be more comfortable with their exalted
status, with the exception of Bill Berry who decided, all
things considered, that he'd rather sit on a tractor than a
drum stool. Despite their misgivings I absolutely loved 'Shiny
Happy People' and knew it was just the kind of off-kilter pop
that I had to include in my first programme.

On top of that there were records put out by Neil Young,
John Prine, The Field Mice, Metallica, Leatherface, Stevie
Ray Vaughan and Arvo Part that I enjoyed very much, and I
wanted to play tracks from all of them on this new show too.
Not only that but I wanted to mix the new stuff with a bit of
everything that had been important to me as I was growing
up. Obviously that meant a bit of punk and prog rock, which
was a mix that would have been unthinkable in the late
seventies. Then there was reggae and psychedelia and particularly the American garage bands featured on the classic
Nuggets compilation assembled by Patti Smith's guitarist
Lenny Kaye. Already this was looking like quite a lot to get
into an hour, as the territory I'd mapped out for myself
appeared to be the entire history of rock.

I remain convinced that this was right. If you love music,
why restrict yourself to certain genres? If you're a real
'foodie', which I'm not, you will presumably sample cuisine
of any nationality and ingredients. If you're a real traveller,
which I'm not, you will want to go to places that feel very
different from where you have been before. Why would
anyone who has music at the centre of their life not want to
go on a similar journey? This is the problem I have with what
are called 'specialist' music shows. I love folk and blues and
rock and soul but I don't want to listen to a solid hour of any
of them. I want a mix of all of it. I mean, I love cheese but I
don't want a four-course meal of goats' cheese roulade,

Cheshire cheese sausages, vanilla cheesecake and then a hearty cheeseboard. Actually, thinking about it, I do, so forget that bit.

You know what I mean, though, don't you? On my current Radio 2 show Stuart Maconie and I spend hours looking through the records we're planning to play and thinking about what would be the perfect track to complete the blend. When Laura Marling was playing live recently we followed her breathtaking rendition of 'Devil's Spoke' with 'The Message' by Grandmaster Flash. It's not rocket science or anything, but it does need thinking about and, again, you'd perhaps be unsurprised to know how many supposedly music-based shows don't bother. It is primarily about playing what we consider to be great music, but it is also about balance, about texture, about the mix. Everyone I know who loves music loves a wide variety of genres, inasmuch as a 'genre' even matters, and most radio still refuses to acknowledge this. Similarly, if you have grown up with a passion for music, how could you ever stop looking for new tunes that will come to mean as much to you as those tracks that defined your formative years? The 'foodie' will always seek out new dishes, the traveller will always need to discover mysterious new places. I am always looking for the new favourite record that I haven't heard yet.

I decided to call the show *Out On Blue Six*. I don't know why, really. I certainly didn't want to call it 'The Mark Radcliffe Show' as that seemed ridiculously self-aggrandising and I was reluctant to stand accused of that. This modesty I was later able to shed as I became more successful and a bit of a bighead. In fact, I was initially hesitant about becoming a minor public figure and 'Z' list celebrity and in early press shots concealed myself beneath what was referred to as a monk's cowl but was in fact a Kilkenny duffel coat bought on holiday in Dublin. I also wore large sunglasses and, whilst you might think this made me look a bit of a pranny, and you may well be right, it did cause a little bit of a stir. I had really been thinking about bands who I'd loved who chose not to appear on their record sleeves, and in particular Joy Division as we have already discussed. It was always accepted that people who became Radio 1 DJs wanted to be celebrities first and musicologists second. Of course there were notable exceptions to this rule, but the vast majority seemed to be passing through en route to a televison quiz show. As a young listener I know I would have been drawn to a new presenter who chose to keep his face hidden.

I'm pretty sure this wasn't driven by modesty. In fact, it may have been just the opposite. I may have thought that I wouldn't get the attention I thought I deserved as just another bloke with an hour on the radio. With this ploy, I thought it would be a way of drawing attention to what might otherwise seem a very minor addition to the schedule. Eventually I had to consign the duffel coat to the wardrobe of oblivion, as it became apparent that you couldn't present the Glastonbury Festival on Channel 4 dressed like that without looking even more of a pranny and quite possibly fainting due to heat exhaustion.

The title *Out On Blue Six* had been the name of an obscure Manchester band in the late seventies I must have seen on a poster, as I don't recall having heard them. I believe Carl Marsh who went on to join Shriekback was a member. There is also a 1989 science fiction novel of the same name by the Irish writer Ian McDonald. I haven't read it, I'm afraid, and wasn't aware of its existence when I decided to use the phrase for this new show. To me, it just seemed to suggest being out on your own on the far edges, almost as if I was a pirate DJ broadcasting from a rusting space station rather than a rusting trawler in the North Sea. It seemed to say that here was the hit parade of a parallel universe.

I made some little jingles from odd records by The Residents and Stackridge and got the actor and comedian John Thompson in from Didsbury to shout things like 'Set the controls for gas mark 7'. I then picked the records and timed them with a BBC standard-issue stopwatch before getting them typed up in order on two sheets of A4. Having done all that I went into a small anteroom off our office and, in tiny scrawl, wrote down every single word I was going to say, not trusting myself to be able to think of anything when the time came.

The first *Out On Blue Six* was broadcast on Monday 8 April 1991 and these are the records I played:

The Damned – 'New Rose'
The Shangri-La's – 'Leader Of The Pack'
Syndicate of Sound – 'Little Girl'
Chapterhouse – 'Pearl'
World of Twist – 'Sons Of The Stage'
Hawkwind – 'Master Of The Universe'
R.E.M. – 'Shiny Happy People'
KLF – 'The White Room'
808 State – 'Nephatiti'
The Raybeats – 'The Calhoun Surf'
Pink Floyd – 'Lucifer Sam'
Sun Dial – 'Plains Of Nazca'
The Lightning Seeds – 'Pure'
Sonic Youth – 'Dirty Boots'
Kitchens of Distinction – 'Railwayed'
Joy Division – 'Atmosphere'

Job done, I put on my duffel coat and went for a pint.

1992

NIRVANA – 'SMELLS LIKE TEEN SPIRIT' (LIVE AT READING)

Having been helicoptered in for his triumphant appearance the main man sits backstage with adrenalin coursing through his veins listening to the roar of the crowd growing ever louder. Standing in their thousands his devotees have been waiting many hours to see their hero stride onto the stage and raise his arms in a victorious salute. There have been engaging acts lower down the bill but there is an overriding sense that this is the moment the entire event has been building towards. For some of the faithful, this will be a first and perhaps only chance to see their idol in the flesh and the mood is one of grinning, feverish excitement. People can scarcely believe that they are actually here to see history in the making. There are also questions about his state of mind and physical health that add an extra piquancy to the anticipation. Will the undoubted pressures of his lifestyle and fame affect his performance?

And then the stage lights go down. The mob are by now teetering on the edge of hysteria. Suddenly, there he is. Surrounded by sturdy henchmen he strides onto the stage and, punching the air, shouts: 'Well, alright! Well, alright!'

So much for Neil Kinnock at the Labour Party 'victory' rally at Sheffield Arena on 1 April 1992. Didn't anyone look at that date and wonder if it was tempting fate in any way? Eight days later John Major's Conservative Party were returned to power, which surprised more or less everyone including, one suspects, John Major. Poor Neil. Still, he wasn't the only one to have an annus horribilis, was he, Ma'am?

Whether Kurt Cobain went through any of the same emotions as Kinnock as he waited to ascend the ramp to the main stage that Sunday night at the Reading Festival we will never know. What is undeniable is that Nirvana dominated a three-day festival in a way no other band has done since.

I don't wish to offend anyone but I've always found the Reading Festival to be a pretty ghastly affair. As an event it has none of the colour and countercultural underbelly of Glastonbury and several other more recent additions to the festival calendar. My abiding memories are of trudging dimly lit muddy fields in the drizzle as packs of wraiths and hobbits in Ned's Atomic Dustbin hoodies huddled by flaming toxic mounds of polystyrene burger cartons as The Sisters of Mercy's gothic grind emanated from a cloud of dry ice some-where in the middle distance. And yet there is a sense that it is perhaps the most 'authentic' event of its kind. It has taken place on the same site since the very early seventies and prides itself on being a strictly musical proposition for young fans who want nothing more than to see a bunch of bands they like, and to hurl bottles of urine at those they don't.

This celebrated Reading tradition is said to have begun in 1988 when the unfortunate recipients of the treatment were Meat Loaf and Bonnie Tyler. You can see why. Both would have represented easy targets to lock on to. Meat is a man as known for his girth as his operatic mock rock and would have been easy to score a direct hit upon having emptied your bladder into a Budweiser bottle. Bonnie, though com-paratively svelte, was known for her big eighties peroxide bouffant, which would have been visible to low-flying air-craft. 'Total Eclipse Of The Heart'? A total eclipse of the sun would have been her only salvation that year. Perhaps not surprisingly, rapper 50 Cent lasted only twenty minutes in 2004 before he had not so much a eureka moment as a ure-thra moment. Teeny-bop duo Daphne and Celeste gamely completed their set in 2000 despite ferocious aerial bom-bardment from the pee artillery. No doubt their rendition of hits such as 'Ooh Stick You' and 'U.G.L.Y.' ('you ain't got no alibi – you ugly') did little to quell the antagonism. The plucky twosome nevertheless brazened it out, having told the rowdy latrine-eschewing revellers to, quoting one of their songs, shove it 'up your butt with a coconut'. The elegant solution.

In 1991 Nirvana had also played at Reading but low down the bill on Friday afternoon. No one, myself included, paid all that much attention. A year later the success of 'Smells Like Teen Spirit' and the accompanying *Nevermind* album had propelled the band into the mainstream as well as making them the biggest 'indie' band in the world. 'Grunge' was a term that had passed into general usage, being used to describe not only music but fashion and lifestyle. The band's personalities had also become closely monitored, particularly the fragile lead singer and guitarist Kurt Cobain. In retrospect the 'grunge' era produced little memorable music but you couldn't say that for Nirvana. In 'All Apologies', 'In Bloom', 'Come As You Are', 'Lithium' and 'Teen Spirit' they created the songs that define the times and managed to combine the ferocity and angst with truly memorable tunes. It's a really good trick if you can pull it off.

Accordingly, that weekend there was talk of little else but their headlining appearance on the Sunday night. Festival Sundays can be a bit of a downer as people start to filter away, shuffling back to the overcrowded railway station or attempting to find their car amidst the gridlock of the outer fields, knowing that they have to go back to their normal lives the next morning. After the weekend-long suspension of the rules of workaday life, reality begins to bite back. At Reading in 1992 it was quite clear that nobody was going anywhere until Dave Grohl had rendered his drums unplayable.

I was there that year in a semi-official capacity and it's still a thrill to look at the poster and read the first three lines:

The 20th Reading Festival
August Bank Holiday Weekend
Comperes John Peel and Mark Radcliffe

I was hosting the second stage, which had been branded the 'Radio 1 FM session tent'. Over the three days I gave minimal and unnecessary introductions to a host of championship contenders who have mostly fallen by rock's stony wayside. At the time a bill consisting of Levitation, Suede, Cardiacs, Spiritualized, Curve, Catherine Wheel, Thousand Yard Stare, Shonen Knife, Midway Still and Leatherface was more than enough to ensure a full marquee, though not many of those names resonate today. Intense Americans Cop Shoot Cop destroyed some very expensive guitars at the end of their set and one can only imagine that they wish they'd saved a bit more money now. Some say that the majestic Suede, whose star continued to rise, were the band of the festival that year. They weren't, though. Not by a long way.

Friday night on the main stage saw a bill of PJ Harvey, Public Image Limited and The Charlatans, with the comparitively cheery Wonderstuff topping the bill. In the backstage bar, however, the main talking point was that Dave Grohl was having a Beck's. I shamelessly set off around the beer tent to find him, just so I could see one of the three most famous men in rock in the flesh. I had expected, given the band's somewhat combative reputation, to encounter a scowling semi-feral creature enclosed by a coterie of bristling bouncers. I was surprised, then, to see him alone, chatting amiably to anyone who approached him. He was also dressed in clothes that seemed casual, practical and largely devoid of standard-issue 'grunge' holes. I was also struck by how handsome he was. He looked rather like Laurence Llewelyn-Bowen might look if the flamboyant interior-design dandy had opted for a career in landscape gardening. He also seemed very tall but that only lasted until you encountered Krist Novoselic, who was the undisputed Peter Crouch of grunge bass.

The weather worsened on Saturday as The Manic Street Preachers, EMF and Ride came and went, grateful that not a single yellow message in a bottle had arrived during their time on stage. Headliners Public Enemy may well have been wondering if the grunge goblins hadn't been crossing their legs and stockpiling receptacles for most of the afternoon.

Still there was talk of nothing but Nirvana. I began to get a little tired of it, to tell you the truth. All right, there hadn't been any bands on who had been truly amazing, though Suede had probably come closest. Even so, it was ridiculous that a single act seemed to be dominating the event to that extent. I mean, there was no way they would be good enough to live up to that level of expectation, right? That sort of build-up can only end in crushing disappointment. Just ask Neil Kinnock.

Sunday's bill looks like hard work on paper now. The Melvins and Screaming Trees kicked things off from noon. Both bands were closely associated with the headliners and, in truth, just sounded like inferior versions. Respected Stateside cult indie rockers Pavement and, at the risk of being unkind, another Netto Nirvana in Mudhoney did little to lighten proceedings. I'm a fan of The Beastie Boys, Teenage Fanclub and Nick Cave and The Bad Seeds, who all appeared that day, and yet the mushy sound made sure any subtleties were lost. The only light relief came from Abba clones Björn Again, who must have been eager to leave the site in search of a dry-cleaners at the earliest opportunity. I knew how they felt. I'd have left myself were it not for this Nirvana lot, but I felt I had to stay just so I could confirm to everyone I knew that they were not worth the hype.

By the nature of my compering role I had a stage pass and decided that I might as well watch the headliners from the closest possible vantage point. These days all the major acts clear the wings of liggers, freeloaders, hangers-on, comperes and other lowlife, and who can blame them? If you're Bruce Springsteen pulling your tripe out for two hours you don't want to be put off by the likes of me flashing my little-deserved 'access all areas' laminate. Astonishingly, on the evening of Sunday, 30 August, I was allowed to stroll right onto the side of the stage to where Big John, formerly of Scottish anarchopunks The Exploited, was tending to Cobain's guitars. Expecting to be asked in no uncertain terms to move on at any moment I was then amazed to be perhaps two feet from the blessed and damned Kurt as he made his now celebrated entrance. He was wearing white surgical robes and a long blond wig and was being ferried onstage in a wheelchair. For a moment there I thought it was Courtney Love.

Immediately they started to play it became apparent that something very special was happening. Grohl has said that they rehearsed only once, the night before, for this performance and 'it wasn't good'. Perhaps sensing the possibility of a high-profile disaster spurred them on. I never got the chance to see John Bonham play live and, as he is generally accepted to have been the greatest rock'n'roll drummer who ever lived, this is something, particularly as a drummer myself, that I greatly regret. However, seeing Dave Grohl drum has to be the second-best thing. It's rare to see that compelling combination of brilliant technique and brute force. He was, and I choose a word that is overused by Americans advisedly, awesome. Combined with the melodic twangy subsonics of Novoselic they were a band in themselves. As regards Cobain, rumours of his death had been greatly exaggerated. He didn't say much but he leaped and pirouetted and can be seen frozen in midair on many of the iconic photographs reprinted many times. Listening to the tracks again now I'm surprised by how together it all sounds. I had assumed that the ferocity of the music and the exhilaration of the moment concealed mistakes and misfirings by the fistful. Across a set of more than twenty songs, though, they are pretty much note perfect and are playing just as thunderously at the end of the night as they were on the first song. Nobody went anywhere until Dave Grohl had rendered his drums unplayable and I remember thinking that it was a miracle the kit hadn't exploded during the set having received that level of continuous pulverisation. Grohl has talked about 'Lithium' being the highlight of that evening for him and certainly it must be amazing to hear your own song sung back to you by 50,000 disciples. Especially as it would turn out to be the last UK gig the band would ever play and Cobain himself would be dead within two years. For me, though, it's 'Teen Spirit' that provides the immortal moment. I said that they were pretty much note perfect. That's not exactly true. On this number the guitar lines are fluffed, but all of us who were there that day are convinced that, far from being bum-notes bashed out by an addled addict, these 'mistakes' were made deliberately. It seemed that at the height of his powers and popularity Kurt Cobain was defacing his own masterpiece and that, perhaps, gives us some insight into the mind of the man whose dream came true only to discover that it didn't make him happy.

1993

STEREOLAB – 'FRENCH DISKO'

As this song appears as track four on the 1993 'Jenny Ondioline' EP, there's a good chance it might be unfamiliar to you, unless you've had nothing better to do than listen to my radio shows with any degree of regularity, in which case you'll have heard it several times.

Stereolab are from London, are led by Tim Gane and have a French lead singer called Laetitia Sadier. Another key member was Mary Hansen, who was very sadly knocked off her bicycle and killed in London in 2002. They've made lots of great records but this, for me, is the one. It is just about my favourite record with which to start a programme. I don't know why, really. I just feel connected to it in some way. Perhaps it runs at the same speed as my heartbeat. It's a fairly simple number but then, when asked what he loved most about rock'n'roll, Lou Reed answered, electric guitar, bass and drums going from E to A 'if it's done right'. I don't even know what the chords are to 'French Disko'. In fact the bulk of it relies on one chord only. It's a good one though. It is 'done right'.

After John Peel died it came to light that he had a special, battered, wooden record box in which he kept 142 extra-special seven-inch singles. These included records by Alan

Price, Bill Oddie, Cat Power, Elmore James, Ken Colyer's Jazzmen, The Move, The Yardbirds, The MC5, Sam and Dave, Pavement, Medicine Head, Ann Peebles, Paul Revere & The Raiders, Nilsson and nine by The White Stripes. The Beatles' 'Come Together' was in there along with 'Ever Fallen In Love' by Buzzcocks and of course 'Teenage Kicks'. Also there was 'Down Down' by Status Quo, which pleased me enormously as we all like a bit of Quo, don't we? Take any classic track of theirs and you're immediately hypnotised by the twin guitars of Rossi and Parfitt, who are the Morecambe and Wise of rock, and I can think of no higher compliment than that. As the double Telecaster chug beds down down, you are just instinctively waiting for the bass and drums to pile in, at which point all's well in the world. It too is done right. Some records just have that effect on you in a physical way. For me, 'French Disko' is one of them. 'Immigrant Song', 'Heroes', 'Fight For Your Right To Party', 'You Can't Hurry Love' and 'Do Anything You Wanna Do' get me in just the same way. As does 'Blitzkrieg Bop' by The Ramones. I've said before that I'm never entirely sure about people who don't like The Ramones. It's not that we can't be civil, but I just know that we will never be close if you can't feel what I feel when 'Blitzkrieg Bop' bursts into life.

Also in Peel's box was '9 to 5' by Sheena Easton. That was a surprise, although John was cherished for his unblinkered attitude to music and my only vaguely negative feeling was that I would have loved him to have suddenly sprung a choice like this on the adoring audience for his radio show. So was Sheena Easton what you might call a guilty pleasure for Peel? No, because no right-minded music lover, unless shackled by the notion of what's 'cool', need feel guilty about liking any record. If you like it, you like it. You don't need to justify it in any other way. I love those classic Nirvana songs we've just revisited but I love records by Supertramp, Steely

Dan, Fleetwood Mac and Genesis just as much. Talking to Alison Goldfrapp recently she expressed a love of Hall & Oates. I'm not keen myself, though I have recently revisited *Abandoned Luncheonette* and been moderately impressed, but it doesn't make me admire her records any the less.

John's record box became the subject of a television documentary and there was something rather touching about the sight of these old discs that had been so precious to him. These days many people, myself not included, choose to download songs instead of owning the physical artefact. Is it possible, then, that an iPod could one day be as mythologised as Peel's little crate or John Lennon's jukebox? Possibly, I suppose, though unlikely as there is no personal stamp on it save the selection of songs. This, of course, will always be the most important thing. I know people with shelves of meticulously alphabeticised CDs and vinyl discs who never seem to play any of them. I know music nuts who own very few actual records, preferring to constantly access different kinds of music online. Fair enough. If you don't need to own it, save your money. Buy more songs from iTunes rather than one CD from the shops. That was the mistake the record companies seemed to make when they tried to prevent the downloading of music. How can it ever be bad for the industry for people to consume more music?

As you would expect, I still need to feel the record in my hand. I can happily play it off the computer on the air, but I want to feel close to it by having a copy I can touch. I also have a record box. It's a long, grey, hessian-covered attaché case issued by the BBC to studio engineers and producers in the sixties to carry away five-inch reels of tape bearing session tracks by the in-house big band or chamber orchestra. It has a small cardboard label on which is written: 'Property of the Stuart Hall Show. Please return to room 4042.' It is the perfect size for CDs and it would probably hold around fifty discs. What I would put in it if assembling my absolute favourite tracks would change from day to day, and would always be subject to review as brilliant new things came out. You'd probably find some Nick Drake in there along with Television, Dr Feelgood, The Who, David Bowie, Joy Division, The Supremes, Black Uhuru, Roxy Music, The Band, Pink Floyd, Radiohead, Kraftwerk, Velvet Underground, The Chi-Lites, Chuck Berry, Neil Young, The Byrds, Fleet Foxes, Kate Bush, Led Zeppelin, Jonathan Richman, Creedence Clearwater Revival, New York Dolls, Patti Smith, Flamin' Groovies, Culture, Robert Parker, Tom Waits, The Smiths, Talk Talk, Emmylou Harris, Hank Williams, Chic and The Ramones naturally. That's today's list, anyway. But 'French Disko' is definitely in. And it's staying in. Why? Because it's done right.

1994

JEFF BUCKLEY – 'HALLELUJAH'

It has become commonplace on the interminable karaoke shows that have come to dominate Saturday night television to talk of contestants having been on 'a journey'. Admittedly they will have been sent a 'SuperSaver' train ticket, which will whisk them to London, unless it's on a Sunday in which case part of their 'journey' will have been by replacement bus service, before taking them back to obscurity in South Shields on the return leg. Fair enough. You can't stay on holiday forever. Unless you're Judith Chalmers or Prince Andrew. However, 'the journey' in question is not to be taken quite so literally. It refers to the transformation the participants undergo from not-always-very-good-though-by-no-means-intrinsically-bad singer with a cheap haircut to not-always-very-good-but-undoubtedly-a-bit-better singer with an expensive haircut they won't be able to afford to maintain for long.

In 1994 there were exciting new ways to make all sorts of journeys. On 6 May the Channel Tunnel opened after having taken 15,000 workers seven years to build. This meant that construction moved at approximately four and a half miles a year, which was still faster than the trains could manage through it during the snows of late 2009. Another life-changing possibility came with the introduction of the National

Lottery. If you were a woman you could be ordained as a vicar in the Church of England for the first time. Even Edvard Munch's *The Scream* went on a trip round Oslo. Mind you, all of these 'journeys' seem fairly inconsequential when compared to the one taken by John Wayne Bobbit's penis.

In that January, John's wife Lorena was acquitted of severing his manhood with a kitchen knife on the grounds of temporary insanity. There was no question that she had carried out the attack, having cracked after years of his drunken womanising. One night in 1993 he returned to their home in Manassas, Virginia, and flopped into the maritial bed clearly having imbibed a great deal of what passes in America for beer. Incensed, his long-suffering wife stood at the kitchen sink drinking a glass of water and perhaps saw the blade of the vegetable knife glinting in the moonlight. Returning upstairs, she put the expertise accrued through years of dicing onions to good use as she lopped off her snoring husband's chopper with her own handy chopper. At what point the comatose John realised that what appeared to be a distinctly pleasant dream during which a small sexual favour was imminent was in fact a more brutal reality is difficult to ascertain. What isn't in doubt is that his matrimonial assailant then fled the scene of the crime with the detached member, which she threw into a cornfield. Miraculously, the authorities were able to later locate it despite one officer having commented that it was like looking for a needle in a haystack. I imagine John thought that was a bit below the belt. Which is more than his penis was.

Why Lorena thought that getting rid of the evidence might help matters is unclear. Even the most cursory examination by the most lackadaisical police surgeon would have revealed that Mr Bobbit was without what it is more or less impossible to avoid calling his 'bobbit', and if that isn't a euphemism it probably should be. Perhaps she was hoping that not-all-that-big John would wake up the following morning unsure where he'd left his keys, wallet and tackle. He would then have had to make a tricky phone call to his favourite bar to ask whether anyone had handed a penis in.

John would later also become separated from his wife but, on the upside, would become reattached to his travelling wilbury, which may well be another euphemism that has yet to pass into common usage. You might think that having been on a 'journey' such as this he might have chosen to keep his, ahem, head down and preserve what was left of his dignity. Sadly not. He became for a time the frontman of underachieving rock band John Wayne Bobbit and The Severed Parts, which is tantamount to calling the group members a bunch of dicks. Inevitably a brief career in adult films followed before, perhaps even more inevitably, he became a minister in the Universal Life Church.

There were great records released that year too in Blur's *Parklife*, Suede's *Dog Man Star*, *Definitely Maybe* by Oasis and *Mellow Gold* by Beck, which yielded the definitive slacker anthem 'Loser'. But good as these albums were, they didn't really take us anywhere we hadn't been before. They were all brilliantly realised revisions of white guitar rock but done, as Lou Reed probably noted, absolutely right. Two other LPs, though, seemed to take us on some kind of 'journey'.

With its vinyl crackles, eerie sci-fi theremins, loping beats and the pained vocals of Beth Gibbons, 'Mysterons' opened Portishead's *Dummy* sounding like music from a subterranean demi-monde.

Jeff Buckley, by comparison, was working with regular rock instruments, but the way he utilised them, combined with arresting compositions and surprising song choices, provided the perfect foundation for that voice to call us from somewhere in the stratosphere. Talking to his mother Mary

Guibert, she confirmed to me that he had a fascination and
deep admiration for the music of the Cocteau Twins. 'It's
amazing, Mom,' he had enthused to her, 'they have their
own language.' And he was right. It was amazing. Robin
Guthrie's dreamlike washes of guitar provided the perfect
setting for the otherworldly vocal stylings of Elizabeth Fraser,
with whom Buckley would later enjoy a short-lived relationship. In contrast, Jeff did use conventional words but his
soaring voice invested them with a wholly distinctive passion
that enabled him to take us far, far away.

Buckley's album *Grace* remains his sole masterpiece due to
his premature passing in May 1997. The subject of much discussion and conjecture, like the demise of Nick Drake with
whom he seems to share certain parallels, Buckley's last
moments appear to be a tragic accident. Certainly that's what
his mother believes. Assembling the band in Memphis to
start work on the next record, Jeff went swimming in Wolf
River Harbor, a Mississippi tributary. He was wearing all his
clothes, including his boots, and appears to have been
dragged down by the wake of a passing tugboat. Not that
those simple facts will ever halt the speculation.

During *Grace*'s gestation Buckley had honed his performance skills in the cafés and bars of New York's East Village
and there was indeed something of the Greenwich Village
troubadour about him. The album was recorded in
Woodstock and though there was a twenty-five-year anniversary revival of that most famous of all festivals this year, Jeff's
ethos seemed to hark back to the simpler, more idealistic
times of the original event. Times perhaps documented in
the records of his biological father, Tim. And yet there was
nothing retro about *Grace*. It was mixed by Andy Wallace,
who had undertaken the same job on the epoch-defining
Nevermind and helped Jeff realise an ambitious sound that
was absolutely of the moment.

I saw Jeff play several times, notably at Glastonbury in 1995, but met him only once. On 22 August 1994 he came to the BBC's studios on Oxford Road in Manchester to perform a session for my late-night Radio 1 'Graveyard Shift' programme. I remember chatting to him in the goods lift amidst the flight cases and finding him charming and funny if slightly lost in his own thoughts. He struck me as someone who took his music very seriously but wasn't overly drawn in to the cult of his own personality. Certainly, no one who took themselves too seriously would have agreed to provide instrumental backing whilst a British disc jockey they'd never met before read out the tour dates in a 'Jeff Buckley voice'. He was also devastatingly beautiful and was wearing a fine trilby.

This in itself was proof that he was one of the good guys, as anyone in a band who wears a trilby is either a gentleman or bald, and quite possibly both. Generally speaking, if there's someone in a rock group wearing a hat there will be some hair-loss issue unless The Edge just really does like the feel of a tea cosy on his head. Jeff Buckley had luxuriant tresses and therefore it followed that he was a gent. The only exception to this rule could possibly be Peter Doherty who, though troubled, struck you as someone who was lost rather than malevolent due to his ever-present Homburg. However, this judgement evaporated when he began to be seen out with La Moss wearing two hats simultaneously, leading to TopMan stocking budget trilbies with a double brim. What sort of madness is this? It's like taking two bottles into the shower which, unless one of them is Black Sheep bitter, conventional wisdom decrees, takes us to the edge of insanity.

Songs like 'Mojo Pin', 'So Real' and the title track that Buckley wrote, or co-wrote, for *Grace* are impassioned, driven, restless and highly sophisticated. It's easy to see why he would become such an influence on Rufus Wainwright.

The choice of cover versions equally demonstrated that here was someone painting from a broad palette. 'Lilac Wine', which I had previously only known by Elkie Brooks, took on a new poise and shimmer. And which other rock artist can you imagine taking on Benjamin Britten's 'Corpus Christi Carol'? Well, Rufus Wainwright, funnily enough. However, it is the version of Leonard Cohen's 'Hallelujah' that is the track that cements the album's, and Jeff's, place in history.

A baffling and yet breathtakingly beautiful song, 'Hallelujah' seems to convey a reflective and deep response to an emotional event that we cannot quite understand. I played Jeff Buckley's version live on air on daytime Radio 1 as we watched dumbfounded as events unfolded at the World Trade Center on 11 September 2001. At that moment there seemed to be nothing that anyone could say to aid the under-standing of what was going on. We were all being taken to a place, a world, we hadn't been to before and the passion and pain of the Buckley voice seemed to express that better than anything else at that instant.

Buckley had apparently been more familiar with the 1991 version of the song (the one that appears in the *Shrek* movie) by John Cale than with the original. In truth, both this and the Buckley rendition are better treatments of the song than the version Cohen recorded, although having seen it per-formed by its composer at Glastonbury with 70,000 people singing along I can testify to its power in the hands of its cre-ator in a live setting. Bizarrely, the song finally entered the mainstream when it became the Christmas number one in 2008 at the climax of Alexandra Burke's *X Factor* 'journey'. There were those who considered her version to be verging on the sacrilegious. I wasn't one of them myself, as I found it intriguing that Simon Cowell, or whoever chose the song, had even been aware of its existence. It certainly made a change from a Westlife cover. And so if we're talking about 'journeys' then the song itself has had even more interesting travels than the phallus of John Wayne Bobbit. Thankfully for John, that came home. And for 'Hallelujah', with the greatest possible respect to Leonard, home will forever be with Jeff.

1995

PULP – 'SORTED FOR E'S & WIZZ'

It was his hand I will always remember. I know it's a cliché to talk about a performer with complete control having the audience 'in the palm of their hand', but if clichés exist because they contain a basic truth then it was perfectly demonstrated that day. Oddly, in a year when Nick Leeson ran amok at Barings Bank and Eric Cantona ran amok at Selhurst Park, utilising all his skill to effect a perfect drop-kick on Crystal Palace fan Matthew Simmons, control was in relatively short supply.

The following year the man himself would have his own moment of wonderful madness when he would bare his bony backside at the Brits to puncture the messianic hubris of Michael Jackson. But that day in June '95 he held all of us in, as I say, the palm of his hand.

Emerging from Sheffield, Arabacus Pulp were an altogether more intriguing prospect than your average indie band. Their musical interests seemed to run beyond standard guitar rock into electro, soul and even the oft-derided disco. Shortening their name to Pulp, they would become the most literate commentators of the Brit-pop era, though never short of killer pop tunes. You could hear a tune like 'Disco 2000' and simply hum along and dance without noticing the melancholic lyric with its talk of woodchip wallpaper and living alone. Or you could watch Jarvis Cocker, in his rumpled vintage suits and Deirdre Barlow glasses, moving with a twitchy grace and hang on to every word of his domestic vignettes and realise that if Morrissey was the missing link between Elvis and Alan Bennett then Cocker had started with Mick Jagger and ended up in the same place.

There were other great records released in 1995 of course. Radiohead upped their game with *The Bends* whilst the fragile beauty of Emmylou Harris's voice was perfectly harnessed by Daniel Lanois on *Wrecking Ball*. Elastica and PJ Harvey turned in terrific LPs and Teenage Fanclub put out their finest moment in *Grand Prix*. For playful exuberance and an irresistible rush of hedonistic abandon you couldn't help but grin every time you heard 'Alright' by Supergrass.

At the end of the previous year The Stone Roses had finally got around to releasing their sophomore album *Second Coming*. I've always wondered to what extent this title was a joke as they had earlier released a song called 'I Am The Resurrection'. Having met John Squire several times I've always found him to be understated and slightly reserved though quietly amusing, so I'm prepared to give him the benefit of the doubt. He was, as writer and musician John Robb once put it, the first non-macho guitar hero. It seems unlikely then that he was being entirely serious about the importance of his admittedly eagerly awaited waxing. Whether Ian Brown considered himself able to walk on water I do not know, although it seems highly unlikely as his simian gait made it look like he was having quite a job walking on dry land and if he could have changed water into wine it might not have been a bad idea to prove it at Spike Island. That record had more weight and bluster than the near perfect debut, but still left the fans eager to see the returning heroes at the 1995 Glastonbury Festival. Sadly there was to be no 'second coming' as Squire broke his collarbone whilst mountain biking, rendering him unable to perform, although

I'm not quite sure why. You don't play the guitar with your collarbone, do you, although Hendrix probably gave it a go. The wait for the return of Jesus therefore went on until, mercifully, he was reincarnated to sing 'Earth Song' at the Brits the following year.

The organisers of the festival were then left needing a headline act in a hurry and found to their enormous relief that Pulp were available. With the release of 'Common People' in the close season that May it was clear that the band had been promoted to the Premier League and so there was no question about their right to a headline slot, although some wondered whether they could really hold a crowd of that size. Chief amongst the doubters was Jarvis Cocker.

'It was,' he tells me, 'the most nervous I have ever been before a concert. I remember sitting on a chair gripping the sides convinced that if I tried to walk I would fall over. I then went to gather my thoughts in a tent, knowing this was a significant moment and scared that when I got up there my mind would go blank.'

The band had arrived on site on the Friday night ahead of their Saturday booking. All the hotels in the area had been booked up months beforehand and so Jarvis and co had no choice but to camp, and there can't be many headliners who've done that. Not that it matters. I've been a regular for many years and I have very rarely camped. I love the event and think there is nowhere else like it, but I don't need to get trench foot to feel better about myself.

Jarvis talks about wandering the fields that Friday night and listening to Oasis, 'that were good', whilst taking in the scale of what lay in front of them, not least because they were going to be playing some songs that no one had heard before which, when confronted with 70,000 people who had booked expecting The Stone Roses, might be seen as a risky strategy.

'We'd browbeaten Island to release "Common People",'
Cocker admits now, 'and then we had no album.' Accordingly
some hurried writing had taken place yielding what would
eventually constitute *Different Class* and one of the songs
debuted that day was 'Sorted For E's And Wizz'. Not released
as a double A-side single with 'Mis-Shapes' until the
September, it caused huge controversy. The cover included
instructions on how to make a 'wrap' for amphetamines or
cocaine and prompted that bastion of the moral high ground
the *Daily Mirror* to run a headline urging the government to
'ban this sick stunt'.

Had they bothered to give the words even the most cursory listen, they would immediately have understood that, far
from being a celebration of the drugs that had been so central to the acid house and rave scenes of the late eighties and
early nineties, Jarvis was observing the desolation at the very
centre of that lifestyle. He talks of the lack of meaningful
conversation as everyone is out of it. He expresses a bleak
loneliness as the night wears on and he finds himself having
lost his friends somewhere in a field in Hampshire. At six in
the morning he wants to go home to his mum. And ahead of
everyone lies the misery of the comedown from the artificial
high. Yes, it came in a sleeve that seemed to encourage illicit
consumption, but there was no point in pretending it wasn't
going on and anyone who knew what it was knew how to
make a wrap anyway. As those of us who knew his lyrics
came to expect, it was sharp, poetic, funny and true. It also
had an association with the Cycling Proficiency Test-eschew-
ing Squire and friends.

'I was trying to get off with this girl at The Leadmill in
Sheffield,' comes the candid admission from Jarv, 'and she
kept saying, "Are you all sorted for E's and wizz?" which was
a phrase she'd picked up at Spike Island.'

He loved the phrase and stored it, knowing it would be

useful somewhere. Again, though the *Daily Mirror* might dis-
approve, there's no point in pretending that there aren't drugs
at the Glastonbury Festival. There are drugs at every festival,
as well as at every football match, in every prison, in every
school, in every bar. Wherever you get a crowd, you will find
drugs. At Woodstock the stage announcers had advised the
revelling hippy hordes which was the best acid to take.
Holding this thought, Jarvis was minded to be a benign presence as he held the spotlight that Saturday night. He talks of
it feeling like 'an act of faith, to try and be nice to people like
a festival in the sixties, like holding their hand and taking
them through an acid trip'.

'I thought it would be appropriate,' he now says, recalling
the decision to play the song. However, shortly before the
performance he admits to feeling paranoid as he realised the
lyrics might not be properly heard and the song risked being
perceived as wholly pro-drugs. 'If they were off their heads,'
he observes, 'the last thing they want is some nobhead up
there singing about it.'

Watching Jarvis perform that night, there was no sign of
the chair-gripping nerves he'd encountered earlier in the day.
Immediately before a show, he says, his body goes into 'shut-
down' and he explained that he 'can slow my heart beat
down like James Coburn in *Our Man Flint*'. The band and
the music were wonderful but it's the ability he had to com-
municate with the audience and direct them with the tiniest
gesture that has stayed with me. I recall Leonard Cohen
appearing to slow the whole event to his own pace and how
impressive an achievement that seemed. Seeing the primal
two-piece The White Stripes own that stage was equally
remarkable and we'll come back to them. But standing stage
left and watching this lanky, bespectacled figure, I became
wholly transfixed. At one point during the number I became
fascinated by his bony fingers as they pointed and twisted to

express the words in some subconscious way. A close-up appeared on the big screens and on the millions of television sets at home it seemed like the whole massive shebang was focused on that one hand. Whether you were 'sorted for E's and wizz' or simply drinking cans of Special Brew didn't matter. The alienation that he'd been singing about was wholly absent for the thousands of people 'standing in a field' that night. And if you think I'm over-romanticising it, well, you may be right, but I wasn't the only person who felt like that, was I, Jarvis?

'It was the culmination of a long period of obscurity,' he says wistfully. 'This was the moment we knew we'd arrived.'

1996

THE PRODIGY – 'FIRESTARTER'

It is still hard to believe, especially in these sanitised PC (Post Cowell) days, that 'Firestarter' got to number one in the hit parade. Incredible to think that this bone-shaking, thunderous explosion of noise and industrial-strength rhythm was a staple of daytime radio for months that year. When *The Fat Of The Land*, the album on which it was included, was released in 1997 it went to the top of the American charts. The Prodigy achieved mainstream success with a record that came from way, way out in the left field.

They came from Braintree in Essex and were the Braintreechild of techno keyboard, errm, prodigy Liam Howlett and fronted by the Johnny Rotten of rave Keith Flint. Flint, once seen, was a vision you couldn't easily forget. He appeared quite small and had a hairstyle that consisted of heavily lacquered fins shooting up on either side of his head. In this respect it's an ideal barnet for the ageing raver with male-pattern baldness as it doesn't need any follicular coverage on the crown. Another ideal style is the monk's tonsure and it may be possible to combine the two. During the week, whilst engaged in monastic business like illuminating letters, not talking much and brewing idiotically potent mead, you can keep the sides smoothed down. Then come the weekend, a bit of the old sugar and water and you're transformed into some banging acid house malevolent goblin.

If you watch the 'Firestarter' video it is still deeply unsettling. As the throb and roar of the track piles in we find the grim-faced Flint deep underground in some long-deserted tunnel or sewer. He is wearing cut-off, ragged trousers, a Stars and Stripes jerkin, has chains round his neck, black rings round his eyes, and that distinctive coiffure that looks likely to collapse into a double combover. Howlett, looking uncannily like the young Eminem, stands motionless behind him as Keith jerks and twitches in some mutant dance whilst spitting out the words. Mad cow disease hit the UK that year and, though none of us quite understood what the effects on our health were likely to be, it seemed eminently feasible that Keith had been exposed to it. At other times in that clip we catch Howlett and fellow members Maxim and Leeroy sprinting down the pipeline to escape, well, we're not quite sure what, but certainly a bovine spongiform encephalopathological Keith Flint does not look like a man you'd want to bump into whilst taking a casual stroll in a corrugated-iron cave complex. It's as if they've been forced underground to escape some apocalyptic event on the surface and have encountered some taciturn troglodyte *enfant terrible*. Albeit one with access to heavy-duty hair gel. Well, you've got to stockpile supplies, haven't you?

So what could have driven The Prodigy down there in the first place? It's hard to say but it seems possible that the appearance of The Spice Girls could have had something to do with it. In the two-tier society of that time 'Firestarter' was the anthem for the downtrodden Borrowers living under the floorboards, but in the sitting room above 'Wannabe' was the parlour song of choice. Like mad cow disease but more skimpily dressed, 'girl power' swept the nation as millions thought that actually all they really did want to do was 'zigazig ah'. They might not have known what that entailed exactly, but it seemed to involve dancing on tables and shouting a lot and looked like it might be a lot more fun than knocking around in combat pants in drains with some techno terrorists from Essex. Everyone, it seemed, could reel off the list of Sporty, Ginger, Scary, Baby and Posh as their faces leered from every media outlet and their records, dolls and primary school lunchboxes dominated every high street.

In truth, even the most cynical found it hard not to be invigorated by their chutzpah and sense of sisterhood. They may very well have been put together by some svengali who saw them as his (mad) cash cow, but since when had that been a problem in pop? Berry Gordy exercised ruthless control over The Supremes but it didn't mean they couldn't make great records and have fun in the process. I'm not suggesting that 'Wannabe' is up there with 'You Can't Hurry Love' but it is a hugely enjoyable record unless you're determined to sneer because they're not playing their own instruments and writing their own songs. Who cares? That's like sneering at John Terry and Ashley Cole for not blowing up their own footballs and there are far better reasons to sneer at that pair than that.

In my glittering show-business career I have met four of the five Girls off the Spice rack. Melanie C seemed well adjusted and fairly serious about her musical career. Emma Bunton struck me as very sweet, though I accept we are barely scratching the surface here. Victoria was a big surprise. Far from the aloofness implied by her 'posh' persona, she was hugely engaging, sharp-witted and very funny. And very thin. I have no doubt that 'Brand Beckham' would not have existed without her drive and savvy. Melanie B I have never encountered so if you're reading this, Scary, and I accept that's unlikely, then I'd appreciate it if you could find a window in your diary for me, then I'll have the set. It doesn't have to be for the whole evening or anything. We could just have a pint of Deuchars IPA and a bag of scratchings or something and I'll even get the first round in.

If there was a female Keith Flint in Spiceworld, though, it was Geri. Of all of them she seemed to be the most feisty, the most boisterous, the most bolshy. In her Union Jack dress at the Brits the following year she would become one of the defining figures of British pop culture of that era. I've interviewed her several times, most recently about her *Ugenia Lavender* series of books for children, and once shared the stage with her for the turning on of the Blackpool Illuminations for Radio 2. Now, I'm a great lover of Blackpool, particularly when 'the lights' are on. I am also an employee of Radio 2 and, though not all of its programmes appeal to me personally, am broadly supportive of the output. And the pay cheque. However, you would have to say that the turning on of some coloured lights, no matter how many million bulbs are involved, is not exactly a riveting spectacle on radio. At the risk of stating the obvious, you can't see it. There we were, Geri and I with a supporting cast including Lemar, McFly, Swing Out Sister and a not-so-little-anymore Jimmy Osmond, whipping the crowd on that windy car park into a pre-switch-on frenzy for the benefit of the listening millions, only for them not to be able to witness the promenade and tower festooned with light. Nor could you see Geri writhing on a plywood plinth and nearly popping out of her glitzy frock, which for the attendant technicians and engineers was just as much of a visual treat as the illuminated tableau on the Golden Mile. The unexpectedly petite Geri, though no doubt eminently capable of diva-like behaviour, emerged from her bus carrying a small dog, greeted me effusively with a kiss, and got on with the show like a real trouper with eminent good grace.

I did take my eldest daughter Holly to see The Spice Girls in concert and it was, of course, a thoroughly enjoyable and professional show. For me, though, it lacked the raw excitement that I always look for in a gig and certainly found when I saw The Prodigy at the 1996 Phoenix Festival. Held, briefly, at Long Marston airfield in Derbyshire, the event was nothing if not scrupulous as regards security. Commendable though this might have been on paper, the reality of letting tens of thousands of revellers in through what looked like a gap in a hedge resulted in gridlock on the surrounding roads for literally days. Due to broadcast my Radio 1 evening show live from the site, my colleagues and I had been stuck for several hours in a queue of standing traffic behind an agitated woman in a Fiat Punto who was ferrying headliner David Bowie's Union Jack 'Earthling' trenchcoat to the backstage compound. The traffic chaos that day resulted in a motorcycle courier being hastily bribed to ferry me and a small bag of records onto the site whilst the rest of the team, including Marc Riley and Stuart Maconie, gallantly forwent the festival experience and selflessly got plastered in the hotel bar.

The Prodigy, who had presumably avoided the road problems by burrowing under the perimeter fence, played before Bowie and produced some of the most exhilarating noise I have ever heard. It was unclear exactly what, if anything, was being played live but the sheer weight and menace of that sound seemed to pummel your intestines and induce a genuinely physical reaction somewhere deep in your gut. It also seemed to present a threat to the structure of the stage and the lighting rig. Flint prowled the stage like a demented demon drunk on the power he exerted over his followers, tripping and twisting across the stage as the cacophony raged around him.

With some degree of synchronicity, a real-life Keith Flint-esque figure also came to public prominence at that time.

Daniel Hooper was an eco-campaigner who was a prominent member of the loosely aligned groups who took an active role in the mid-nineties in attempting to prevent the completion of several major road-building projects. Known as Swampy, he was a tunnelling specialist, having lived for a week underground during protests against the construction of the A30 from Honiton to Exeter through the village of Fairmile. He was the last man standing, or more likely crouching, in the rat-run of passageways burrowed by human moles beneath the site. He would also be a significant presence during works on the Newbury bypass and the second runway at Manchester Airport.

Swampy appeared in the papers on more or less a daily basis as he was not only the representative of what the *Sunday Times* dubbed 'the rediscovery of rebelliousness among Britain's bourgeoisie' but also quite cute. With his cheeky smile and organic knitwear, he resembled some Netherlandish Breugel-esque serf up to no good in *The Fight Between Carnival and Lent* painting. He was, without doubt, a man of sincere beliefs prepared to risk his own life in pursuit of what he considered to be the common good, but there was an unmistakable air of the mischievous imp about him. With his dishevelled crusty hair framing his elfin features and a little light attached to his head as it poked out of his latest bunker, he was like the character Kenneth Grahame couldn't quite fit into *The Wind in the Willows* and made all of us yearn for simpler, more bucolic times as we drove past his encampment in our cars tooting the horns in support, seemingly unaware of the irony of that action.

Such was his notoriety that he became a panellist on *Have I Got News For You* and thereby matched the achievement of The Prodigy in taking the alternative into the mainstream. If Keith Flint had left the band then it seemed that Swampy would have been an ideal applicant for the job as described in the small ad that Liam Howlett would have placed in the *Braintree Evening Gazette*'s situations vacant section: 'Wanted. Techno frontman. Would suit scruffy bloke in jumper with funny hairstyle. Salary and vocal ability negotiable. Cave dwelling experience desirable.'

1997

RADIOHEAD – 'PARANOID ANDROID'

In 1997 a government-backed campaign to raise road safety awareness featured a pair of animated hedgehogs. Brilliant. The hedgehog is, of course, legendary for its ability to avoid traffic, but this was the newly elected Tony Blair's Cool Britannia. Yachtsman Tony Bullimore was found alive and well, if a bit wet and distinctly peckish, and was praised by the Queen for his 'extraordinary act of survival'. As this was by no means the only time he had summoned the emergency services it would have been better if he hadn't gone at all and been later praised for his 'extraordinary act of staying at home'. But El Presidente Blair was in the chair and things could 'only get better' according to D:Ream featuring Peter Cunnah and Brian Cox, who is possibly the only ex-member of a pop group to be working at the Large Hadron Collider near Geneva and is, as far as I'm aware, the sole particle physicist ever to reach number one on the UK charts, unless Lady Gaga has kept her expertise on the interaction between matter and radiation a very closely guarded secret.

Noel Gallagher went to 10 Downing Street to chat to the Strat-toting, strutting PM about the finer points of Brit-pop and the new Oasis album *Be Here Now*, a record so long that you could 'Be Here Anytime In The Next Hour And A Half' and it would still be playing. At the same mid-paced tempo. In fact a great deal of Brit-pop was similarly unhurried as, unlike punk or grunge, its originators had nothing much to rail against and so produced music lacking any sense of fury. Geri wore that dress at the Brits. Katrina and The Waves won the Eurovision Song Contest. The first *Harry Potter* book came out. Hedgehogs could avoid juggernauts.

These were heady times and though dissenting voices to the New Labour Order seemed rare, there were those who saw darker forces at work. One of these may well have been Thom Yorke, who watched quizzically as the Cool Britannia carnival gathered momentum. Voicing his concerns saw him howled down by those who told him he was being paranoid. Some probably called him an android, but that was just plain rude. But that same sense of suspicion, of judgement being reserved, was also tangible in records like 'Into My Arms' by Nick Cave, Spiritualized's 'Ladies And Gentlemen We Are Floating In Space', 'Tiny Tears' by Tindersticks and The Verve's 'The Drugs Don't Work' and 'Bitter Sweet Symphony' that year but it was *OK Computer* most of all that kept us on our guard. There was always a danger of complacency. Look at Ferdinand Marcos. Serenely lying in cryogenically frozen state, safe in the knowledge that he would return one day to his fridge stocked with Heinz sandwich spread and his palace built entirely of coconuts, he was discovered to be thawing like a deep-frozen pizza in a power cut due to the electricity having been cut off. Apparently Imelda had forgotten to pay the bill and owed in the region of £135,000. This came as a surprise, quite possibly to Ferdinand himself as some nerve endings and brain cells began to twitch somewhat prematurely, as Imelda had always seemed to financial prudency what hedgehogs are to road safety.

These were the kinds of things that Radiohead were able to convey in their thoughtfully melancholic and yet stately songs, though admittedly they never referred to them explicitly. But if there was a party going on, Thom and the guys were in the kitchen watching from a distance and shaking their heads, waiting for the dream to sour.

In 2010 the hard winter resulted in fourteen hedgehogs being taken into care at the Wildlife Rescue Centre in Fife. Whilst they were there, being fed at the taxpayers' expense, they got so fat they could no longer roll into a ball and had therefore lost their main means of survival when faced by the oncoming HGV tyre. If that's not a symbol of broken Britain then I don't know what is. The road safety standard bearers of the mid-nineties had become the obese benefit scroungers of the Noughties and no one could say Thom Yorke hadn't warned us. No one is calling him paranoid now.

1998

CORNERSHOP – 'BRIMFUL OF ASHA'

Anglo-Asian indie popsters Cornershop first released 'Brimful Of Asha' in 1997 when it got to a measly number sixty in the charts. Thankfully lanky mixologist Norman Cook agreed to sprinkle a bit of Fatboy fairy dust on it, and they found themselves with a number one the following year. Marc Riley and I had always had great affection for the band and such 'lost' classics as 'Kawasaki (More Heat Than Chapati)', which I considered to be the best song title since Half Man Half Biscuit's '99% Of Gargoyles Look Like Bob Todd' and 'Fat Lad Exam Failure' by Hebden Bridge's Bogshed, formerly The Amazing Roy North Penis Band, although why they named themselves after the appendage of one of Basil Brush's redoubtable sidekicks remains unclear. Had there been a John Wayne Bobbit-inspired episode of that TV series I'd missed? 'Hey, Mr Roy, check your family jewels. Boom, boom.'

Cornershop weren't overly blessed with musical ability when we booked them for a session on our Radio 5 programme in 1993, although we'd never worried too much about that. We weren't musical Luddites, and still retained a deeply unfashionable love of Peter Gabriel-era Genesis which, again, we didn't worry too much about as we were contentedly deeply unfashionable. But we had both lived through the punk years when the notion of 'do-it-yourself' was sacrosanct. In fact, this is something I have continued to believe in ever since: if you feel like you want to have a go at something, do so, even though you might think you don't have the ability, qualifications or experience. Strangely, the only area of my life in which I am reluctant to apply the DIY ethic is in the area of home DIY, in which case the letters are short for 'don't involve yourself'. I remain speechless with admiration for friends of mine who can make their own fitted wardrobes, tile an en-suite or replace the carburettor on a Suzuki Jimny whilst simultaneously wondering whether their expertise is entirely fair on the nation's chippies, tilers and grease monkeys. If we could all do everything then we wouldn't need to hire anyone to do anything and therefore none of us would ever work except for ourselves and no tax would be paid and so VAT would have to be put up to 98.5 per cent so that we could keep the potholes in the roads filled in. Is that what you want? No. Well, you might want to think about that next time you get out your powerdrill or Dremel.

My job, if you can call it that, is to find good records to play on the radio and then talk in between them. Now clearly, anyone can do that and it's therefore a source of continued amazement and gratitude to me that anyone bothers to listen at all. If all music lovers took the selfish DIY option I'd be unemployed and so you'd have it on your conscience that my children would be forced to move to a more modest *palazzo* and send those ponies to the glue factory. Well, thanks very much. I should really say here that we don't actually have any ponies because it seems much easier and cheaper to hire them by the hour. My youngest, Rose, is very keen on being in the saddle, which is fair enough, but there's always the donkeys on Blackpool beach, isn't there? We don't need to keep a horse on standby permanently.

Apart from anything else, it's just such a ludicrously huge animal to keep as a pet. I mean, why stop there? Why not keep a rhinoceros in a shed at the end of your garden as well?

In terms of bands, though, Marc and I were very much of the opinion that to stay true to our punk roots, we would never shy away from booking someone just because they didn't know a D-sharp from an E-flat. Well, there is no difference between a D-sharp and an E-flat, but the fact that Tjinder, Ben and the rest of Cornershop probably didn't know that didn't make hearing them play 'Summer Fun In A Beat-Up Datsun' any the less joyous.

When we started our Radio 1 afternoon programme in 1997, following our ignominious ejection from the breakfast show, we needed a piece of music we could use as background whilst we were talking. The loping groove of Cornershop's 'Sleep On The Left Side' from their album *When I Was Born For The 7th Time* seemed ideal. I imagine it would have been ideal for Cornershop too, as they would have been paid royalties on this track every weekday for the next seven years. Quite right too.

I can't hear that music without immediately being taken back to that show and it prompts very happy memories of being on air messing around, and yet nightmares about sitting at the opposite desk to Marc watching the clock tick round as we stared at a blank computer screen where that day's jokes were supposed to be.

When I look back at the content of our shows now I really don't know where it all came from. Again, it never occurred to us that we weren't qualified to write, produce and perform comedy for the reasons I've outlined above and, anyway, we thought we were hilarious. I know that sounds arrogant, and it may well be, but there's no way you can be so racked with self-doubt that you think it's rubbish before you even start. We never allowed ourselves to think that until afterwards. And making each other laugh seemed to us to be the most important thing. If we found it funny, then there was always a chance that somewhere out there people fitting wardrobes, tiling shower cubicles and swapping carburettors might find it vaguely amusing too, although we didn't think about this overmuch. In truth, I've never really thought much about the audience for any of the shows I've presented. First and foremost I've tried to please myself, which might seem selfish, but I've had to sit through a lot more of it than you have so I think it's only fair that my needs should come first.

The 'quality items' that peppered that show I remember with some affection and, in some cases, a sort of paternalistic pride. Fat Harry White, the blubbery soul man and king of the double entendre, I still miss as if he had been a real person. He was clearly based on the lascivious love-handled Love Unlimited ladies' manatee Barry White. I had heard him interviewed about his sex life which, though not a subject in which I felt I was lacking detail, contained the admission that he pleasured Mrs White on their dining table. There you go. Game over. It was Mr White, in the dining room with the chopper. But this seemed to me an enormous boast for the manufacturers of that table. That their product, designed to hold tea and cakes, could actually withstand the weight of Big Bazza in flagrante delicto would surely be something they would want to include in future publicity. And so I asked Chris the engineer to put an effect on my voice that would lower it to the bowels of Barry-dom and approximated the likely advert myself. We immediately loved this basso profundo priapic porpoise so much that we coupled him with another spherical soulman, Fat Larry from 'Zoom' hitmakers Fat Larry's Band, in 'When Harry Met Larry'. Harry's voice, initially due to my inability to stick to one accent, wavered between a mid-Atlantic drawl and broad Lancashire. The comparatively skilled mimic Marc Riley bestowed on Philadelphia-born Fat Larry the voice of Bernard Manning for reasons that evade me even now.

Once it became clear that the doo-wop whopper Mr White had considerable mileage for our daytime show, we thought it politic to change his name to Harry just in case his increasingly lurid adventures should cause offence to the XXL lothario of the drop-leaf table himself, and so Fat Harry White was born. Following an ill-fated role as an astrologist on the ill-fated breakfast show, Harry settled happily into regaling the afternoon audience with tales of his everyday life as he pottered around town on various errands in his soft-top Bedford Rascal. In this he was ably assisted by our friend and co-writer Patrick Gallagher, who has since gone on to better and more intelligent things as he's been scripting *Basil Brush*. Which, knowing what passes for his sense of humour, makes that Bobbit scenario more than likely.

For Harry there was joy to be had in every situation. On one occasion he was working at the gents' outfitters 'Slacks-R-Us' when Foxy Fiona, one of several 'very sexy ladyfriends', arrived looking to purchase some trousers for her conveniently long-legged father's birthday. After asking to see what Harry 'had in the trouser department', the obliging Mr White felt sure that he had something with 'enough length to satisfy' Fiona. After some deliberation, Harry reports that Fiona was 'very interested in the big pink pair I had as she particularly liked the way they swung loosely when I walked. I laid them out on the counter so she could have a good look and run her fingers admiringly down the crease.' Naturally there was some haggling over the price, which involved some 'backwards and forwards action over the counter' as you might reasonably expect. As if that wasn't enough, the very same day, which had turned extremely cold apparently, Harry decided to buy a fur hat from his 'very sexy ladyfriend salesgirl Sexy Selena' who kept them, wouldn't you know it, downstairs. Well, you can probably work the rest out. We were often asked how we got away with this on daytime radio and we always, rather disingenuously, maintained that Harry had no idea what he was saying. As far as he was concerned he was just telling you what he'd been up to. The innocent ramblings of a fat bloke going about his business. It was just that something had got lost, or perhaps added, in translation. His daily ramblings were broadcast around three-fifteen and many people have told me how they would sit listening to him in the car at the school gates waiting to pick up their children and seeing several other parents jump out of their cars as Harry bid them farewell for another day.

Harry would later go on to make a classic and indeed classy album entitled *Hmmm Baby – The Seduction Selection* on which he was accompanied by his Love Limited Orchestra consisting of Marc and I sharing a Yamaha DJX keyboard. We slaved over that album for a period of up to five or perhaps even six hours and the work we put in certainly shows, I think. Even now tracks like 'Callin' Dr Love' (Fatboy Slimfast mix), 'Rummagin' For Love', 'Amore En Vacances' (featuring DJ 5 O'Clock Shadow), 'Working Out With My Lady' (Chemical Toilet Brothers edit), 'The Animal In Me' (Roni Outsize club version) and, of course, the poignant 'My Baby Stroked Me Beard' still sound like classics of the genre. Whatever the genre is. You will also be pleased to know that Marc and I still receive royalties for the help we gave Harry in composing those classics, and how gratifying it is to look through the statement and see that in the last twelve months we earned fourteen pence off 'Strokin' My Feline Baby' alone. And that's each.

Many other characters populated those programmes.

Butch Schlong and Snatch Friggit joined us from our sister station W.A.N.K. Cincinnati to bring us the latest impenetrable bulletin from the American Sports Network with their histrionic reporting of baseball, basketball, dodgeball, codball and something-else-ball. The woodland squirrels with 'urban' attitude Slim and Shady wreaked havoc as they chased Madonna magpie and wound up John Peel the partridge. Idle firefighters lounged around the station ordering takeaways in 'London's Not Burning'. The members of Radiohead, including the Greenwoods Major and Minor, found themselves back in the classroom in 'Thom Yorke's School Days'. Welsh Countdown seemed to feature suspiciously high numbers of Ls and Ws. 'Slipknot's Army' featured the masked American panto-rockers reviving the roles of Arthur Lowe, John Le Mesurier and Clive Dunn with Clown as Captain Mainwaring. 'Mouse News' brought you highly detailed information on stories concerning mice that had appeared in the press whilst, by way of contrast, the 'Vague News' left you no wiser than you were before you listened to it. Irish contestants ran out of time before being able to claim a prize on 'Oh Lucky You'.

Marc, as Lard, brought us his classic cuts, animal sanctuary and a 'where are they now?' feature which asked the whereabouts of various pop stars, most of whom would be found to be hiding away at the top of the charts. A garden building was erected in the studio so that contestants, i.e. Lard, could confront their worst fears in the 'Shed of Dread'. Were all these sketches works of genius? No. Did they always make us laugh while we were doing them? Yes. Is it right to laugh at your own jokes? Of course.

Fat Harry aside, perhaps my favourite character from those days was Scoff Cruddle, the West Country commentator and pundit on 'One Man and His Frog'. I conceived this item in the corridor whilst Marc and I were on our way to a meeting with then controller of BBC2 Jane Root. Thinking it might be wise to have an idea to throw at her, though, with our television track record, having no expectations of hatching a series that would make it to the screen, a version of *One Man and His Dog* called 'One Man and His Frog' popped into my head. For this prospective televisual feast keen country froggers would use their prize 'bitches' to herd tadpoles around a pond. Inspired.

Now, several things happened following this brilliant concept being pitched to Root, albeit in a manner which may have led her to believe that it wasn't an entirely serious proposition. The following year the long-running programme celebrating the art of the shepherd and sheepdog and their ability to manoeuvre the flock into a little fenced area was, for no apparent reason, cancelled. I must confess to some feelings of guilt at this decision because my new postmodern spin on the classic format must have sown doubt in Root's mind about the relevance of the old show. Even more sinister, though, was the subsequent appointment of Jane as President of the Discovery Channels in the USA. A great deal of their programming is, naturally, devoted to animal matters and I'm not privy to what ideas Jane presented to the big cheeses at her interview, but I wouldn't have been at all surprised to learn that talk of frogs and taddies had arisen. With no commission for 'One Man and His Frog' we had no option but to re-create it for radio.

We invented a whole world of pond-side enthusiasts who would be riveted to hear the latest rounds taking place in the most prestigious event of the frogging calendar 'The Anusol Masters'. This rectal preparation had long been a favoured comedy item of ours due to its unnecessarily blunt name. Whilst on tour with The Shirehorses we would always put two tubes of Anusol on the rider along with three pairs of white towelling socks and Ovaltine for one. Often we would specify whether the soothing ointment should be in the green or blue tubes.

Back on the radio I would welcome the deliciously fruity yokel Scoff Cruddle to join me daily in the commentary box to describe for the rapt listeners goings-on pond-side. Scoff was played by our producer Will Saunders who, astoundingly, actually talked like that in real life. Every morning I would pull up a floral deckchair next to his desk and together we would create another contestant and another heat. The competitors were all given names that we came up with by blurting out random syllables and then joining them together. For many years the 'Anusol' was dominated by Frarge Boffle Nurp and Crynovulin Spang. On air the eager contender (Marc) would coax his frog bitch, usually called Shirley or Denise or somesuch, through the pond's regular obstacles including the feared jirrup hurdle with barked commands such as 'come by, bitch'. I would offer a running commentary of events as the splashing continued in the background, after which Scoff Cruddle would offer expert analysis. 'Well, Mark,' he would intone, stretching vowel sounds beyond all previously suspected elasticity, 'young Boffle Nurp had bongied the bitch like a dandelion in a suckle yarm. I'm not saying he's burfed the crow daddy but it'll be no pork belly till beanflow this Misery-tide.' We worked incredibly hard to make sure that whilst it made no sense at all, it did seem to reflect old country ways that were in danger of fading away.

I occasionally talk to Will, who had a complete career change after his time with us as he went to work on comedy programmes. Whenever I hear his voice I get nostalgic for the Anusol and wish the frogging season was starting all over again. And, like Rupert Bear, who I can't quite bring myself to accept is not walking around through the next airy glade in some distant Nutwood, I like to think that Scoff Cruddle is out there somewhere. Perhaps he's running a flag-floored village inn where he regales the regulars with yarns from his days as the BBC's voice of frogging as Cornershop play on the jukebox and he waits for the distinctive revs of the Bedford Rascal as his regular drayman Fat Harry squeezes up his back passage.

1999

THE FLAMING LIPS –
'RACE FOR THE PRIZE'

With his overtight, grubby suit and unruly grey hair and beard Wayne Coyne resembles less the lead singer of a proper grown-up rock group than a lecturer in metallurgy at a university that used to be a polytechnic. And yet he fronts The Flaming Lips, a band whose uplifting and fantastical records are re-created in live concerts involving puppets, animal costumes, projections, lasers, confetti cannons, blood capsules and a giant plastic hamster ball enabling Wayne to scuttle over the heads of the faithful. Their euphoric musing on mortality 'Do You Realize??' has been adopted as the official rock'n'roll song of their home state of Oklahoma after being voted in by the public. Naturally a few local politicians tried to veto the choice on account of the band's 'communism'. Is that really how far we've come? Thankfully Governor Brad Henry vetoed the veto to honour the choice of the people.

'Race For The Prize' from the album *The Soft Bulletin* is a song that only Wayne Coyne would really write. There were, of course, other great songs released the same year. Blondie returned to the top of the charts with a characteristically breezy slice of power pop in 'Maria'. Moby's album *Play* was heard on adverts everywhere. Blur unveiled one of their most heartfelt moments with 'Tender', a piece of music that brings a lump to the throat when seen in the documentary film *No Distance Left To Run* capturing their emotional reunion headline appearance at Glastonbury in 2009. Eminem emerged with his unsettling view of the world from downtown Detroit, of which more shortly. The Chemical Brothers issued the *Surrender* LP featuring 'Music: Response' and 'Hey Boy Hey Girl', tracks with such a rampaging rush that they managed to appeal to the old blokes like myself who would never hear those tracks at four in the morning in what I believe was referred to as 'a banging nightspot'.

Of course, Sting made his own valuable contribution to the cultural life of the nation with his *Brand New Day* album containing the unforgettable song 'Perfect Love ... Gone Wrong'. This is a heartfelt vignette of the relationship between a man and his dog, but written from the dog's point of view when the master has the audacity to get a new puppy. This, I think, was a long overdue attempt to really bring some deeper canine understanding to the world of coffee-table jazz pop. And, as if that concept doesn't sound remarkable enough already, and once heard it is never forgotten, there is also a rap section. In French. Of course there is.

Now, it's conceivable that the blessed Kate Bush might be able to pull something like this off, and one imagines that for all its ridiculousness, or perhaps because of it, the puckish Wayne Coyne might be drawn to the idea. Many of The Flaming Lips' most memorable songs have lyrical inspirations other bands wouldn't think of. 'Race For The Prize' talks of two scientists trying to outdo each other in the search for the 'cure for all mankind'. Whatever that might be. Lost in their research, the rivals plough on knowing that exposure to the things they're working with might well result in their own deaths and yet, undeterred, they continue with their hazardous experiments for the greater good. The track is reflective and tinged with sadness and yet hugely joyful. And pretty funny. You can listen to the words and try to work out just how serious Wayne is on the subject of scientific research, or you can just sit back and let it wash over you like the sweeping pop epic it is.

How the search for the cure for all mankind is going I have been unable to verify at the time of going to press. I did ask Wayne the last time I saw him and he confessed that he wasn't sure either, having been too busy shooting a video in the nude with a bunch, if that's the correct collective noun, of naturists. That seems reasonable enough. One man can't be expected to do everything and if you're tied up charging through dense woodland with your gonads on display then you need your wits about you. Especially in the vicinity of briars and, no doubt, there being nudists involved, volleyball and frying bacon and eggs in senselessly low-level frying pans. Look, I have no beef with those in the buff but, not to beat around the bush, why do they have to take up sports that involve so much flapping about? Surely a game of chess would be more suitable for all but the most pert. Similarly their insistence on getting that close to hot fat seems fool-hardy to say the least. We all know that fried food clogs the arteries but frankly that would seem to be the least of your worries if you're dangling rashers into molten lard at groin height. What's wrong with a pre-baked cocktail sausage, eh?

And so, wrapped up with his bare-bottomed brethren, Wayne could give me no further updates on the 'cure'. My own view is that they probably have found it but are having it suppressed by big business. This is by no means a unique situation. With all the scientific brainboxes in the world they must surely have sorted out the everlasting light bulb, the razor blade that stays sharp and the cure for the common cold by now. The truth must be that they are being paid by major manufacturers of lighting, razors and cold remedies not to make their findings public. Sadly, these boffins are unable to find a solution to every problem and so, for the time being, Alex Ferguson's nose is going to have to stay that colour.

In 1999, the scientific problem that the general populus was most concerned with was the millenium bug. Well, that and the Millennium Dome. The crisis at the Dome hinged on the covering. Apparently, and every camper will sympathise with this, every time they tried to stretch the tarpaulin, or whatever it was, over the poles, it ripped. Nightmare. Where was Tony Blair going to hold hands with the Queen if this big tent wasn't finished? The Dome was the object of much derision at the time as it cost about a hundred billion pounds or something and everyone was agreed that the money could have been much better spent on crisps and pop for everyone planning a millennium street party. And yet, the Millennium Dome regenerated a pretty grim part of the capital and is now a spanking concert venue. I went there to see Leonard Cohen on the Jubilee Line from Bond Street and thought it was all a marvellous example of integrated urban living, but then I live in a field near Runcorn and don't get out much.

Sometimes I think we just have to accept that things cost a lot. Look at Joleon Lescott. My club Manchester City signed him from Everton for, well, you can never actually get anyone to confirm the actual price with football transfers, but by common consensus, too much. Somewhere between 25 and 35 million pounds seems to be an approximate figure and this after consulting several leading experts in the field such as Big Paul and Baz who work behind the bar at The Spinner and Bergamot public house in Comberbach. I know what you're thinking. Can that survey, carried out at length over several pints of Unicorn and Ward's pork pies, really be taken as credible? Well, Paul is a City fanatic and Baz similarly devoted to all things Evertonian, so you can't say it isn't a balanced view. But what I don't understand is why City are criticised for coughing up all this cash. If we've paid too much, that's good for Everton, isn't it? They should be thanking us, not slagging us off.

And it's not like our owner Sheikh Mansour cares about how many millions over the odds we've paid for Joleon. He comes from a world where money, as you or I understand it, doesn't really exist as it's something that just flows from the ground continuously. The price of things is irrelevant as the supply of money is infinite. For him to worry about the price of Lescott is the same as you thinking you'd better have a smaller cup of tea as the water supply might run out. Of course, the real issue here is that there are several big football clubs who like to enjoy the privileges of their own little cartel at the top of the Premiership and they don't like the status quo threatened. They will try and tell you that situations like the one that exists currently at Manchester City are 'bad for football'. Whatever. All I'm going to say is that if you're involved in a game that revolves around money, you might as well have more than anyone else.

For most of us, however, the price of things will continue to be a cause of concern, as I remarked to Babs at the butty shop when she attempted to charge me twenty pence just to have Branston Pickle on a cheese barm. Where's Sheikh Mansour when you really need him, eh?

Unlike my personal condiment cash-flow crisis, the Millennium Bug was going to affect us all. We were led to believe that at midnight on New Year's Eve all our computers were going to cease functioning and would most probably explode, threatening the foundations of our houses. All banks would lose track of all our money and a financial meltdown would follow. (Funnily enough this did later happen but for a whole other set of reasons.) Not only that, but planes were going to fall out of the sky as their navigation systems would fail once the computers tried to get their heads around a year that was represented as '00'. It was referred to as the Y2K problem. Except it didn't seem much of a problem, really. Now perhaps top computer scientists, marshalled by Wayne Coyne, had been searching for a 'cure for all mankind' in the event of this viral problem and had quietly succeeded. Or perhaps they were just trying to scare us to keep us in our places. Yes, you can have your minimum wage, introduced this year at £3.30 per hour, but see how easy it is for us to control you now that you've become wholly dependent on your computers. Which leads us to . . .

2000

GRANDADDY – 'THE CRYSTAL LAKE'

Grandaddy were a bunch of chinstrap-bearded misfits from Modesto, California who made some of the most achingly beautiful Americana you will ever hear. Their home town they described to me as consisting pretty much entirely of 'computer stores and taco outlets'. I'm sure that wasn't really the case; I've looked it up and there seems to be a symphony orchestra and a winery and all kinds of other stuff, but that was how it seemed to the band's main writer Jason Lytle and that was the vision that infused their masterpiece *The Sophtware Slump*. The album portrays a world obsessed with technology that will ultimately let you down once you've come to depend on it. There's a track called 'Broken Household Appliance National Forest' in which the landscape has itself been altered by the dumping of redundant white goods and if it seems to be stretching a point to think of it as a 'national forest' then perhaps you've never seen a mountain made of retired fridge-freezers.

The sleeve of *The Sophtware Slump* features photographs of discarded computer keyboards shedding keys and gradually being covered by the sand and gravel as if nature is somehow reclaiming territory. Again, if this seems a little alarmist one viewing of Julien Temple's elegiac film *Requiem for Detroit* will leave you appreciating Jason's prescient vision.

In the development of popular music Detroit is as important as any city has ever been. It was the home of Tamla
Motown and can lay claim to having given birth to punk
through Iggy and The Stooges and the MC5. Immortalised
by Kiss as 'Detroit Rock City', it spawned Ted Nugent and
Alice Cooper as well as perpetuating its soul heritage in the
seventies with acts like The Emeralds and The Spinners.
Techno is generally accepted to have its roots in the city and
The White Stripes originated their 21st-century mutant
blues there. However, if there is indigenous music that most
closely mirrors the Detroit of 2010 it is in the restless, testy,
disaffected documentation of the 8 Mile district by Eminem.
Since the wholesale demise of the car industry, huge swathes
of the downtown area have been abandoned. Schools, industrial units, housing projects, roads, automobile plants all lie
dormant and derelict as the greener kind of plants return to
the pastures that were originally theirs.

On the upside there is very little traffic congestion these
days as there is very little traffic, which for 'Motor City' is the
ultimate irony. You'll get home from where you've been very
quickly but that might not seem important if you've nowhere
to get back from. A conurbation built for 2 million people,
it's now home to 800,000. The literacy rate amongst young
people in Detroit is estimated to be around 53 per cent. In
modern Ethiopia it's over 90 per cent.

When Hurricane Katrina hit New Orleans the most striking thing for those of us watching from the outside was how
many of the poorest residents, devoid of health care, cars or
friends who could offer them out-of-town refuge, were left to
fend, forage and find shelter as best they could. And this in the
centre of a major American city in the twenty-first century.
For the impoverished residents of modern-day Detroit there
isn't even a natural disaster they can blame. They've been
abandoned by their own country in the first post-industrial

city. Many of them are the families of workers drawn from the deep South to man the car plants who find themselves marooned now the production lines have stopped. There is no way out and nowhere to go and a subsistence economy, with food being grown on urban smallholdings on what were once car parks, is beginning to take shape. *The Road* of Cormac McCarthy must seem very close to reality for many of those people. Except there's no cinema in which to see the film and no bookshop in which to buy the book. And even if you could, there's only a 47 per cent chance you could read it.

Temple's movie, with footage of limitless numbers of automobiles rolling off the lines projected onto crumbling factory facades, makes the point poignantly and beautifully. Was this the world Jason Lytle foresaw? A world where the lost Eldorado of 'The Crystal Lake' had, like everything else we take for granted, slipped away.

If that was what Lytle was saying one can imagine that he was, if not a lone voice, then certainly one of a very small group who would be labelled 'cranks' despite the dotcom bubble bursting. The appearance of his band, part religious cult, part backwoods hillbilly, wouldn't have exactly led anyone to consider what they had to say with any degree of seriousness. Their live shows would often see them struggling with ageing analogue synths, leading to charges of Luddism. Behind them they projected hypnotically turning wind turbines. We get it, said the logged-on mainstream, they're 'alternative', right?

About an hour's drive from Modesto is Palo Alto. In a suburban garage in 1938, and with a start-up budget of just over five hundred dollars, Bill Hewlett and Dave Packard began to tinker with bits and bobs in order to start making gadgets. Their first devices were actually audio oscillators which, despite selling a few to Walt Disney, failed to really take off.

Undoubtedly they were ahead of their time. If they'd been able to hang about until the seventies and the advent of Hawkwind and Krautrock, they'd have made a killing. That, however, is an academic point as the corporation they founded turned over 104 billion dollars in 2007 thanks to getting stuck into computers. Just fifteen minutes away is another garage where Steve Jobs and Stephen Wozniak cobbled together the first Apple gear. The Hewlett-Packard garage is on the National Register of Historic Places, which seems fair enough although it's a shame you can't go inside. You can see it from the pavement, apparently, but it seems an awfully long way to go to look down a driveway at a shed. There's a song on *The Sophtware Slump* called 'Hewlett's Daughter' in which Jason plaintively sings of his love for this girl, who also loved her father, amidst the detritus of what seems to be a world where technology has failed. Is it that Hewlett? Could be, but the song describes a society where the industry at the core has spiralled into decline.

In 2003 'Second Life' was launched. A virtual world where you lived, loved, shopped and even banked, it seemed desperately close to a nightmare vision of some future dystopia. Wasn't it conceivable that the gregarious, attractive, happy avatars locked in there were being manipulated by participants who were growing ever more sedentary and misanthropic in real life? You could be a sexy, scintillating, sun-kissed honey on screen whilst being an obese loner perched on a commode, locked away in a squalid room with only the flicker of the screen permeating the half-light. Couldn't you decide to give up what you had become and choose to be forever beautiful online? In other words, could 'Second Life' become real life, and vice versa? And where would that leave you when the power ran out?

Of course, computers haven't deserted us, though the Internet does close at lunchtime on Wednesdays in Northwich, the town closest to where I live. A friend of mine's mother gleefully told him that the World Wide Web was being shut down permanently. Thankfully it turned out she meant Teletext. But Jason Lytle seems to have been expressing thoughts that the plight of Detroit proves to have been not far off the mark. After all, civilisations have disappeared before. What makes us so sure that we're here forever? In 79 AD people were getting ready to go out for a pint and a bite to eat in Pompeii, you know.

2001

RADIOHEAD – 'PYRAMID SONG'

Mon.
Hi love, arrived safely. Staying on a little square with a church in same hotel as band. Discreet and posh and nicely antiquey. And the hotel. Ha-ha. Verona is lovely. The picture on the other side is the Ponte Pietra 'cos there's a big river called the Adige here. Who knew? Miss you (a bit). See you Sat. Mx

Tues.
Went for walkabout this a.m. This pic is Juliet's balcony as in 'Romeo and . . .' Knew old Bill Shakey had done some stuff about 'Two Gentlemen of . . .' but didn't realise the Montagues and Catapults were from round here. Of course, press officer wants me and Marc do a 'Lard, Lard, wherefore art thou Lard' pic. Told 'em to piss off. Morecambe and Wise have a lot to answer for sharing that bed. Mx

Weds.
Went out last night with Ed. You know, the tall one you met in Barcelona. He is a full foot taller than Thom! That must be the biggest gap between members of the same band, eh? Unless Nicky is that much bigger than Sean in The Manics. We had pizza! When in Rome . . .! Show went great. Johnny is lovely but doesn't want to talk and so is communicating

through my electronic drum pad. Very funny. At least, we think so. Concert tonight in the Roman amphitheatre. Can't wait. Mx

Thurs.
Brilliant gig last night. Sun going down over this coliseum thing which gave the stone a lovely glow. Dead warm too. Sat outside under the stars listening to 'Lucky'. Wow! There's opera on usually and so there was still a stage set with some castle ramparts. *Rigoletto*? You'd know better than me. I s'pose you'd rather see that than the guys, wouldn't you? Thom played 'Pyramid Song' on the old hotel upright piano today. Brought tears to the eyes. As bad as that, eh? Ha-ha. He is some kind of genius to be sure. Mx

Fri.
Went to Venice on train with Marc and Michelle today. Took about four hours and we had about 90 mins there. Still, when in Rome! We'll have to go back, eh? So, how's the foot and mouth there? Can you pick me up at 3 from T2? Had top trip tho'. Love you, Mx

2002

JOHNNY CASH – 'HURT'

It's my birthday and I am forty-three. Not, you might think, any kind of landmark. And yet I lie in bed in the spare room at the top of the narrow house overlooking the canal in Ghent where my brother-in-law was living at the time, sinking into a deep blue fug. The kids have gone downstairs to let me have a bit of a lie-in but there's no chance of going back to sleep. The voiles that pass for curtains block no light and, in any case, the cockerel who's been crowing and bothering his harem since dawn is now engaged in a noisy stand-off with some passing grebes. And anyway, the only thing I can think of is that I am forty-three.

Age has never bothered me. I have never lied about it, at least not since trying to get served with a half of dark mild in the The Blue Boar on Deansgate in Bolton in 1975. I've known several people who also bob along in this often stagnant backwater pop-radio tributary of show business who are desperate for you to believe they are ten years younger than they really are. I've never seen the point myself. All that happens is that people think you look a bit rough for your age.

I wasn't the slightest bit traumatised by turning forty, except by the torrential rain which threatened to wash out the cheese, beer and dodgy folk music gathering I'd organised in the garden. You know how it is. You invite all the friends and family members who love you and then the weather means you have to cancel everything. I mean, you don't want to let down thirteen people like that, do you? Neither did I suffer any angst on my fiftieth. Standing at the side of the stage at Glastonbury watching Leonard Cohen singing 'Hallelujah', where you left me at the end of the last book, seemed to me a quite wonderful way to celebrate half a century. I look forward to becoming sixty without the slightest qualm.

But that fiercely hot day in Belgium I cannot stop thinking about being forty-three. I cannot stop scratching my mosquito bites either, but in a few days' time my legs will be back to normal. They will be as they were before those vicious Flemish midges gorged on good English blood enriched by decades of quality real ales. To be absolutely fair to that marauding horde of Wallonian gnats, I think a lifetime of continental lager might well induce me to turn vampire if I thought I could imbibe some residue of Jennings Cumberland nectar. However, though my skin will revert back to what it was, my age will not. I will never be not forty-three ever again.

Why should this bother me? Because I cannot pull away from the thought that I might be more than halfway through, that's why. Even at that moment I realised how ridiculous this was. I might live many years beyond, or shy, of that arbitrary figure. Still, I couldn't shake the notion that I'd passed the marker post it had taken over forty years to reach, turned and was now on the way back.

Why my own mortality should obsess me like never before or since is hard to say. I'd been listening to a lot of Sigur Rós, particularly the new album ( ). Their extraterrestrial cascades of sound, laden with wistful laments, despite being sung in their own invented language Hopelandish, might have put me into something of a trance. ( ). Brackets with nothing in them. D'you see? There's nothing at the centre. It's the futility of human existence. These are the big questions. How long do I have left? What am I here for? Is it too early for a bottle of Black Sheep? Oh no, we're in Belgium. Is it too early for a bottle of Stella?

Reflections on the transitory nature of life were also considered by Bruce Springsteen on *The Rising*. His best LP for many years it was, in part, his response to events seen on 11 September at the World Trade Center the previous year.

The most heartbreakingly personal record dealing with life slipping away, though, came when Johnny Cash released 'Hurt'. The song was written by Trent Reznor, one of those American names like Meryl Streep that you feel sure must be an anagram, of frat-boy electro-industrial shock rockers Nine Inch Nails.

I've never had much time for them, myself. I went to see them at the Manchester International 2 and found it all a bit pathetic, really. The drummer was in a cage as if, unleashed, he was going to bite you on the ankle. Keyboards were trashed as drinks were poured over them by the band which, as an act of wilful destruction and display of nihilistic intent, lost some of its potency when you knew they'd been in Johnny Roadhouse's music shop earlier the same day buying up the cheapest second-hand gear available. Reznor fronted the whole pantomime with bug-eyed intensity but I could never bring myself to buy into it. This was a man who recorded an album at 10050 Cielo Drive, where acolytes of Charles Manson butchered Sharon Tate and friends. As the house was due to be demolished after the completion of *The Downward Spiral* album, Trent kept the front door. The one that had had 'PIG' marked out on it in blood. Call me picky, but I find it difficult to warm to a guy like that.

His song 'Hurt', however, turned into something hugely affecting when it was selected for inclusion on Johnny Cash's

American IV: The Man Comes Around record. One of the pared-down series of albums recorded with Rick Rubin in the producer's chair, songs such as Depeche Mode's 'Personal Jesus', Ewan MacColl's 'The First Time Ever I Saw Your Face', 'In My Life' by The Beatles and Hank Williams' 'I'm So Lonesome I Could Cry' take on an emotional intensity as they are growled by a giant of American popular culture whose life is clearly ebbing away.

It's not a perfect LP – the version of 'Bridge Over Troubled Water' I have never been sure of – but it really does do justice to the ballad of The Man In Black as he approaches the final verse. The song 'Hurt', taking stock of what he has become in that tortured husk of a voice, would be moving enough on its own, but the accompanying video added even more potency. Old photographs of Cash and his family in their hell-raising heyday flash by as he sits motionless, ruined head shrouded in wispy white hair, and stares into the camera like a proud Native American chieftain in the aftermath of some bloody defeat. June Carter Cash stands stony-faced with a hand on the once strong shoulder. It is hard to think of a more fitting epitaph for one of the true giants of popular music.

Whether any of these factors came into play that day I couldn't say for sure. Perhaps I was just a bit down in the dumps because I was in Belgium. I've also wondered whether the palindromic significance of 2002 had something to do with it. Years that read the same forwards and backwards have had a peculiar association with my birthdays. I once spent a 29 June on the island of Gozo in the Maltese archipelago. The Ottomans and Barbary pirates once invaded Gozo. And the year? 1551. Postmarks, without which I wouldn't have received many cards, were introduced in 1661 and postal orders, which I was given annually by Aunty

Mary, in 1881. Whilst still at junior school I once received a birthday gift of a Ladybird book documenting the life of Captain Cook. When did his first voyage finish? 1771. Now this has got to be more than a coincidence. Perhaps momentous feelings arise in palindromic years and if that is the case then I, like you quite possibly, have had more than my fair share. In the normal order of things they only come up once every 110 years and so each of us will generally only have to contend with one at most. I've had two thanks to that pesky millennium and so, having sailed blissfully through 1991, I got emotionally clobbered in 2002. Thankfully 2112 won't be a problem. However far I go, I won't be around for that one.

Johnny Cash died the following year.

2003

THE WHITE STRIPES –
'SEVEN NATION ARMY'

This year saw the release of the Led Zeppelin live album *How The West Was Won*. The Gandalf of the guitar the Rt. Hon. Jimmy Page paid a visit to our studio to talk about it on afternoon Radio 1, which is, after all, the home of classic rock. White-haired and twinkly, he was charming company, but I became fascinated by his leg.

Seasoned Zep watchers will be aware of a peculiar little kick that Page executes at moments of high musical drama. It's a sort of slightly backwards, slightly sideways jerk from the knee. As we sat on-air listening to the full glory of 'Stairway To Heaven' he remained serene and beatific and pretty much motionless and yet when the guitar solo kicked in, Jimmy Page's leg kicked out. He was sitting down and so it wasn't as if someone had suddenly scissor-kicked in midair or anything, but that leg reacted as if it was still clad in velveteen, oriental-dragon-emblazoned loons at Madison Square Garden.

This struck me as an interesting example of the primal force of music and the way the body reacts to it. Unless he had sciatica, of course, in which case, Jim, I hope it's all sorted out.

There is something of the same primal power about the music of The White Stripes, I think, and in particular the much discussed drumming of Meg White. It has always been my belief that there are no great bands who don't have a great drummer. You can have an average singer, guitarist, bass player or keyboardist and still be right up there. In fact, the way a group absorbs and responds to their deficiences is often what gives them their uniqueness. Joy Division sound that way because Peter Hook was struggling manfully to get to grips with how to play the bass. If Jaco Pastorius had been their bassist, and I acknowledge it's unlikely as he was rarely seen in the Salford or Macclesfield locales and anyway Hooky would probably have chased him out of town to make sure he hung on to his job, then they would have been very different. And crap. Was Jaco more technically advanced than Peter? Of course. Would he have brought the same supreme subsonic melodies to the table? Of course not. He'd have been too busy slapping the fretboard to make that sound like wet kippers being packed into a box that highly proficient bass players are so desperately fond of. Hooky's trademark lines were all he could play, and were all that they needed.

Necessity can indeed be the mother of invention and could quite conceivably have resulted in The Mothers of Invention. Put four brilliant musicians together and you can guarantee that they will produce clinically accurate music of no emotional value. Or jazz rock, as it's known, which we discussed at the start of this book. Well, I discussed it myself, and you read it, unless you skipped that bit in which case you're going to have to go back and read it now, which serves you right for not taking this seriously enough. How you think you're going to pass the exam with a haphazard approach to reading the set texts I'll never know.

But drums are different. Whatever kind of music you're playing, the rhythm has to be solid or people feel instinctively uncomfortable. They might not be musically informed enough to know why they can't lock into it, but they will know that there is something amiss. At the end of the day, people like to dance to music and you can't dance if the beat is wrong. The drummer is also a far more distinctive player than most of the members of the audience realise. Playing the drums involves combining every limb, and each drummer will coordinate in a slightly different way, giving their band a wholly individual rhythm. It might not differ radically to the untutored ear, but the rhythmic quirks of that drummer playing those drums on that song will affect the way all the other instruments and voices relate to each other. This is why changing a drummer is just about the hardest thing to do for a band after replacing the lead singer.

You might think that playing the drums for AC/DC is just about the best job it's possible to imagine. You fly round the world first class staying in the best hotels to play straight 4/4 for an hour a night before going home with a million pounds. It's still slightly harder work than being the bass player in AC/DC, for which you fly round the world first class staying in the best hotels to play root notes in 4/4 for an hour a night before going home with a million pounds and, on most songs, you don't usually have to play until the chorus. And yet, simple as it seems, and we're back to Lou Reed and the E to A theory here, it needs to be 'done right', and Angus and Malcolm Young say they don't feel it's 'right' unless it's Phil Rudd on the drum stool. This may be the case but if you want to put that theory to the test, lads, in the interests of saving you a bob or two, I'll give it a go for £750,000.

So, every top band has a top drummer. Which leads us to Ringo. Poor old Ringo gets trotted out every time to disprove this theory and I think it's unfair. For a start, The Beatles weren't really a band in the sense that we're discussing it. They never had the chance, or wanted, to be a proven live act. Did they make several visionary masterpieces in the studio? Yes, they did. Only a fool would argue otherwise. But their early dates were opportunities for teenyboppers to scream and wet their pants, it wasn't primarily the music that was the important thing. Once their *oeuvre* became more complex, they retired from the live arena for good. Having said all that, if you listen to the records the drums are pretty much perfect.

The same can be said for Pink Floyd. They are a truly great band, have created some of the finest rock music the world has ever known, and yet anyone in possession of a drum kit can play what Nick Mason is playing and still have a spare hand to hold a pint. Now, is this because Nick Mason is not much of a drummer, or that he's sensitive to the music and is holding all his wild tendencies in check? I don't know. He is certainly atuned to the track and I've read interviews where he appears to be candid about his musical limitations, and yet what else could he play? I love the drumming of Phil Collins and Stewart Copeland, but their style would be wholly unsuited to the music of Floyd. Nick Mason and Ringo Starr were the perfect drummers for the bands they were in and that's what matters the most. You wouldn't have wanted Keith Moon in The Rolling Stones. Or indeed your guest bedroom.

Sometimes this theory presents a problem. We all have a romantic notion that a band should be a group of mates who've been that way for years. This way they're able to operate from a position of mutually shared security and trust. Naturally we all fall out with our friends from time to time. I have been in and out of beat combos with my great friend Philip 'Shimmy' Walmsley since we met during our first week at university in 1976. That hasn't stopped us having our disagreements. Apportioning blame is often a pointless exercise in these situations as it's just one person's word against another and anyway, Phil, it's just a car. And a duckpond. And some ducks, admittedly, but for goodness' sake let it go.

However, what do you do if your band takes off and you realise that one member is not as good as the rest of you? Well, either you have to take a brutal decision very early on before you get famous, or you just accept it. This is tricky if the dodgy player is the drummer. U2's Larry Mullen Jr. is a fine drummer and, as he put the notice up at school in the first place, it is arguably his band, so no problem there.

For Coldplay the situation was more problematic. Their drummer Will Champion couldn't play the drums when they started out, which didn't seem too much of an issue as he was the rhythm guitarist and took over behind the kit when the original drummer failed to turn up for rehearsals. Is he the best drummer in the world? He wouldn't claim to be and in fact seems not to have all that much interest in drumming at all. I was once doing a live session with them at the BBC's Maida Vale studios. After the sound check I asked him if I could have a go on his drums, being a drummer myself. He said I was welcome though they weren't 'his' drums. He explained that every night when he walked out on stage the kit was there but that was the only time he saw it. He was, he said, 'the only drummer I know who doesn't own any drums'. What about practising, I enquired? He responded with customary good humour and candour by saying that he played two hundred gigs a year, which seemed to be practice enough because, frankly, 'how hard can it be'?

This brings us back to Meg White. The other half of The White Stripes, who may well be easily three-quarters, is Jack White. Originally they told the world they were siblings, which proved to be 'spin' as it seems generally accepted now that they were former lovers. Both are now happily married, Jack to a girl from Oldham (hence *Icky Thump*, which is Northern parlance for 'cripes'), and Meg to Patti Smith's son Jackson.

Jack White's guitar-playing, songwriting and 21st-century take on swamp blues has seen him rightly recognised and lauded as one of the most distinctive voices to emerge in rock in recent times. He is as much of a guitar hero, with a sound as distinctive, as The Edge or James 'Leggy' Page with whom he made a film called *It Might Get Loud* in 2008. Page's musical vision was made real by the construction of the greatest rock band of all time with Robert Plant, John Paul Jones and John Bonham. The Edge has Bono, Larry and Adam. Jack White created this maelstrom of noise with just Meg on the drums. Not only that, she provides only the most basic of beats. And not only that, she looks like she thinks she's doing Jack a favour by doing it.

Her laconic approach provided a compelling contrast to his virtuoso *tour de force* and made them one of the most extraordinary live acts I have ever seen. I watched absolutely spellbound at Glastonbury in 2005 and marvelled at how just two people, and one of those with minimal musical talent if maximum effortless charisma, could hold a crowd of that size in thrall. Their instruments and stage adornments were all painted in their trademark red and black, and as we watched the ballet between them unfold as they hopped between aspidistras from guitars and drum kits to marimbas and timpani it was as if we were peering through the keyhole of some dusty Victorian nursery watching two errant brats locked in a bizarre game of their own devising. They have a greatness which, as the journalist Andy Gill put it when reviewing their live album *Under Great White Northern Lights*, 'goes against the common practice of concert performance'.

During the accompanying DVD Jack White explains that they have always made things more difficult for themselves on purpose. There is no bass player to fall back on. They persist in using old guitars that go out of tune. The organ will deliberately be placed a bit too far away to reach easily. And yet despite and also because of this they have, as Gill perfectly sums it up, 'squeezed maximum impact from minimal resources, Meg rarely straying from the simplest, most starkly dynamic of pulses'. Quite so.

Of course, there are those who feel uncomfortable with this. They think that every successful rock act should have a large sweating man at the rear rather than a fresh-faced girl who seems content to use just one hand half the time, and I'm aware that there's a punch line there that I'm leaving out. Jack, having chosen to embark on selling over 12 million albums with what seemed initially like such thin resources, is adamant that their approach was the right one. 'She can do what those with technical prowess can't,' he told esteemed musical publication the *Daily Star*. 'She bangs on pots and pans. For that, they repay her with gossip and judgement. In the end she's laughing to the Prada handbag store. She wins every time. Her extreme minimalism is too much to take for some metal heads and reverse-contrarian hipsters.'

These were thoughts I tried to hold in my mind as I sat onstage at the Manchester Apollo, where I'd also seen Meg drum, ready to play the drums for Rufus Wainwright on 22 April 2010. As a venue, the Apollo is one I hold in high regard. Like Hammersmith Odeon and Edinburgh Playhouse, it's one of the great old atmospheric rock theatres in the UK. When I was growing up, and before the existence of the arena circuit, the Apollo was as good as it got. If a band were playing there, they had cracked it. Over the years I have seen Genesis and The Clash and The Ramones and Captain Beefheart and Radiohead and Bruce Springsteen there, and so to tread those hallowed boards really felt like something special.

The performance came as a result of a programme I was taking part in for SkyArts as part of a series called *First Love*.

The basic premise was that someone known for something, for example gibbering between records on the radio, would undertake a performance demonstrating their musical ability in another area, such as banging on pots and pans in the name of extreme minimalism. Lenny Henry and Meera Syal did some singing. Newsreader Katie Derham played the violin. And Janet Street-Porter joined a baroque recorder ensemble. As you might expect.

I was mentored in my drumming by the amiable and pretty much ambidextrous Steve White, one of England's finest drummers who's played with all sorts of people, most notably Paul Weller and The Who. Whitey took me right back to basics, which was a far greater distance for him than it was for me. We began by tapping in strict tempo to an electronic metronome in order to build up what he called 'muscle memory'. It occurred to me at this point that there could be other areas of my physical existence that might benefit from that too. He taught me to sit up and breathe properly and, in particular, to minimise my range of motion. Most self-taught drummers actually use up far too much energy waving the sticks around rather than actually hitting the drums. This is because when we start out we're desperately trying to show off, and flailing wildly about is a good way of making it look difficult and arduous. It can also distract the bass player to the extent that he plays wrong notes, which is always a good way of ensuring that as the drummer you're not at the bottom of the band food chain.

The climax of this programme was to be a public performance. Several acts were approached and astoundingly Rufus Wainwright said yes. What made this even more remarkable was that he was doing a solo tour with just him and his grand piano. How his prodigious musical ability would be complemented by some idiot off the radio thumping away on the drums was hard to imagine, even if that same idiot had had the odd Whitey masterclass and a session with Richard Jupp of Elbow.

The track we were going to be doing was 'Going To A Town'. A beautiful song, this came as something of a relief, as it seemed at first to be fairly straightforward in percussive terms. However, when I met up with Steve he'd mapped out a chart stretching across two sheets of A4 paper detailing all the odd bar lengths, tacits, rallentandos and other features that sounded as if they should have been on the menu at a local trattoria. Initially this was somewhat daunting, but as I began to really think about playing the kit, being aware of how a touch on each drum or cymbal could affect the sound of the song, I became obsessed with getting it right. All my life I'd just sat on the stool and hit things, and for the first time I began to see the difference between playing the instrument and mindless violence.

We tried it once at Rufus's sound check and he could not have been more welcoming and generous. I sat behind my beautiful new Gretsch Millennium Maple drums – you know, like Charlie Watts uses – and with firm eye contact ran through the number. I think, though I don't know for sure, that Rufus was immediately relieved and perhaps a little surprised that I had obviously learned it. I imagine he thought that it would be a bit of fun, which indeed it was, but I was aiming higher than that. Here we go with that Lou Reed thing again. I wanted to 'do it right'. We got through the number safely and then went back to run the rallentando section again. Or the bit where it slows down to you, and until a couple of weeks earlier, me too. 'I'll watch you for that bit, then,' said the maestro, 'if you know what a rallentando is then that's good enough for me.' And this from a man who's written an opera.

Rufus's show was one of two very different halves. The first was a recital of his new album *All Days Are Nights: Songs*

For Lulu. In large part a tribute to his recently deceased mother, the folk singer and songwriter Kate McGarrigle, it was a performance of compelling intensity. The atmosphere in the hall was suitably charged, not least because Rufus had asked the audience not only to refrain from applauding between the numbers, as it was intended to be heard in one piece as a song cycle, but also to remain silent for his funereal approach to and departure from the keyboard. This he did in a black cowl with a long train sweeping the stage behind him. I sat on the end of Row N and marvelled at what he was doing. Apart from the poignant beauty of the material it was an awesome feat of memory. I mean, he was playing an awful lot of notes up there, as well as singing an awful lot of words. It was like simultaneously playing a piano concerto whilst reciting a one-man show. It wasn't particularly crying out for drums.

After the interval he emerged in what for Rufus passes as more casual garb. A fitted tunic, skinny green trousers and white patent trainers. He then encouraged the crowd to 'clap to your heart's content' as he ran through some of his most popular songs and chatted easily about, amongst other things, his love of Yorkshire Gold tea. I stood behind the monitor desk in a chalk-stripe suit borrowed from a bespoke tailors in Brighton, and waited for the nod.

Finishing the second half, Rufus left the stage to tumultuous applause, at which point my drums were wheeled out on a riser, which probably took away the element of uncertainty about whether there was going to be an encore or not. He came back out and sat at the Bechstein and told the crowd that a special guest was coming on. I shuddered slightly at this as that seemed to give me a bigger build-up than I was entirely comfortable with. If I had been in the audience and heard him say the words 'special' and 'guest' I would have been hoping for his friend and fan Elton John or his sister Martha, though in fairness, neither of them would have much use for a drum kit. Seeing the Gretsch perhaps they were hoping for Charlie Watts. But they got me. Mind you, it would be disingenuous of me to pretend that I didn't get an extraordinarily warm welcome, not least because Rufus had been so inordinately kind to me during his intro-duction, saying that I'd always supported him from the early days of his career. This was true, but that didn't mean he owed me anything. If anything the debt was mine, as his records made my show better on the occasions I played them.

The opening chords chimed from the piano and I took a deep breath, glanced at the 'cheat sheet' I had gaffer-taped to the top of the bass drum and congratulated myself on only having consumed one of the four bottles of London Pride that had been left in the dressing room as my backstage rider. Strangely, I wasn't nervous at all, which is unusual for me. People are always surprised by my stage fright as my job involves talking on the radio to several hundred thousand and, even if it's usually slightly less than the size of the audi-ence the show had before I took it over, it's still a sizable number. But you can't see them. To me, the listeners are the three or four people through the glass in the control room, and I use the word 'listener' in the most general sense as Chris the engineer will normally be watching the football highlights on telly.

But as Rufus and I began our one-off duet I found myself relaxing into it and experiencing genuine enjoyment. We smiled at each other when the rallentando went to plan, struck up eye contact at several points and embraced when it was all done. As I left the stage Rufus said it had been really good fun and that I was 'a really cute guy'. Now, to be nice is one thing, to lie another entirely, but it was well meant and helped to create a memorable moment. For me, I mean. I doubt it lived long for anyone else.

Afterwards Rufus, Whitey and Jupp all proclaimed it a triumph and, suitably proud, I went back to the remaining three bottles of London Pride only to find that Elbow's chancer of a sticksman had beaten me to it.

The next day I returned to Lostock Tennis Club in Bolton where I played my debut gig in 1972. My band was called The Berlin Airlift and I went back with two old friends who'd also played that night, guitarist Ross Warburton and bassist Andy Wright. None of us had been back there in the intevening years and our thoughts were obviously of the fourth member, Jim Leslie, who was sadly no longer with us. As I arrived on the car park I felt my stomach knot. The last time I was standing on the gravel outside that club house I was fourteen. I remember being almost incapacitated with nerves, as we were playing in public for the very first time. If it had gone badly, how different my life could have been. As it was, I emerged after that little concert knowing what I wanted to be. I was going to be a drummer. And one day, I would play at the Manchester Apollo.

THE SHIREHORSES AND TRAVIS –
'WHY IS IT ALWAYS DAIRYLEA?' (LIVE)

Hello boys. This is David. David Bowie calling from
Tokyo. No, that's wrong, Osaka. In Japan. I'd just like to
bring up a little story from September '95, which was the
first time I did your show. I remember you collected me
from my hotel by sleigh with bells on. Very pretty. Drawn
by retired players of Manchester United. I'll never forget.
How the people laughed and cheered our little procession
as we made our way through the streets to your studio.
That September there was little snow so I lost most of my
teeth due to the bumping and rattling over the cobbles and
the odd pedestrian. I don't think we'll ever see the like of
that again. Yours was THE show on the wireless, Mark
and Lard, and I'll be listening out for that sleigh maybe just
one more time and it'll take me to the studio again where
we'll laugh and play good tunes and split the odd atom.
Goodbye, chaps. It was all for the best. All of it.

So began the last Mark and Lard show on Radio 1 on 26
March 2004. Listening to that programme now it's hard not
to be deeply affected by the outpourings of emotion that
were in evidence that day. At one point I refer to a crowd of
six people who had assembled of their own accord, although

a light shower had brought this down to five. A look out of the window enabled Lard to confirm that numbers swelled as the programme progressed, reaching up to thirteen at one point. In reality there were perhaps fifty or sixty souls intent on being there for our last day but the nature of the beast, the perennial underdog kept outside in the yard, we had created meant that it suited our needs to round the figure substantially down.

Appearing in the show that day were many characters and friends that regular listeners had come to expect. Fat Harry White made his last ever appearance, regaling us with tales of his latest job as a milkman whose float, laden with a creamy load of full-fat milk and yoghurt, ended up over his ladyfriend Foxy Fiona's entry. As expected. Further anecdotes involved a camping trip where some of his party had been billeted in small shelters made of twigs and branches called, ahem, 'benders', and a meal out during which an unfortunate incident occurred with a rump steak and some Eton Mess. Naturally.

A suitably thought-provoking 'Thought for the Day' was provided by our resident spiritual adviser the Rabbi Lionel Blair, who professed to not being much of a fan of the pair of us as he liked *Steve Wright in the Afternoon* himself. He went on to tell us that he had recently taken on some voluntary work in a charity shop so he 'could have a good rummage through the stuff before it got to the shelves'. On his way home from his good works he had chanced upon a man living in a shop doorway with only a painfully thin dog for company. This the Rabbi, sounding not unlike Lard, took to be a cipher for the wider human existence as, after all, weren't we all 'simply dossing down in the doorway of eternity'? Profound stuff, indeed. Touched by the plight of this unfortunate individual, forced out of necessity to wear a Lighthouse Family T-shirt and 'stinking like Ann Widdecombe's jock-strap' apparently,

Lionel escorted him back to his own residence. Here, out of the goodness of his heart, he installed the bewildered street urchin into accommodation in a hastily converted coal bunker in order to get 'a ton a week off the DSS'. There wasn't a dry eye in the house. The dog unfortunately had to be put down, which Blair had paid for himself and was receiving back in instalments. With interest. I think that's what's known as 'tough love'. It would have been for his own good. The dropout, that is, not the dog.

Lard returned to his enviable collection of vinyl to treat the enthralled listeners to another of his 'classic cuts'. These were scratched and crackling discs that 'jumped' repeatedly, changing the lyrics in the process. Painstakingly created by Marc and our engineer Chris Lee, who spent hours hunched over the latest Pro-Tools technology which the BBC had heavily invested in so that some tosspots could get some rude words out on the air. Money well spent and no mistake. On this occasion the track in question was 'Mull Of Kintyre' which, due to surface gremlins, became 'Mull Of ★★★kintyre'. You can still hear it online if that doesn't make sense. It's still very funny and I can say that because it was nothing to do with me. Were people offended? Well, if they were then Paul McCartney wasn't one of them. He sent us a huge bouquet that morning with a card that read: 'Wishing you all the best for your last show and thanks for all the fun times we had together.' I've still got the card pinned up in the office today.

Other celebrity messages, often in song form, came from Coldplay, Damon Albarn, Neil Hannon of The Divine Comedy, Doves, Starsailor, Stuart Pearce and Robbie Fowler of Manchester City FC, Peter Kay and 'your ever loving' Kylie. Perhaps the most touching farewell toast came from Kelly and Richard of The Stereophonics. Neither Marc or I were particular fans of the band and they, along with Craig

David, were the butt of many of what passed for jokes. Craig in particular was pilloried on almost a daily basis and was finally cleaved in two to become the gormless Craig and David, a foul-mouthed pair of urban drongos who ran a sandwich shop to the stars noted for the rudeness of the proprietors and a very lax attitude to environmental health. The Stereophonics were afforded similar disrespect and so when they agreed to contribute to our final show we were pleased but genuinely surprised. Kelly did most of the talking, with Richard giggling and chipping in from time to time.

'Who are we going to tune into to be insulted?' they asked. 'We are really going to miss your original, witty comedy and slagging us off all the time. Who else is going to do it? We wish you all the best in your future. If you've got one.'

We took that on the chin. We thought it was very big of them to take the trouble to get involved at all and the sound of a score being settled seemed entirely appropriate. Craig David was invited to take part as well but declined. I can't honestly say I blame him.

Elsewhere, that two hours, and a bit, featured the Mystery Man quiz where two listeners were fed clues by a mystery celebrity until one guessed that it was Thom Yorke putting on a silly voice. 'Great Moments in Pop' recalled The Shirehorses appearance at Glastonbury in 1997 when the stage on which we stood began to sink into the mud. The affable gentlemen of Travis were in the studio to act as house band and it must have felt like *Jim'll Fix It* for those lads when they got to perform with us on 'Why Is It Always Dairylea?' a song that they say bears an uncanny similarity to their own 'Why Does It Always Rain On Me', though I've never seen it myself.

The final record was 'Crazy, Crazy Nights' by lumbering 'Black and White Minstrels' of panto-metal Kiss. After it faded away the familiar sound effect of the studio door creaking open appeared as Lard wandered aimlessly around the studio mumbling to himself. A second creak heralded the arrival of myself to enquire of Marc what he was doing.

'We've spent a lot of time in here,' he quivered, 'and I was just having a last look round.'

I consoled him and told him not to beat himself up before suggesting we go to the pub where he can buy me a pint.

'One last catchphrase?' he pleaded.

'A swift half of a catchphrase, then,' I conceded. Lard had been known for his battery of catchphrases including 'Biggedy Biggedy Bong', 'Five pounds – it's a lot of cash' and in particular 'Stop ... carry on'.

Accordingly, the final word spoken on the Mark and Lard show was:

'Stop . . . . '

Followed not by a 'carry on' but by the sound of the studio door slamming shut. It's the stuff of heartbreak, isn't it? Weirdly, though, due to some kind of technical difficulty, this in turn was followed by a Radio 1 jingle which just faded into a silence lasting several minutes. Many were impressed that we'd managed to arrange this as an audio representation of the hole that was going to be left in all of our lives. As if. You only get a minute's silence on Remembrance Day. It was just a monumental cock-up, and not on our part, though it did provide a memorable signing-off.

After the show we went to a party that had been arranged in the show's honour at The Living Room on Deansgate. None of us stayed all that late as I recall.

The next morning it was Saturday and we wouldn't have been going into work anyway, and so it wasn't until the following Monday that it hit me. The thing I'd devoted the last seven years of my working life to doing was over. And the people I'd been doing it with weren't going to be working with me anymore. Lots of people asked me if Marc and I had fallen out and I can honestly say we never have. Those who suggested it must have felt like a divorce were wide of the mark, as you don't generally split up with someone you still like.

In truth, it was the BBC's decision to break the partnership, but neither of us resisted. They opened two doors, and we walked through them. Neither of us wanted to feel that we were shackled together for eternity and we were worried that there was a limit to how far we could change things if we stayed together. Whatever we did, people would want us to be Mark and Lard, with all the baggage that involved. Of course, we were also aware that countless hundreds of thousands were quite pleased we were being removed, and the vast majority of the population of the UK had never realised we were ever there. I think we also both felt that we'd sat at opposite desks trying to think of jokes and sketches on a daily basis for long enough. Without the slightest disrespect to Marc, who I know felt the same way, it was a relief not to have to do it anymore.

Hearing the programme again I'm struck by the energy and creativity and also by the presence of words you couldn't say on the radio now. To hear 'shite' in the middle of the afternoon seems mildly shocking by today's standards and who's to say that the move to more tempered vocabulary isn't a good thing? I was also surprised that the records seemed to come from a fairly narrow band of styles. Admittedly we were just playing out some of our favourites on this occasion, but they were pretty much all alternative white guitar rock acts such as Jane's Addiction, Radiohead, Doves, Grandaddy, Travis, Elbow and Ten Benson. Johnny Cash, The Divine Comedy, Black Box Recorder and The White Stripes were in there as well, but you don't half find yourself yearning for a bit of Tamla Motown or something when you hear that selection.

Or a bit of Craig David, maybe. Heaven knows, we had our battles with management over music, and I don't think that was wrong, but things were clearly not as clear cut as they seemed to be at the time. I still think we were right, though we could have been a bit wrong too, and whilst I still don't think they were as right as they thought they were they probably weren't as wrong as we thought they were.

I still get people who come up to me all the time and say, 'Why are you looking in my bin?' But there are also frequent occasions when people tell me how much they enjoyed listening to that afternoon show and ask when Marc and I are going to get back together. We will never get back together as we know that it was over that day and can never be re-created. Unless we both find ourselves out of work, of course, in which case the most likely scenario is that I'd be up for it and Marc would get the window-cleaning round he's always talked about. We had a very good innings and enjoyed it hugely and if there's one regret it's that we really saw it as our mission to change, remould, convolute and distort what a daytime radio programme could be and no one seems to have done the same since.

2005

RICHARD HAWLEY – 'COLES CORNER'

In every city and every town there's a place, a special place where people meet. In my city there's a place just like that. You won't see a street sign for it and you can't find it on a map, but it's there, right under everyone's feet. Thousands of feet have stood there, waiting in the warm morning sunshine or stamping bored and impatient in the freezing winter night annoyed at someone who's late or will never come.

So writes the Sheffield troubadour and unabashed romantic Richard Hawley on the inner sleeve of his 2005 *Coles Corner* album. Richard's journey from guitarist in Pulp and Longpigs to beloved crooner has been an unexpected pleasure, not least to him, but there are few other artists working in music today who have so effectively used their home town as the inspiration for their songs and given them swoonsome orchestral settings to create such melancholic grandeur.

The titular corner in question was outside Cole Brothers department store in Sheffield. The shop itself was closed down in 1969, but the name lingers. On the LP cover we see Hawley positioned there, looking expectant and clutching a bunch of lilies. Inside he is photographed checking his watch and then making a call from a pay phone with the bouquet propped up on the little shelf where you used to stack your twopence pieces. The final picture in the sequence, on the rear of the CD case, sees the flowers in the bin. She hasn't turned up. Richard is nowhere to be seen but, knowing him as I do, I think of him halfway down his third pint propping up the bar at the nearest hostelry. We've all been there. Well, not Coles Corner specifically, but our own local equivalent and, in fact, these pictures had to be shot at Alan Ayckbourn's Stephen Joseph Theatre in Scarborough due to the absence of the original landmark.

Chatting to Richard about the importance of Coles Corner to the oral history of Sheffield, he recalls a few of the many stories he was told whilst making the record. 'There was a café opposite,' he says, 'where people could weigh up a date and see if they were a looker or not. There were these two sisters and one was as blind as a bat but wouldn't wear glasses so she used to sit with her sister who had good eyesight and she'd tell her if he was nice or if he was a minger.'

He tells me about the couple who took a similarly cautious approach and found themselves sitting in the same booth at the café looking for each other across the street. They got married and had six kids apparently.

More than the love stories, though, Richard finds the notion of Coles Corner to be the touchstone for the nostalgia he has for civic and retail pride. I must confess that this is something close to my own heart. When I occasionally wander through Primark in Manchester, on the assumption that clothes whether expensive or ludicrously cheap are always going to look less than spectacular on a frame like mine, I can't help but notice the brass rail that runs alongside the staircase that takes you from the ground floor to the basement. When this was the grand department store Lewis's it would have been someone's job to shine that so you could see your face in it before the store opened for business that day. It's still there, but some Brasso wouldn't go amiss.

'I can imagine there being four corporations in the world,' muses Hawley. 'It is shocking how similar high streets are becoming and I have a sense of that otherness being lost. Maybe it's sentimental, I am a hopeless romantic, but I can't join in the fervour for newness. My dad used to say that "every paving stone tells a story" and we lose more than we gain. Everywhere is becoming the same and if a little herbert songwriter with glasses from Sheffield can try in some way to slow it down then I'm going to do it.'

With these thoughts in my head I wait on the Town Hall steps, the Coles Corner of my home town Bolton, and wait for my sister Jaine. I haven't brought a bunch of flowers but I do take her for lunch in the café of Whitakers department store. We have the roast chicken dinner on a two for ten pounds deal. The pair of old ladies in the queue in front of us want to pay separately until they learn that this will negate the 'two for one' offer and cost them seven pounds fifty each. They reluctantly agree to pay together, which then involves much agitated rummaging in purses at their table as the generous platefuls rapidly cool. The last time I was in here would have been more than thirty-five years ago when, having met her on the steps, I treated Hilary Wardle to cheese on toast with spaghetti hoops. I knew how to impress a girl.

I don't live far from Bolton but though I visit family in the suburbs I rarely venture into the town centre. I'd been told that I would find it somewhat faded. I was warned that many of the once rather fine emporia had become pound shops and charity stores and that the once bustling streets were a far cry from how I would remember them. In some ways this was true. Like many other towns, Woolworths sits

crumbling on one of the main intersections. On the opposite corner the branch of Boots the Chemists where my
mum used to dispense prescriptions and where I'd wait for
her to finish work by browsing in the record department
upstairs sits vacant with the clock on the wall outside frozen
at twenty past one.

Boots are still present in the town centre but, like all the
other major chains, have taken premises which afford the
luxury of covered shopping. With the prevailing climate of
the Northwest of England this is perhaps understandable but
it has undoubtedly created as many problems as it has solved.
Bolton boasts not only a great outdoor market but is also
home to the Market Hall. Opened in 1855, it was once the
largest covered shopping area in the country, showing that
the concept is by no means a new one. When I was a child
the Market Hall was full of myriad tiny stalls selling pretty
much anything you needed from handkerchiefs to horse
brasses, hat-pins to humbugs. I would wander those clam-
orous aisles, hanging on to Grandma Goad's hand, as leaving
go would surely result in being lost forever amidst the haber-
dashery and hardware, until we arrived at John Hoole's stall
where we could stand and drink sarsaparilla from tiny
Duralex glasses.

The Market Hall is still there with its magnificent iron-
work restored and maintained. But it's now home to the
major chains, the little independent stalls consigned to the
past. As Richard would have it, the otherness has been lost.
Wouldn't it have been better to let the stalls stay where they
were and let the big names take up positions on the high
street?

I nip into the Nat West bank and suddenly I am jolted
back to my childhood. In the doorway is a fireplace surrounded by highly polished oak panelling and for some
reason I remember this vividly from going in there with my

dad. I know for a fact that there was a piece of coloured paper folded into a concertina that used to sit as decoration in that grate. Why would something like that stay in your mind for the best part of fifty years? It's a mystery really, as is why banks seem to employ so few cashiers in relation to the numbers of cashier stations they have available. On this occasion, although the staff are nothing if not friendly and efficient, the ratio is two to eleven, leading to the inescapable conclusion that somewhere round the back nine of them are bingeing on mugs of tea and Jammie Dodgers. As I await my turn I glance up at the fabulous stained-glass dome that serves as a reminder of how we used to build things. I'm there quite a while and note that one of the leaded lights bears a Latin motto: 'supera moras'. When I come home I check its meaning. Ironically, it is 'overcome delays'.

As I walk those streets, expecting at any moment to meet my fifteen-year-old self coming the other way, I'm struck by how wide the streets are and how grand the municipal buildings. These things were proud declarations of our cotton-fuelled prosperity and independence and were built to last. The Post Office is like a cross between a Greek temple and Buckingham Palace, the Town Hall and accompanying crescent of law courts and museums spectacular in the spring sunshine. I go into the art gallery and there with her breasts bared still sits Zeda, sculpted in cast bronze by Jacob Epstein in 1927 and imprisoned in a perspex case for generations of schoolboys, my own included, to titter at.

Walking past the Octagon Theatre, which has happily survived as an independent provincial repertory, I walk across Victoria Square and down Oxford Street, passing the statue of 'revered son of Bolton' Fred Dibnah, and turn right heading for Churchgate. In my adolescence I could spend the whole of a Saturday on this one street between the parish church and Preston's of Bolton, 'the diamond centre of the

North', at the traffic lights. There was the Capitol cinema, one of three in the town centre along with the Odeon and ABC, two great pubs in The Swan and Ye Olde Man and Scythe, Sabini's ice cream parlour, a Berni Inn, Ye Olde Pastie Shoppe and two music shops in Booth's and Harker and Howarth. Sabini's and the Berni Inn are both bars now, as many units in this part of town seem to be. The cinema is long gone, The Swan partially closed down, Harker and Howarth located out of town and a couple of large shop fronts crowned with the familiar 'To Let' signs. And yet it is still a street that retains some sense of the past and a whiff of elegance and pride. Ye Olde Pastie Shoppe remains and their cheese and onion is still the best there is bar none. Booth's music shop is still there too, under a sign proclaiming that 'Richard Arkwright inventor of the water frame for cotton spinning occupied a shop on this site as a barber and peruke maker 1760–68'. I wander in and find that Tony Aspinall, in the company of his good lady Jean, is still in charge. It is, he tells me, the oldest music shop on the same site anywhere in the world. This sounds like quite a boast but so much do I want it to be true that I determinedly avoid doing any research that could disprove it. He gives me a postcard show-ing the shop around the time it opened in 1832. Two formally suited assistants, one heavily bearded, the other droopily moustached, stand erect in the doorway. To one side is a window where brass instruments hang, making you wonder exactly how many tubas were sold on a daily basis in pre-Victorian Bolton. Tony takes me downstairs to where he and I once rehearsed with a band and, once again, I'm sure that I will encounter my teenage self trying to unravel the chords to 'Virginia Plain'.

Across the road the quite beautiful half-timbered facade of Ye Olde Man and Scythe watches over comings and goings as it has done since 1251, though it was substantially rebuilt in

1636. It is now conjoined with a small jewellery store called, rather wittily, Ye Olde Wench and Trinkets. At the table in the front window of the pub sit two elderly gentlemen having halves of cask bitter and eating pasties out of paper bags from the shop down the street. Perhaps they, like Richard Hawley and me, have made their way back there to reassure themselves that not all the 'otherness' has been lost.

2006

JENNY LEWIS – 'YOU ARE WHAT YOU LOVE'

You are what you love,
And not what loves you back.

Hmmm.

2007

FLEET FOXES – 'MYKONOS' (DEMO)

2008

ELBOW – 'ONE DAY LIKE THIS'

2009

THE UNTHANKS – 'TAR BARREL IN DALE'

Somewhere in a rundown suburban house in Seattle an indie kid with marked grunge tendencies hunches over his acoustic guitar and writes a song about an island he has never visited because he likes the sound of the name. There is something about the romantic and mysterious images it conjures up that fuels the creative spurt. Stroking his straggly beard and pushing his lank mousey-blond hair behind his ears he pushes his chair back and smiles, knowing he has crafted something special. His name is Robin Pecknold and he is the lead singer and songwriter of the as yet largely uncelebrated and unknown Fleet Foxes. That situation is about to change and within months a quarter of a million songs will have been downloaded from their MySpace site.

Life changes in a moment for Elbow too. It is the night of 9 September 2008 in that there London and the judges have retired to consider their verdict as to who will be the recipients of the Mercury Music Prize at the swanky Grosvenor House Hotel. Y'know, just across the street from that big park. I am there with Stuart Maconie, broadcasting to the nation, having interviewed many of the contenders including Laura Marling, The Last Shadow Puppets, Colin and Ed from Radiohead and a wonderfully giggly and lubricated Adele. Robert Plant and Alison Krauss, nominated for their stupendous *Raising Sand* album, provide us with evidence that their rich partnership extends beyond the perfect entwining of their voices into improvised comedy. Perhaps this kind of connection is a crucial element of vocal blend at its most compelling. Rachel Unthank and The Winterset are there to showcase their record *The Bairns*, and their harmonies, with the added sibling ingredient, are utterly spine-tingling. I am later told by one of the judging panel that though the final decision was unanimous, The Unthanks made it to the final two.

Oh, and we talk to Elbow, of course. The lovable, lovely, laughing lads of Elbow. Secretly we're all delighted yet amazed they have come this far. The quality of their music has never been in doubt but they didn't seem to be the stuff that huge bands were made of. They had an approach to styling that might politely be said to be scruffily eccentric. They looked good, but then you occasionally see a street sweeper who manages to exude a little style. They were of no fixed haircut. They weren't what you might call obvious pin-up material. They were no oil paintings unless you wanted to delve into cubism. They were from Bury. They were called Elbow. Not the kind of group that wins the big awards.

As the moment approached, when Jools Holland milked the moment with the golden envelope, I told myself I didn't really care who won. I imagine most of the people in that room were similarly relaxed about the verdict. And yet when Jools squeaked: 'And the winner is Elbow', there was the hugest cheer and spontaneous eruption of goodwill I have ever encountered at an event of that kind. I realised straight away that I had wanted them to win all along, as they were not only friends but richly deserving of the recognition and it seemed as though all assembled, even the other nominees, felt a similar sense of joy. They returned to the studio euphoric and toting bottles of cheap champagne sold at ludicrous hotel prices to toast and savour the moment and to sing out our show with 'One Day Like This', performed in the Cockernee knees-up Chas and Dave idiom so beloved of all residents of the capital from Mayfair to the Old Kent Road and other places on the Monopoly board.

Talking to Elbow's Guy Garvey about that moment he describes it as: 'not so much being catapulted to Mars but more like being invited to come and take your place at the table. We had always felt on the fringes of things due to the nature of our insecurity but we felt, on that night, like we'd actually done something. I suppose we felt like we'd made it.'

Undoubtedly the song that was most responsible for this was 'One Day Like This' but in typically perverse fashion the band decided at the last moment not to play it as the judges sat chewing on their guinea fowl and listening to final persuasive performances. Elbow chose to showcase the stately and emotional 'The Loneliness Of A Tower Crane Driver', a decision which did not please everyone. 'The organisers of the television side of things really wanted us to play "One Day",' Guy recalls, 'but it had already got so much attention that we thought we'd use the platform to play one of our still passionate but less obvious ones. We had quite a battle with them and in the end we just said, "Well, we're playing this or we're not playing".' Of course, there was no chance of that programme being broadcast without Elbow and whilst the band ultimately held the trump cards, and could have been seen as being difficult, it has to be up to the artist to play what they want. Elbow, you suspect, came hopeful though not optimistic about winning, and so were quite rightly keen to let people taste the breadth of *The Seldom Seen Kid* record.

Nevertheless, the power of 'One Day Like This' was perhaps the key factor in the result. It was a song that the band had given birth to but which had grown up and left home, got its own flat and taken on a life of its own very quickly. Guy says he now thinks of it as 'an old friend. We also think of "New Born" as an old friend, as you guys were the first to play it and we all sat around pissing ourselves 'cos you played the full version on Radio 1 in the afternoon.'

I talk to Guy about the writing of 'One Day' on a chilly but beautifully clear spring day in the Northwest of England where there is little evidence of ash from an Icelandic volcano save the absence of aeroplanes bright in the Northern sky. 'It was,' he says, 'a day just like this funnily enough. And it was about the morning after being with someone and waking up with them for the first time. I had three or four versions of it in my head but I had always had the idea of a big simple string section as part of the melody.'

He said that often one of the other members of the band would come up with the melody but on this occasion it sprang into his head and, to ensure it didn't evaporate just as quickly as it came, he sang it into a dictaphone and still has that tape. If there was a piece of music in his mind at the point of creation it was, he revealed, Aaron Copeland's *Fanfare For The Common Man*. 'I wanted it to be simple and elevating and enobling,' he recalls with a grin, 'and when we got to the refrain Mark (Potter, guitarist) said, "Hey, that sounds like 'Hey Jude', can we do that?" at which point we thought, fuck it, let's go the whole hog for once, as we'd usually stop at something that celebratory.'

That song did indeed become a 'Hey Jude' of its time and began to pop up in all kinds of places. Guy says he realised they had created something that existed far out of their own sphere when he saw it used as the music to accompany footage of that day's achievements for the television coverage of the Beijing Olympics. He also tells me that the late Manchester singer-songwriter Bryan Glancy, a great friend of Elbow's and to whom *The Seldom Seen Kid* is dedicated, told him that his dad used to cry at the athletics. 'It was something to do with the emotion and effort involved. Bryan was prone to sending out cryptic texts and I got one from him once that said "chip off the old block". I wondered what it could mean but the Commonwealth Games was on and it clicked. I rang him and said, "You're crying at the athletics, aren't you?" Well I was like that. Tears in my eyes at the Olympic round-up and immensely proud.'

It has also become a song which people use at weddings a lot, which pleases Guy but perhaps not quite as much as seeing it feature at the climax of a campanology competition, used by 'big beery blokes at their moment of victory'.

It's impossible to find anyone who begrudged Elbow their moment of victory, nor the success and respect that has come their way since. Whether the same level of success would have happened to Rachel Unthank and The Winterset is hard to say, though it seems unlikely. Their music, starkly beautiful as it is, lacks the widescreen appeal of 'One Day Like This', even if it has the same degree of passion and ravishing harmonies.

The blend of human voices is the music that machines will

never be able to reproduce. From the earliest choirs through doo-wop and The Everly Brothers and Simon and Garfunkel and The Beach Boys and Crosby, Stills and Nash and Le Mystère des Voix Bulgares and The Carpenters and Plant and Krauss to the Fisherman's Friends and their 2010 album of shanties, the sound of voices locked in an embrace will always provide moments of inextinguishable unique beauty. Often, it seems to be something that happens by chance. If a great band is more than the sum total of its parts, then that is especially true of great vocal acts.

When Robin Pecknold recruited Christian Wargo, Casey Wescott and Josh Tillman to his band Fleet Foxes he cannot possibly have known that their voices would complement each other in such a stunning way. He also recruited Skyler Skjelset to play guitar. Skyler, though, doesn't sing and it's the singing that is the thing. When I first heard their records I was stopped in my tracks as I hadn't heard a band harmonise like that for decades, if ever. When I played their eponymous debut album to my then ten-year-old daughter Mia she listened intently and then said, 'How are they doing that?' It's a perfectly good question, and one you suspect not even the band themselves could effectively answer. When they came to our studio in Manchester to perform on our radio show they were quietly polite and unassuming with the exception of effervescent keyboardist Wescott. They were dressed in the manner of vaguely stylish landscape gardeners. Shabby chic might describe it. They shuffled around semi-aimlessly for a while until gradually, in their own time, they took their places, manned their minimalistic equipment, opened their mouths and this wondrous noise emerged. I was sitting in the room with them and it was still more or less impossible to believe that this heavenly music was emanating from these earthbound scruffs. How were they doing it? Pecknold has described himself as lacking in social skills and says that the members of Fleet Foxes are pretty much his only friends. This makes it even more remarkable. That your only friends turn out to be able to create this wonderful vocal blend is way beyond good luck.

The vocal blend achieved by The Unthanks has a more obvious root. At their core are the sisters Rachel and Becky, who were raised by their folk-singing parents in the folk clubs and village festivals close to their home village of Ryton in the Northeast of England. The songs of the sea and the border country were part of their upbringing as was a bit of the old clog dancing.

For our last programme of 2008 they came to perform some suitably festive music live in the studio. At that time they were still known as Rachel Unthank and The Winterset and the line-up consisted of the sisters along with violinist Niopha Keegan and pianist Stef Conner. Their first number was performed by the quartet a capella and was called 'Tar Barrel In Dale'. Written by their father George, the song records the tradition in their home village of carrying tubs of flaming pitch from pub to pub to bring in the New Year. Icy pavements, beer and molten tar in a bucket on your head. What could possibly go wrong?

Again, the sound of those voices entwining in that room was magical. It was an absolute privilege to be there at such close quarters as there was the certain knowledge that you were hearing something very special, and something that no one else in the whole world could exactly reproduce.

In 2009 I spent one of the happiest and most invigorating weeks I've ever had in broadcasting as we took *The Radcliffe and Maconie Show* to Hadrian's Wall. As a trail walk it is simply beautiful, particularly over the exhilarating high craggy ground of the most unforgettable section between Banks and Chollerford, taking in the Roman forts at

Birdoswald, Housesteads and Chesters. The landscape is ever changing and you're never far from tangible reminders of the history and heritage of the path you're treading. Blessed with fine weather our West to East crossing from Bowness-on-Solway to Segedunum Fort at Wallsend was so utterly absorbing and companionable that I just wanted to turn round and go back the other way at journey's end. It was not, however, without incident.

On the Tuesday night the programme was due to be broadcast from the High House Farm Brewery, close to Chollerford. The Unthanks were booked to provide us with some suitably evocative, locally sourced music. Unfortunately, the ISDN lines that should have been installed at the micro-brewery to enable the programme to be carried to the national airwaves had not materialised. This resulted in a frank exchange of views between our executive producer 'Fish' John and engineer Nick about who was responsible for this less than ideal scenario. Having said that, they were agreed on one thing: each thought it was the other's fault.

While this high-level production meeting raged, the rest of us, having walked around fourteen miles, began to take all the equipment back down the narrow stairs from the High House Farm Brewery café bar and load it back into the vans, as it was quite clear that notwithstanding which of John or Nick would come off worse once they started to hurl bottles of bitter at each other, there was going to be no programme broadcast from there that night. Meanwhile, our other engineer and fellow walker Chris had ascertained that the luxurious hotel and spa we were staying in that night had ISDN lines in its conference suite.

Accordingly the whole party relocated to Matfen Hall, where three vanloads of equipment were quickly reassembled. The massed ranks of the newly expanded Unthanks then arrived, were informed of the change of plans, and cheerfully started to set up. The utterly charming and unfazed proprietors of the High House Farm Brewery just brought all the food and beer, including cask ales, down to the new venue. Simple. What's more, the good people and management of Matfen Hall benignly turned a blind eye to the fact that we were eschewing their hospitality facilities in favour of creating our own pub on the premises.

Satisfied that a new plan was in place and that, having moved the equipment twice, there was nothing more we could usefully do, Stuart, our producer Lizzie and I slipped into the white dressing gowns we found hanging in our rooms and made our way to the pool and spa to ease the aches and pains of the rambling day.

The spa complex was located in the same area of the hotel as the hospitality suite and the comings and goings were easily viewable through the plate-glass windows separating us aquatic types from the rest of the team. From the feverish pacings, puce complexions and wagging fingers it became clear that, contrary to what had been assumed, all was far from well. Not wanting to get involved, the three of us sniggered and crouched behind pillars so as not to be seen. At one point, as John stormed past waving a walking pole in the direction of the back of Nick's head we hid, and I swear this is true, underwater. We held our breath and ducked under the surface of the swimming pool until we thought the coast was clear. What we didn't know was that though the hotel had ISDN, it was the wrong sort of ISDN. We also had a satellite truck with us but, and I'm glossing over several important technical issues here, it was the wrong sort of satellite. John and Nick were of the opinion we had the wrong kind of engineer and exec producer respectively. On a brighter note, the sauna was working perfectly.

Stuart, Lizzie and I, sensing that we should probably go and see what was going on, put our robes back on and made moves to return to our rooms. Unfortunately, the corridor that would enable us to do this led through reception, where the latest production/engineering stand-off was taking place. We waited for several minutes in the hope that the warring factions would disperse, but once it became clear that things could rage on for some time we had no choice but to shuffle in and enquire what was going on. The looks on the faces of those trying to manage the crisis at the sight of the three of us in those dressing gowns is as withering as I have ever encountered.

Eventually it was decided that Stuart and I would be driven into town to put the show out from the studios of Radio Newcastle whilst The Unthanks would stay at Matfen Hall to record their session before jumping in a car themselves and bringing the results to the studio. Ironically, that Tuesday night we broadcast what we all later considered to be the best programme we made that week.

After we came off-air we returned to the conference suite, where the expansive High House Farm buffet and bar appeared admirably stocked. As the tensions ebbed away we sang songs into the night, whilst never quite escaping the knowledge that we would be walking fifteen miles the next day with another programme to follow. One of the many guests present that night was George Unthank and how joyous it was to hear him lead a hugely spirited and rumbustious rendition of 'Tar Barrel In Dale' as we destroyed the all-important vocal blend of his daughters and their band by piling in for the choruses. But thinking about that collective performance brings me to the end of this book and the only two truths that are contained herein:

1. A song, like 'Tar Barrel In Dale', 'Mykonos', 'One Day Like This' or any of the others included here – with the

possible exception of 'Why Is It Always Dairylea?' – can capture a moment as well as any photograph.

And 2. It is impossible to exude an air of authority, concern or opprobrium whilst wearing a white fluffy towelling robe and mules bearing the insignia of a hotel and spa.

AFTERWORD

2010 BAND OF HORSES – 'FACTORY'

This is my most recent favourite record. I don't know as yet what it will mean to me when I hear it again nostalgically sometime in the future. It's too soon to tell. It sounds wonderful, though, and that's all that really matters.

This much I know. That right now someone somewhere in the world is making my next new favourite record.

ACKNOWLEDGEMENTS

Thanks to those who generously gave of their time to talk during the writing of this book: Simon Armitage, Jarvis Cocker, Brian Eno, Guy Garvey, Richard Hawley, Mike Heron, Noddy Holder, Ralf Hutter, Cahill O'Doherty and Sir Cliff Richard.

Thanks for continued support and encouragement to: Caroline Chignell and Emily Rees Jones at PBJ, Lizzie Hoskin and Lorna Skingley at Smooth Operations and Kerri Sharp at Simon and Schuster.

Love, always, to Rose, Mimi, Holly and Bella.

ABOUT THE AUTHOR

Mark Radcliffe was born in Bolton and went to Manchester University. He has been employed by the BBC to talk between records for over twenty years. He has won six Sony Gold Awards and recorded six albums. Sometimes he is on the telly. He is married with three daughters, one granddaughter, a dog called Toto and lives in the badlands of Cheshire.